Quality by Design

Taguchi Methods and U.S. Industry

Quality by Design

Taguchi Methods and U.S. Industry

Lance A. Ealey

ASI Press

Dearborn, Michigan

Published by the ASI Press, a division of the American Supplier Institute, Inc.

Printed in the United States of America

Library of Congress Cataloging-in-Publication Data

Ealey, Lance A.
Quality by design : Taguchi Methods and U.S. industry / Lance A. Ealey.
p. cm.
Includes index.
ISBN 0-941243-05-2
1. Quality control—United States—Statistical methods.
2. Production management—United States—Quality control.
I. Title.
TS156.E25 1988
658.5'62—dc19

88-22239
CIP

Contents

Preface

On average, one in every four purchases made by consumers in the United States causes problems, according to the U.S. Office of Consumer Affairs. A proliferation of poor products and services helped create the consumer-protection movement in the 1970s and earned many sectors of U.S. industry abysmal reputations. Worldwide, the United States was gaining a reputation as a first-class nation that produced second-rate goods.

In too many industries, the essence of a company—its product or service—was getting lost in a shuffle of high technology and feeble management. Excellence was measured in profits, not market share, and profits were becoming harder and harder to achieve.

For many Americans, the 1970s (and, indeed, the 1980s) were the dark ages of quality. Quality virtually went into hiding at many U.S. companies during this period. When the United States was a net exporter of goods, the relative nature of quality among U.S. companies was unimportant in a paradoxical sort of way. American companies were, in effect, the only game in town, so quality was defined by the reliability and durability of the products these companies made. Today (the late 1980s), America is a net importer, and American quality is judged by competitive, world-class standards. By the 1970s, Japan had begun a massive consumer-products push in the United States, which showed the American consumer that there was indeed a higher level of quality available at a lower cost. The 1980s brought increased shipments from overseas, a recession, and even stronger competitive pressures. It has been an exciting and sometimes terrifying two decades.

Today, many of the top U.S. corporations have begun a strategic counterattack in terms of world-class quality products and services, driven by innovative leadership that focuses its attention not simply on the bottom line, but on the product line as well. In the process, these companies find themselves increasing both profits and market share—and they've also discovered that high quality and low costs aren't mutually exclusive goals.

This book, the result of observations, interviews, and studies I have conducted during the past year regarding the Japanese and American automotive industries, is about how that change in thinking came about. I share with most American managers a growing irritation with the ubiquitous comparisons of Japanese and American management styles—rest assured, this book is not a study in such comparisons.

I could not help but be impressed, however, with just how much the Japanese have accomplished in the manufacture of automobiles, especially considering that their rise to become the largest automobile producer in the world has been achieved within the short span of some 30 years. And, as so many other observers have noted, what has happened with automobiles (and with cameras, TV sets, audio equipment, and so forth) can also happen in other industrial sectors.

Like other observers, I, too, have looked for miracles of technology, unique cultural factors, government-industry cooperation, and economic factors such as dollar/yen imbalances to explain just how the Japanese have managed to undermine what used to be a domestic automotive monopoly in the United States ruled by three corporations.

All of the above factors were involved, but there is another factor in Japan's "new industrial revolution" that has, until this decade, been largely ignored by contemporary observers. That other factor is Japanese industrial management's commitment to quality as a way to lower costs and ensure a more rational use of human resources and skills at all levels. Many readers are doubtlessly aware that Japan educates more engineers today in absolute numbers than the United States, despite having only half our population. The importance of engineering skills—whether on the factory floor, in the product-design office, or in corporate management itself—can never be overstated. Major Japanese manufacturing companies will typically employ more engineers than even larger American companies in the same industries. That's not to say that Japan's engineering talent is better than that found in the United States—Japanese engineers I've talked to would usually rate American engineering staffs either technically superior to or on a par with their own staffs. The difference is that Japanese engineers typically focus very keenly on the product in terms of what the customer wants—namely, low cost and high quality.

That's because the management at Japanese companies judges success in terms of market share. The differences that evolve from such a strategy, compared with the American obsession with next-quarter profits, can be startling. Suddenly, management is totally focused on the need for sound, reliable products that serve real needs and wants: products that serve "the voice of the customer." That's the only way a company can sustain market share, or see it grow, over the long term. And the only way to meet the voice of the customer is to design and build products that deliver high quality at low cost.

While researching how Japan developed such superior industrial engineering, I came across the name of Genichi Taguchi, a man of many interests and skills who perhaps symbolizes the strength and pragmatic character of post-World War II Japanese industry. He is by no means the only outstanding Japanese industrial engineer, and would be the first to deny any such pretensions. In fact, getting Taguchi to discuss his work and achievements is a rather difficult task, given his innate sense of modesty and intelligent recognition that much of what he has achieved has resulted from cooperation with others. However, Taguchi's contribution to low-cost quality improvement—combined engineering and statistical methods that achieve rapid improvements in cost and quality by optimizing product design and manufacturing processes—has been well-documented.

Taguchi's system of Quality Engineering is often referred to as Taguchi Methods in the United States. Taguchi did not come up with the name, and is not even particularly fond of it. However, for the sake of editorial convenience—and because America has come to associate the two—Taguchi Methods is used as a synonym for Quality Engineering in this book. As Taguchi himself has noted, the designation has helped spread the idea of designing to reduce variability in the United States, although he makes no claim to its origination.

Having been an automotive journalist for more than eight years, my frame of reference is naturally inclined toward things automotive. That inclination has actually worked to my favor in the writing of this book, as the U.S. auto industry and its supplier base have been at the forefront of industries embracing Taguchi's methodology. This phenomenon is, to a large extent, the result of Ford Motor Co.'s activities in promoting Taguchi Methods among its engineers, as well as those of its supplier companies. Ford created the Ford Supplier Institute, now the American Supplier Institute (ASI), Inc., a nonprofit organization that teaches and promotes new concepts in quality, including Taguchi Methods, Statistical Process Control, and Quality Function Deployment. To Ford's credit, it created a resource not only for the entire U.S. auto industry to use (General Motors Corp. and Chrysler Corp. also train their engineers through ASI), but for all of American industry to benefit from. In fact, the U.S. defense industry is now beginning a massive training effort that could improve the reliability and cost-effectiveness of U.S. military hardware. Ford deserves recognition for this—no other company has done quite as much, quite as well.

In an effort to put the issue of quality into perspective, the first chapter of this book deals with the historical events that brought the U.S. and Japanese automotive industries to their present positions. The comparative view of courses of action taken by the Big Three automakers and their Japanese rivals is enlightening in many respects. By 1957, some Japanese companies had already been using Taguchi's

Quality Engineering methodology for almost ten years. By the late 1980s, they had been using it for more than 30 years. American companies, by comparison, have been aware of Taguchi's system for less than a decade, although striking results are already being seen from their use of Quality Engineering.

While the U.S. auto industry is in the vanguard in terms of promotion and propagation of Taguchi Methods in the United States, many other industries are moving toward the system in increasing numbers—Taguchi's methodology is applicable to almost all industrial enterprises. And while quality improvement is the most visible effect of application of Taguchi Methods, the real power of the system is its steadfast focus on bottom-line results, both in terms of capital outlay and the cost of quality.

Although I discount any kind of racial or ethnic predisposition that might give a society an "edge," it has been suggested that the longer history of cultural development in Asia might lead to a broader approach to problems than is common in the West. Western technologists and engineers like linear problems with linear solutions. They like to define discrete problems and then develop elegant solutions within the boundaries so established. The goal of American technology has been to control all aspects of an industrial environment, including error, to produce quality products. The Japanese industry that arose from the ashes of World War II, however, saw error, or "noise," to use Taguchi's term, as something that could not be contained. It was a reality that was too expensive and too widespread to control; it was, to extend Taguchi's metaphor, deafening. Japan faced a reality that could only be subdued by building products and processes that were robust against noise.

Thus did Taguchi's system of Quality Engineering come into prominence. Taguchi's focus is holistic and entirely pragmatic. He has developed a philosophy and a means to track the cost of variation, as well as a system to reduce that cost as much as possible. With this book, I have attempted to describe some aspects of Taguchi's methodology in terms that a nontechnical manager could readily understand, and I have tried to keep jargon and special language to a bare minimum. Appendices on major parts of Taguchi's methods and ideas, such as the Quality Loss Function (QLF) and the Signal-to-Noise (S/N) Ratio, have been included at the end of the book.

A major problem in quality development has been knowing where one is early enough in the product-development cycle to make cost-effective decisions for continuing actions. The "traditional" approach of problem identification and problem solving is too slow and too uncertain for success in highly competitive industrial markets. The QLF and the S/N Ratio (a communications-industry index of transmission quality that Taguchi uses to measure the level of quality in a product or process) can tell an engineer where he is early on in the product-development phase, while there is still time to make major improvements without incurring significant costs.

In the traditional American approach, an engineer evolves a design through almost countless iterations, and problems are identified and corrected along the way. This design technique is very similar in effect to reliance on inspection during the manufacturing process, and carries with it many of the same quality and cost problems. Corrections are usually made too late to be economical or fully effective. In contrast, Taguchi's methods of off-line (or "upstream") quality control help achieve major improvements at the completion of the first major design cycle.

The tools used in Quality Engineering are not, as a rule, exclusive to Taguchi's methodology; rather, they are adapted to meet the needs of industrial research. Taguchi Methods differ from classical design of experiments in that they are designed to be used by engineers, not statisticians. Taguchi Methods are applicable in scientific research, but they are especially attractive to industrial engineers because they do not seek to identify cause and effect relationships. Rather, they seek to design products and processes that are robust against variation-causing influences. To quote from a recent translation of an article by Taguchi, "Taguchi Methods provide a way of thinking and a method of using small-scale experiments in the laboratory to find optimum designs for large-scale production and the marketplace."

Here the term "optimum" refers to the best factor levels (highest S/N Ratio, etc.) *for a particular experiment.* These may not necessarily be the optimum levels out of all possible factor-level combinations, which would appear in a full-factorial experiment. However, while full factorials cover all possible test conditions, they are not efficient when the number of factors and levels becomes even moderately large. Optimum levels for Taguchi Methods experiments represent a substantial improvement in quality that can be determined efficiently and cost-effectively, although it may not be *the* optimum factor-level combination.

In addition to tangible and rapid improvement of products and processes, Taguchi Methods have major intangible benefits that especially appeal to engineers. As I will explain in the following pages, Taguchi is an engineer first. His methods evolved during a time of drastic scarcities in postwar Japan, when there was extreme competitive pressure to bring new products to market rapidly and economically. The Japanese had studied the methods of classical experimental design developed by R. A. Fisher of England, but concluded that they were inadequate for competitive industrial applications. Fisher's ideas, which I will review briefly in Chapter 5, are excellent for scientific research, but they require much time and use of advanced statistics. Typically, a statistician controls the experiments and the data analysis while the engineer assumes a subservient role. Since the engineer is really the expert in the design of the product or process, not the statistician, communication problems frequently occur.

Fisher's methods have never been widely adopted in industry by engineers. Taguchi's methods, on the other hand, are easy to teach and to learn. After a week of solid instruction, a good engineer can begin designing, executing, and analyzing his own experiments using Taguchi Methods—without the need for expert statistical advice or support.

Additionally, Taguchi Methods, especially the QLF and the S/N Ratio, provide a common language and approach that improve the integration of product design and manufacturing, either within original equipment manufacturers or within their suppliers. Training product-design engineers and manufacturing or process engineers in Taguchi Methods provides common perspectives and objectives—a major step in breaking down traditional barriers between the two groups.

The discovery of Taguchi Methods by U.S. industry is causing a revolution in product and process design. What has been called the "NASA approach" to quality—quality improvement no matter what the cost—is being replaced by a *productive* product-development process. Taguchi defines cost and quality, jointly, as productivity, and stresses that the task of the engineer is not simply to make products that work, but to strive for quality improvement under cost conditions that yield competitive power. It is a revolution that will undoubtedly rank with the development of Henry Ford's moving assembly line in terms of the cultural changes it forces American industry to undergo. The challenges will be great—but the rewards will be, too.

Since my initial exposure to Taguchi Methods last year, and the industrial engineers and managers who have adopted them, I have been amazed to further observe that what began at Ford Motor Co., AT&T Bell Laboratories, and Xerox Corp. in the United States has extended to Canada, Mexico and Latin America, Europe, the People's Republic of China, and such Southeast Asian nations as Singapore and the Philippines.

ASI has established joint or cooperative licensing arrangements in countries such as Canada (the Canadian Supplier Institute), Mexico (the Monterrey Institute of Technology), England (ASI International U.K.), France (the Taguchi Methods Institute in cooperation with Velez Consultants), Italy (Elea S.p.A., Olivetti Consulting/Training), and West Germany.

All of these institutions or organizations are (or will soon be) providing a full range of instruction in Taguchi Methods, as well as implementation consulting services. ASI has also established the ASI Press, publisher of this book. The ASI Press is now developing many new books on Taguchi Methods, including a seven-volume series on the methodology in cooperation with the Japanese Standards Association (JSA). All of the publications that the ASI Press has published, or will publish, will also be published in the

French, Spanish, and Italian languages. The JSA will undertake to develop Chinese and Korean language editions of the forthcoming series as well.

This development of a "literature" on Taguchi Methods in languages other than Japanese will undoubtedly further accelerate what is already a rapidly growing interest, and one can only speculate on the resulting impact on industry, industrial management, and scientific research. The latter two subjects are mentioned because, while time did not permit proper research and discussion, Taguchi has also helped apply his ideas and methods to the analysis of "business data," medical diagnosis and data analysis, and pharmaceutical research.

I am confident that this broad exposure of Taguchi's ideas and their various applications will provide new ways to improve research and the results of research, as well as the management and productivity of industry. Perhaps it will be my good fortune to report on these future changes and developments.

Lance Ealey
Edison, New Jersey
May 1988

Acknowledgments

The people who helped and encouraged me to write this book are many, and if I included them all, my list of acknowledgments would be long indeed. However, I would like to thank Dr. Genichi Taguchi himself for granting me several interviews; his son, Shin Taguchi, for his insight and skill in explaining his father's craft; and his friend and colleague, Yuin Wu, for providing additional background information. I would also like to thank John McElroy, my former editor-in-chief at *Automotive Industries*, for offering excellent advice, and for generally encouraging me to undertake this project.

Others who have contributed a great deal include Madhav Phadke of AT&T Bell Laboratories, who provided significant insight into Taguchi's work at Bell Labs, and J. K. (Jim) Pratt of ITT, who, in a very fatherlike way, pointed out that most conventional thinking on quality in the United States is bunk—and then proceeded to explain why this is so. I would also like to thank Lawrence P. Sullivan of the

American Supplier Institute, Inc., for his special insight and in appreciation of his very real courage in promoting Taguchi Methods and other quality-control technologies among U.S. manufacturers. I thank my wife, Sharon, for reading and critiquing various sections of this book. And I thank the people I met with at AT&T, Bell Labs, and Bell Communications Research for their help and kindness, including Roshan Chaddha, Ram Gnanadesikan, Erold Hinds, and Donald Speeney, among many others.

Additionally, I would like to thank Don Clausing for his insight into not only Taguchi Methods, but also into modern industrial dynamics, and Wayland Hicks of Xerox Corp. and James McMunigal of McDonnell-Douglas Corp. for their insights. Others who have been helpful include Dana Cound of Diversitech General; Roberta Dika of Chrysler Corp.; James Kowalick of Aerojet Ordnance Co.; Willie Hobbs Moore of Ford Motor Co.; Norman Morrell of The Budd Co.; Hasan Mutlu and Michael Chupa of ITT; and Thomas Stuelpnagel, a defense industry consultant.

Finally, I would like to thank John Kennedy of ASI for his encouragement, efforts, and unfailing enthusiasm to spread the word on Taguchi's Quality Engineering system.

1

Where We've Been: 1957 vs. 1987

Two events in 1957 shook the United States to its core. The first, the Soviet launch of Sputnik, created an immediate furor—suddenly, American technology was second best. The effects of the second incident took longer to coalesce in the American psyche, but their eventual implications regarding U.S. industry were even more profound than Sputnik's.

On August 25, 1957, several executives of Toyota Motor Corp. stood on a sunny dock in Yokohama, Japan, and watched as two unassuming little cars were hoisted aboard an American President Lines ship headed for Los Angeles, California. One executive later remarked that he felt as though he were seeing his children off on a long journey. He should have added the word "perilous" to his statement.[1]

With hindsight, we see just how much historical weight those two little cars warming in the sun on that Yokohama dock carried. They were among the very first Japanese automobiles exported to the United States, and there was a certain yin-yang symmetry to the scene, with the pearl-white Toyopet Crown offset by an identical black model.

At the time, however, the two cars—looking for all the world like a pair of downsized Packards—heralded a five-year span of ceaseless disaster for the Japanese company.

The Crown, introduced in Japan in 1955, was the first true Japanese automobile. To that point, most Japanese cars had been copies of British and American designs. Nissan Motor Corp., for example, exported its first cars to the United States in 1958—but they were copies of the British Austin A40.

The Crown was a heavy, underpowered little car with a maximum speed of 50 mph in a tailwind. In Japan, the Crown was perceived as a car with a higher order of reliability and efficiency than its predecessors. In America, the Crown wasn't really perceived at all.

The Crown was clearly outclassed in the United States, unable to take the rigorous driving demands of the wide open Western states and keep up with the giant American-made cars. Engines literally melted under the strain; brakes turned to butter from overuse.

It wasn't a dynamic beginning: Following its beachhead struggle in 1957, Toyota shipped 703 vehicles in 1958 and 1,171 in 1959.[2] In the fall of 1960, disaster of another kind struck: The Big Three automakers simultaneously introduced their first compact cars. The action began a string of events that forced Toyota out of the U.S. passenger-car market until 1964. If Toyota were to launch its first U.S.-bound vehicles in such a manner today, it would be laughed out of the market. In 1957, however, few people in the industry even noticed.

More than 30 years later, Toyota's prowess as a car-building combine is fully recognized. The company is capable of introducing new models every three years compared to Detroit's average five-to-seven-year timetable, and Toyota's cars consistently rank at the top of the list in independent customer-satisfaction ratings.[3] In addition, Toyota accomplished this feat while becoming the most efficient automaker in the world.

Since 1980, Japan has built more cars each year than any other country, and Japanese methods—most of them borrowed from U.S. industry and modified to fit the country's needs and culture—have rewritten the book on quality and managing for quality. The newly revised quality bible has only one rule—produce the highest quality at the lowest cost, on time, year in, year out.

The Japanese automotive industry is symbolic of the turnaround in quality thinking that's taken place in Japan over the last three decades. The swing in quality from abysmal to world-class is nowhere as striking as in Japan's automobile production. The effects of that swing on U.S. automakers have been both devastating and enlightening.

The historical marketing approaches of the United States and Japan differ dramatically, much the way the mind-set of a participant at a grand ball differs from that of a beggar viewing the scene from outside. In recent years, it's become more difficult to discern which country is the one outside looking in. One thing is certain, however: The Japanese have considered the world their marketplace since the late 1950s, while American companies have been satisfied to stay at home. Recent Japanese automotive exports have accounted for about 55% of total sales, which is a phenomenal amount of product destined for overseas markets. And, much of it comes to America.

Reaping the World Market

In 1957, when Toyota made its first tentative foray into the U.S. market, 6,120,029 passenger cars were built here. It wasn't a record year—not like 1955, when the industry cranked up its lines to the tune of 7,950,377 cars—but compared to the year before and the year after, the recession year of 1957 was good enough.[4]

Imports in 1957, mostly from Europe, amounted to less than 3.5% of total vehicles sold in the United States. Eleven of those imports, including eight Toyopet Crowns, were from Japan. Imports, which hovered below 1% of total sales through the mid-1950s, were of such slight interest in 1957 that few automotive trade journals even bothered to include them when tallying up total cars sold.

America was a separate market in the 1950s, and to the American way of thinking, that separation was natural. When an American car from that era passes on the street today, it looks enormous, weighing two tons and riding on an 11-foot wheelbase with a total length of almost 19 feet. Engines to power such vehicles were also massive, as well as costly to operate by world standards—V8s that had an average displacement of 5.0 liters, three times that of a typical Japanese engine. The typical car in Europe or Japan rode on an eight-foot wheelbase and was fully five feet shorter than its American counterpart.

In rueful hindsight, Americans look at the 1950s not as the continuum they believed the decade to be at the time, but as a blip in history, a time when it seemed more things were within the grasp of more people in the United States than at any time before or after.

In 1957, America didn't design cars with export in mind because American cars were different. Rather, American auto companies played at exporting automobiles to the rest of the world, shipping more cars when the dollar was weak to maximize profits and ending their forays when the dollar's strength made the attempt less attractive. In the minds of many in the American auto industry, it didn't really matter if U.S. automakers bothered to export cars at all; the home market was the only one worth sustained attention.[5]

The U.S. auto industry was insulated from the world by the uniqueness of its products—in a sense, that uniqueness was a more effective and brilliant market protector than any a government could ever devise. America's affluence and wide-open spaces, combined with the low price of fuel, resulted in the appeal of an imposing automobile that was, for a while at least, the embodiment of the American dream.

Thus could General Motors Corp., averaging a dramatic 50%+ of the total U.S. car market, dictate prices and preferences for the entire industry.[6] American industry would remain insulated for more than 20 years hence, until the second of two oil crises and a devastating recession forced the Big Three to acknowledge the threads of productivity with which Japanese automakers were webbing the world.

In contrast, the Japanese, hungry for the hard currency the U.S. market could provide, made plans to export cars to America at a time when total Japanese passenger-car production worked out to slightly more than 47,000 vehicles per year. A single American assembly plant could build as many vehicles in ten weeks!

The American market is the pearl of world commerce and for Japan, that pearl has always been worth cultivating. Japan's domestic market has never been an easy target for Japanese car companies. Competition has been of the cutthroat, price-slashing variety for years. The only Japanese company that makes a profit selling cars in Japan is Toyota; other companies either break even or lose money. Likewise, profits are traditionally hard-won for companies in the European market.

By comparison, the U.S. market was a gravy train until recently, and Japanese automakers earmarked up to 40% of their exports for the United States.[7]

Small Cars, Big Profits

American automakers have historically paid little more than lip service to the entry-level, small-car segment of the market—the segment that gave Japan its U.S. foothold. Before 1960, the Big Three usually filled their small-car niches with products imported from European subsidiaries. It wasn't until the 1961 model year that the Big Three introduced their first modern, domestically built small cars. Less than 30 years later, the Big Three had begun their apparent final withdrawal from this segment, once again going offshore or turning to subsidiaries for their entry-level small-car needs (see **Table 1-1**). The American companies didn't want to bother with small cars, which, under the standard manufacturing and accounting methods of the Big Three, lose money.[8]

The Japanese exploited this tactical weakness by concentrating their initial efforts on the small-car segment. Only since 1986 have Japanese companies begun moving into the higher segments of the market.

Toyota and other Japanese automakers may have fallen on their faces when first tackling the U.S. market, but they have learned quickly and adapted their products to thrive in this initially hostile environment.

Table 1-1.
U.S. Automakers Outsource Small Cars

U.S. Company	*Sourced from*	*Type*
General Motors	Suzuki/Japan	Minicar
	Isuzu/Japan	Subcompact
	GM-Toyota/U.S.A.	Subcompact
	Daewoo/Korea	Subcompact
Ford	KIA/Korea	Minicar
	Ford/Australia	Sporty car
	Mazda/U.S.A.	Compact
	Ford/Mexico	Subcompact
Chrysler	Mitsubishi/Japan	Chrysler imports an entire range of small passenger cars from Mitsubishi.

(Source: *Automotive Industries*)

The late Shotaro Kamiya, the dynamic head of Toyota's now integrated sales organization, was the driving force behind Toyota's first entry into the American market. Kamiya, a dapper man with a rigid sense of self-discipline and more than a touch of Samurai spirit, realized that the cars Toyota was then building were inferior to American-made automobiles. Still, he saw Toyota's American initiative as a chance to compete in a world-class market. It wasn't until 1966, when Toyota introduced the Corolla, that the company had its first true overseas success.[9]

The Corolla was the first car Toyota designed specifically to be a large-volume seller in overseas markets. After eight years of hardship and humiliation, Toyota had finally

> **Quality: Born in the U.S.A.**
>
> The irony in the way that Japan rose to such heights in so short a time shouldn't be lost on American manufacturers. Just about every one of the quality tools used by the Japanese today—Statistical Process Control, Just-in-Time (JIT), Taguchi Methods, Total Quality Control, preventive maintenance, employee involvement, quick machine-tool and press setup and die-change times, process smoothing, group technology—have their roots in Western science and technology.
>
> In 1915, for example, Ford Motor Co.'s Highland Park, Michigan, Model T plant was already using a primitive form of group technology, where all the machines necessary to make a part or component were placed next to each other.
>
> The plant was also using what amounted to a JIT production system. On a daily basis, it received 70 carloads of freight from outside suppliers and sent out 175 carloads of shiny black Model Ts. The plant theoretically carried a four-week inventory of components, although only five days' supply was typically on hand. Some 1,000 cars were produced per day, and the assembly line operated under a pull-through JIT system, with the stated goal of

found the key that unlocked the American market. The following year, Toyota's exports to the United States passed rival Nissan Motor Co.'s for the first time.[10]

Changing Perceptions

Today, American cars are much smaller than those of the 1950s and '60s; the term used to describe them is "international size." Still, U.S. exports account for a tiny amount of total domestic production.

lowering overhead expenses caused by warehousing parts and supplies.

Ford's hand-to-mouth production system was used to maximize productivity, although it didn't feature the elegant yet simple closed-loop kanban card procurement system developed by Toyota Motor Corp. in the early 1950s, and it didn't flow out from Highland Park to Ford's many component suppliers. What it *did* do was build Model Ts so efficiently that Ford was able to reduce the price of each car by more than 50%.

Granted, Ford only built one type of product in one color at the plant, and it didn't have to deal with the complexity of models, colors, and option packages found in the industry today. Still, by 1915 Ford was able to produce more than 300,000 Model Ts a year—more cars than Japan would build in a year's time until 1960.

Ford's River Rouge plant, the model upon which Toyota based its vertically integrated Toyota City complex, was self-contained down to having its own steel-making facilities. It featured an even more efficient JIT production system.

Why? In 1957, it was a matter of size. Years later, American car manufacturers still didn't consider exports to be worth the trouble. In late 1986, domestic manufacturers finally began what could be considered the first serious attempts to market U.S.-built cars around the world. This push was again driven by a weak dollar.

Ford Motor Co. and GM have historically set up overseas organizations to build and sell cars in Europe and elsewhere, including Australia, and, for a brief period before World War II, in Japan. While these operations began building cars attuned to local expectations, very little of the knowledge or engineering innovation fostered in these subsidiary companies found its way back to the American organizations. Ford in particular has since realigned its worldwide operations to nurture the growth of design and engineering among its international companies, to the extent of creating "centers of excellence." This plan gives individual segments of the worldwide organization full responsibility for the design of cars that will be sold internationally.

Still, the Big Three do not now build (and never have built) cars equipped to meet the specifications and unique requirements (right-hand drive, etc.) of other countries. The Japanese have built right- and left-hand-drive cars for years, meeting the specifications of 140 different countries, and they've usually built all versions of a model *on the same assembly line.*

The focus of Japanese industry has always been outward. Yet with the help of the Japanese government, the Japanese auto industry has usually hampered attempts by outside markets to sell products in Japan. There have been some success stories, however. Tiny BMW, a West German performance automaker, sells more than *seven times as many* cars in Japan as the Big Three do combined!

Things may be turning around for American automakers, however. GM, Ford, and Chrysler Corp. have begun strengthened programs to sell U.S.-made cars, minivans, and trucks in Europe, and Ford is actively marketing several U.S.-built models for sale in Japan. For the foreseeable future, however, the road still seems rocky.

Clearly, there's a new realization among American automakers and their suppliers that being competitive worldwide is the best way to sell products in the United States. That realization comes at a time of tremendous uncertainty, not only for domestic automakers, but for their traditional suppliers as well.

The Japanese will be able to build more than two million cars in North America by the early 1990s (see **Table 1-2**). If you add in the 2.3 million cars they can export from Japan to the United States under the Voluntary Restraint Agreement, even in a solid, 11-million-car sales year, the Japanese could grab more than 40% of the total U.S. market. It's entirely possible that the U.S. market will continue to be burdened by an additional 25% vehicle capacity—a full five million cars—over what will be needed to fully serve the market through the 1990s.[11]

Which companies are going to survive in that cutthroat market? They will be winners, companies able to adapt quickly and cost-effectively to the market. The only real question is this: Will they be U.S. or foreign?

Cost-Driven Productivity

In terms of real productivity, many Japanese automakers continue to outpace their American rivals by almost two to one. What's even more astounding is that the plants Japanese automakers have set up in the United States, using American workers, outproduce some Big Three facilities by more than two to one![12] (See **Table 1-3.**)

While the Japanese are the most obvious threat to the domestic auto industry, they are by no means the only one. By the 1990s, there will be more than 40 foreign car companies from all over the world selling automobiles in America. In 1984, the total number of car companies, including U.S. domestic automakers, stood at 29. The seller's market is over for all companies in the U.S. auto industry.

It's interesting to note the different tacks Japanese and

Table 1-2. Japanese Transplants in North America

Company	*Name*	*Location*
U.S.		
Honda	Honda of America Manufacturing Inc.	Marysville, Ohio
Nissan	Nissan Motor Manufacturing Corp. U.S.A.	Smyrna, Tenn.
Toyota/GM	New United Motor Manufacturing Inc.	Fremont, Calif.
Toyota	Toyota Motor Manufacturing U.S.A. Inc.	Georgetown, Ky.
Mazda	Mazda Motor Manufacturing (U.S.A.) Inc.	Flat Rock, Mich.
Mitsubishi/Chrysler	Diamond-Star Motors Corp.	Bloomington, Ill.
Fuji/Isuzu	Subaru-Isuzu Automotive Inc.	Lafayette, Ind.
Total U.S.		
Canada		
Honda	Honda of Canada Manufacturing Inc.	Alliston, Ont.
Toyota	Toyota Motor Manufacturing Canada	Cambridge, Ont.
Suzuki/GM	Cami Automotive Inc.	Ingersoll, Ont.
Total Canada		
Total North America		

Date Open	*Projected Capacity*	*Investment*	*Employment*	*Products*
Nov. '82	360,000	$615 million	3,600	Accord, Civic
June '83	265,000	$850 million	3,000	Sentra, Pickup
Dec. '84	250,000	$450 million	2,500	Nova, FX16
Spring '88	200,000	$800 million	3,000	Camry
Fall '87	240,000	$550 million	3,500	626, Mustang IV
Fall '88	240,000	$700 million	2,900	H2X hatchback
Fall '89	240,000	$600 million	3,000	Leone, P'up/Trooper
	1,795,000	$4,565 million	21,500	
Nov. '86	80,000	$150 million	700	Accord, Civic
Fall '88	50,000	$300 million	1,000	Corolla
Fall '88	200,000	$350 million	2,000	Sprint, Forsa, Samurai
	330,000	$800 million	3,700	
	$2,125,000	$5,365 million	25,200	

(Source: *Automotive Industries*)

Table 1-3.
Home Court Advantage Fizzles as Japanese Beat Big Three in U.S. Productivity

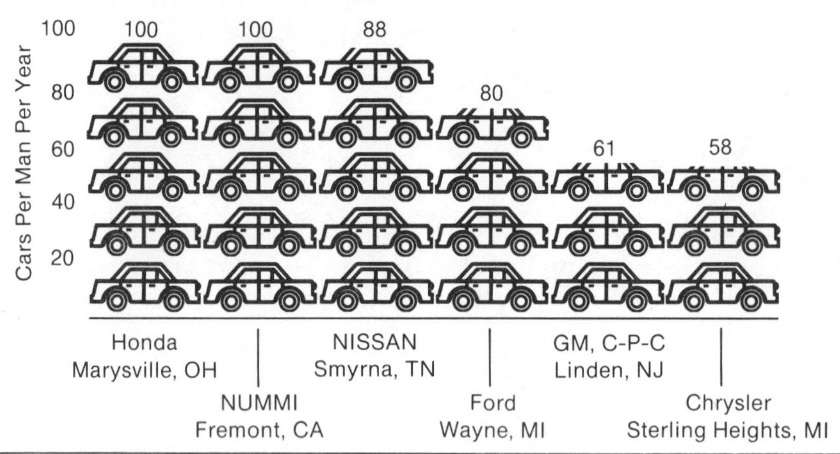

(Source: *Automotive Industries*)

U.S. automakers are taking in response to the rapid saturation of the U.S. automobile market. Japan took quite a thumping in the late 1980s as the value of the yen appreciated by more than 80% compared to the dollar, dropping from more than 250 yen to the dollar to less than 130.

Japanese automakers were forced to raise prices by 25%—in some cases more than $2,000—in the span of one model year. But, it wasn't until January 1987—two years later—that the first Japanese auto company felt compelled to adopt rebate cash incentives to maintain sales levels, whereas U.S. automakers had been using them for years.

In the face of escalating costs and the potential of lost sales, Japanese companies, almost without exception, announced plans to make their operations even more productive.

Honda Motor Co.'s goal was to be profitable when the

yen is trading at 120 to the dollar. Toyota, whose export break-even point was believed to be in the 140 yen/dollar range, began working to increase productivity above its normal, although still phenomenal, 6% annual rate, and the efforts were paying off. In 1986, productivity was up an astounding 7.8%.[13]*

By way of comparison, American automaker productivity historically increases at a 2.0–3.0% annual rate. Recently, U.S. automakers, most notably Ford and Chrysler, have increased their productivity rates at a much higher level through extensive cost-cutting and efficiency programs.[14]

Still, American automakers, who were handed their first big pricing break against the Japanese for free (in the form of a much stronger yen), saw fit to raise their own prices instead of holding the line on increases to maximize their competitiveness. One auto company president even complained that the yen was still too strong and should fall to 125 (at the time, it was at 140) to the dollar before parity is reached—while his company was earning the largest profits in its history.

The Great Supplier Shakeout

American automotive suppliers seem headed toward a shakeout of major proportions, as domestic automakers opt for single sources of parts and components rather than the double- and triple-source strategies that were the norm

*Unlike the gains recently registered at some U.S. auto companies, which reflect a high percentage of employee and program cutbacks, Toyota has been running a lean operation for many years. In this frame of reference, its annual 6% productivity improvement average is truly extraordinary.

just ten years ago. A major cause for concern among U.S. automotive suppliers is what has been called "the third wave" of Japan's attack on the U.S. market.

The first wave began in 1957, when Toyota started shipping automobiles to the United States. The second wave started in the early 1980s, when Japanese automakers first began planning to build vehicle assembly plants in the United States.* The third wave, which began in the second half of the 1980s, involves the systematic relocation of captive Japanese suppliers to supply the seven U.S. and three Canadian assembly plants Japanese automakers will be operating in North America by the 1990s. Indeed, many Japanese supplier companies in the late 1980s were rapidly either building or buying U.S. parts and component plants to remain competitive against the shrinking dollar.

U.S. auto-supplier companies face a particularly perilous future. The Big Three automakers continue to place significant pressures on suppliers for annual price cuts, even while, as several supplier executives have noted, the car companies continue to raise their own prices.

The car companies tend to see it from a different perspective. Noted a Ford spokesman in late 1987, "We are still

---

*Several of the Japanese-transplant automotive companies have complained publicly regarding the lax quality performance by many U.S.-based suppliers. A Mazda Motor Corp. senior executive complained in *Automotive News* that U.S. suppliers can't or won't meet the company's demands for first-time quality, and would rather continue by simply replacing defective goods returned by Mazda's Flat Rock, Michigan, transplant assembly operation. Initially, Toyota's joint-venture assembly plant with GM—New United Motors Manufacturing, Inc. (NUMMI), in Fremont, California—also experienced production problems regarding U.S.-sourced sheet steel. The material was of inconsistent quality and was packaged improperly for shipping, which caused damage. NUMMI's scrap rate shot up, and the inconsistent source hampered the plant's modified "Just-in-Time" production schedule.

over cost, compared to the competition. We have to cut costs by $5 billion in the next five years, because the only vehicles that will be sold in 1990 will be the best ones with the lowest cost."[15]

Another very real challenge for suppliers is the fact that they are increasingly called upon by the automakers to shoulder much (in some cases, all) of the design burden for parts and components. In moving to single sources of supply, the automakers have also decided to use suppliers much earlier in the design process. Car companies are making it clear that they want real contributions in engineering and design. The days are apparently over when a supplier could simply bid on designs supplied by manufacturers and then, if their bid was lowest, build the part exactly as specified. With the drastic reductions in engineering manpower all three of the domestic carmakers have experienced since 1980, they no longer have the resources to design entire cars from bumper to bumper. Instead, they're seeking more and more help from supplier engineering teams. This is going to require that suppliers develop significant product-design capabilities.

Finally, suppliers are being asked to become "system" suppliers, a notion I was introduced to several years ago in, of all places, Australia. It seems an Australian company was bidding for work from an American automaker for a subsystem, only to learn that the automaker was more interested in finding a company that could design, manufacture, and build the entire system, sourcing parts from other subcontractors and delivering a totally finished product to the car company's receiving dock. The entire system could thus simply be wheeled up to the assembly line and attached to the car in modular form. Such systems would include interiors, entire heating/air conditioning systems, and so forth. The Big Three are pursuing the systems concept with vigor. Ford, for example, has given the brake division of Bendix Corp. total responsibility for the brake system on the 1989 Ford Thunderbird.[16]

Some industry observers foresee the day when certain major suppliers will become strongly linked to individual auto companies, much the way the suppliers are in Japan. This assumption is based on the fact that after a supplier designs a system or subsystem, an auto company has very little control over the knowledge and experience gained by the supplier's engineering staff. A supplier engineer could, even without realizing it, refer mentally to a design he worked on for a competitor company, and give the current client full benefit of that experience—to the obvious detriment of the first automaker.

More and more suppliers are becoming not simply suppliers of parts and components, but also suppliers of ideas and innovations. There is an intriguing parallel here between tapping into the creativity of a company's own work force and tapping into the creativity of the company's suppliers.

Obviously, the only automakers and suppliers that will survive to see the year 2000 will be the ones with the highest quality levels, the lowest possible costs, and the best customer-satisfaction ratings. Achieving these goals takes more than a snappy slogan or a shiny lapel pin, as any company executive who's gone the route will tell you—and quite a few have gone the route.

What it takes is a new ethic in quality. From conversations with many enlightened American managers and engineers, it has become clear that, in their minds, it's just as unethical to add tremendous cost to ensure products are of good quality as it is to ship defective goods.

The Boondoggle Dilemma

Recently, a study mission composed of American automotive and automotive-supplier engineers and managers took a two-week tour of Japanese manufacturing facilities. Most of the engineers were specialists in quality—how to measure it, how to improve it, how to find it in the first place.

A supplier-company top executive, one of the few along on the trip, saw the mission from an unusual perspective. "These aren't the guys who should be here," he said. "Most of them will go back to their companies and get, 'So, how was your latest boondoggle?' thrown in their faces."

He was probably right: At most Japanese companies the mission visited, the company's president was either an expert in or at least very familiar with many of the latest quality-improvement and quality-control methods. And, in companies that were actively pursuing significantly higher quality levels, either because their market share was slipping or because they were building an unacceptable number of defective products, the president himself often monitored the company's progress in reaching its quality goals.

In other words, the idea that quality is very important in a world-class Japanese company flows from the most important operating officer on down—all the way to the shop floor. On the other hand, few American executives know how to pursue quality, and fewer are interested or brave enough to teach what they know.

The higher some executives climb in American companies, the more they rely on generalizations concerning the products their companies make. These same executives can usually recite company finance and profit/loss data on a line-by-line basis. Such executives usually approach the task of "getting competitive" not by focusing on improving product and process capabilities, but by wielding a sharp pencil and cutting out programs and people.

While this sort of action is many times rightfully necessary, once the cuts are made, the executive often feels his job is complete. He doesn't pursue the implementation of positive quality and productivity programs to uplift the corporation's competitive position and build the kind of world-beating worker morale that's necessary to become a world-class operation. This basically negative, short-term, bottom-line mentality is being challenged at America's best corporations.

What these American companies are rediscovering is that quality begins at the top. You pour it into a company from the top and it flows down through middle management, finance, product design, engineering, manufacturing and assembly—through the supervisors and foremen right down to the most important person, the line worker.

You can't pour quality in from the bottom and expect it to flow to the top or, for that matter, in from the middle and expect it to flow in both directions. Our boondoggled top executive was thinking in terms of the latter pathway.

If your company's quality person comes back dancing a jig over some new quality concept called Company-Wide Quality Control (CWQC) he picked up in Japan, that's fine. He's supposed to get excited about that stuff—that's his job. If he pushes too hard to have the concept incorporated into your processes, however, he's going to find out fairly quickly just how far his sphere of influence extends—usually just about to the end of his cubicle.

Now, suppose the company president announces that he's decided to begin a CWQC program and that everybody, from executive VPs on down, will be involved. The program will encompass all the quality-control and quality-improvement systems and techniques necessary to improve product quality, with special emphasis on those techniques that address the company's major problems, including product design and unplugging bottlenecks in the manufacturing process. The president himself will monitor the program's progress and personally meet with managers who aren't adopting the program to find out why. This is true leadership.

Which quality program has the best chance of being implemented, the quality engineer's concept or the president's CWQC program? Obviously, the company president's program is the one with enough horsepower behind it to become a reality.

Fast-Tracking Pitfall

Granted, Japanese manufacturing companies have an advantage over their U.S. rivals. Managers and workers rarely change companies: They move only within the organization, and—in the top manufacturing companies, at least—are ensured of lifelong employment. This means that the bright young engineer you hire this year will carry all the training and on-the-job experience he acquires over his lifetime of service with the company right into the president's office, if he rises that far. By that time, he's well-schooled in how the company functions, what its problems are, and where its strengths lie. Right now, we're seeing Japanese executives who've spent a lifetime learning their companies' CWQC methods ascending into executive positions. Who's in a better position to teach quality control or efficient production techniques?

U.S. executives, on the other hand, are groomed to ride the fast track, to make a big impact quickly and then jump into the next up-and-coming position. In fact, under the current rules of engagement fostered by many U.S. corporations, a manager is valued on how many different positions he's had, both inside and outside the company. Also, the emphasis is generally on having a wide range of positions with a wide range of companies, which supposedly means you've been exposed to many different organizational systems and can react flexibly to change.

In the game of musical chairs executives at many American companies are playing, few top-level people have been in their present positions for more than three or four years. Think about that. It takes five to seven years for a domestic company to take a new product such as an automobile from planning to production; many of these fleet-footed executives are jumping into projects begun by their predecessors. Once there, they do whatever is necessary to make a quick, positive impact. So they add a few wrinkles to the project to give it their stamp, possibly changing the entire vision of the plan, and then jump to another assignment before the fruits of their labors (no matter how wonderful or rotten they may be) see light.

Business thrives on change; it's how you create energy within an organization. Being exposed to many different jobs and ways of doing things is essential to the development of a well-rounded executive. It gives him depth of knowledge and understanding about how the company operates. But problems occur when too many key people jump too far too fast. Changing key executives often disrupts the company-wide programs they're fostering, including quality-improvement programs. If the company doesn't have a clearly defined and well-communicated policy on quality, and the executive who has thrown his weight behind the company's quality program is replaced by a bottom-line-at-any-cost manager, chances are that the quality program will disappear almost as quickly as the executive who was championing it. The need for a company-wide, company-acknowledged quality program has never been greater.

Notes

1. Shotaro Kamiya, *My Life With Toyota,* 1976, p. 78.
2. *Ibid.,* p. 126.
3. J. D. Power Customer Satisfaction Indices, 1984–87.
4. Most of the historical sales data were culled from Statistics and Specifications Issues, *Automotive Industries* (hereafter to be known as *AI*), 1956–86, and from Motor Vehicle Manufacturers Association data.
5. *Automotive News,* June 8, 1987, p. 1, and Paul Linert, "The Yanks are Coming," *Car,* March 1988, p. 100.
6. *AI,* Statistics and Specifications Issue, March 1959, p. 77.
7. Roger Schreffler, "Japan's Rise," *AI,* May 1985, p. 124.
8. It is interesting to note that both Honda Motor Co. and Nissan Motor Co. build their entry-level cars at their U.S. transplant assembly facilities. Depending on whom you believe, between 40% and 60% of the content of these cars is shipped from Japan—and thus carries the significant currency disadvantages such parts and components have compared to U.S.-made goods.
9. Kamiya, *My Life With Toyota,* p. 82.
10. *AI,* Statistics and Specifications Issue, March 1968, p. 64.
11. Many sources allude to this overcapacity, including William Pochiluk of *AutoFact,* as well as many U.S. auto industry executives. Also see "Overcapacity Crunch," *AI,* March 1986, p. 6.

12. John Lippert, "Racing to Cut Time on Assembly Line," *Detroit Free Press*, Feb. 7, 1988, p. G1.
13. Schreffler, "Toyota Productivity: The Yen Won't Stop Here," *AI*, June 1987, p. 63.
14. John McElroy, "1986 Industry Report Card," *AI*, April 1987, p. 40.
15. McElroy, "We're Ready to Deal," *AI*, Dec. 1987, p. 39.
16. *Ibid.*, p. 40.

2

Looking for the Quick Fix

Ever since Britain invented the power plant that drove the Industrial Revolution, technological advances have been associated with improvements in quality and competitive position. James Watt's powerful steam engine was the "Great Leap Forward," an example of the brilliant, strategic industrial mechanism that Western nations have sought ever since to gain market advantage.

Watt's engine wasn't the first steam engine, but it was almost immeasurably better than those before it. Thomas Newcomen had developed a successful steam pump some 40 years earlier. But Watt added a state-of-the-art refinement: a separate condenser system that allowed the engine to complete its cycle more efficiently.

Because of Watt's steam-snorting engine, Britain quickly conquered the world with its industrial might; British industrial muscle was supreme. Britain's strength in industry has traditionally been based on the "Big Idea," from Watt's steam engine to the British boffins, scientific experts renowned during World War II for myriad inventions, including radar. Even today, American and Japanese automotive companies war for possession of the small, highly successful British automotive engineering and design houses: Lotus, which General Motors Corp. bought out from under Toyota Motor Corp.; Cosworth, which to date remains independent; and many others.

The United States inherited much from Britain's Great Leap Forward mentality. Bigger, faster, stronger, and usually more expensive—these words best describe American manufacturing and, indeed, America itself. They are pinned to the inventive ideal that is an American enterprise hallmark. This philosophy has historically stood very soundly, although recent attempts to pursue it have led to perversions of our inventive ideal. To discover why, we should go back to Watt's original prime mover.

The legend of Watt's steam engine includes one of those "blinding flashes" of original thinking we love so dearly. Watt was brewing tea one day and noticed the force with which steam escaped from the whistling pot. More quickly than you could say "Eureka!", he'd hit upon the idea for his steam engine—or so the story goes. It's a shame the story isn't true, because it contains the element we've come to expect from industrial drama: the technology pill.

The technology pill comes in many guises. These days, it's usually computer-based; in the more distant past, it was mechanical or a vacuum-tube-equipped "black box" that could replace manpower and cost with gleaming productivity. The beauty of the technology pill is that it's usually a turnkey device: Most often a business doesn't have to change its ways of doing business or thinking, and the technology pill is usually painless to implement.

That's not to belittle the technology behind the pill. The breathtaking sweep of American technology has illuminated the world and put men on the moon. There's a problem with the technology pill, however: A company often buys one without recognizing the dynamic that allows the pill to work efficiently. That dynamic almost always involves people.

"Some of our friends in the automobile business are learning that you can't just throw money and high technology at a problem and hope for the best, because the human mind can't absorb it that quickly." These are the words of the president of a large automotive-supplier company, and he's talking about technology pills. "We've got a lot of automation that we bought second-hand from the car companies that they were going to throw out," he explained. "It's very nice automation. We cleaned it up and took some time to get it to work properly. Before you go racing off to buy a new machine, you ought to try putting your old one in shape."

A prominent Ford Motor Co. executive recently echoed that sentiment in *Automotive Industries*. "You can go out and spend yourself blind," he said. "We've done it in a couple of cases. I can cite instances where we've spent a lot of money for high technology, and I can take you to another plant with low technology that outproduces the high-tech plant."[1]

Make no mistake, our technology can be mind-boggling in what it can do: it's one of the main reasons the domestic auto industry has traditionally topped the rest of America's industrial sector in terms of productivity.[2] The best Japanese companies, however, as noted in Chapter 1, have been improving their productivity levels at a historical rate more than double ours.* Clearly, the technology pill by itself is not stretching the productivity envelope. Even its extreme forms, such as flexible manufacturing, aren't close on the horizon for most U.S. industries, because they require even more manufacturing discipline and control, not to mention worker involvement, than conventional methods.

There's another shortcoming to technology pills: They're so damned transferable. Your competition needs only the capital to buy one (or the nerve to steal one) to erase your entire competitive advantage. It happened in the 19th century when New England industrialists stole British technology, and it happens today. Think about that in terms of flexible manufacturing. America invents the systems, but who do you think will make the most of them?

The domestic auto industry searched for years to discover the secret behind certain Japanese automakers' incredible quality gains. Honda Motor Co., for example, was building horrible little cars in 1972. A short ten years later, it was establishing itself as the benchmark maker of small cars. We've already talked of Toyota, and it's clear that, historically, the Japanese have bypassed high technology in favor of easily understood systems that require more common sense than computers. America develops systems, too, systems with computer-driven architectures so complex that only experts can really understand them, much less use them effectively.

---

*American industry is beginning to catch up with the Japanese, but not on the strength of technology alone. In some cases, American companies seem to be succeeding almost in spite of their high technology. Rather, American workers are being more actively courted by management in terms of ideas and efficiencies and, in some industries, in terms of paycuts.

What could be more simple than using cardboard tags to control your manufacturing flow? That's basically what Toyota does with its kanban cards during Just-in-Time (JIT) production. From these cards, machine operators know exactly how much product to build and when it must be delivered to the next station. The Japanese approach forces responsibility down through a company to the people who know the most about a given machine or process—the people doing the work. These are the people responsible for productivity and quality.

The historical American approach, which apparently began with Frederick Taylor's time and motion studies in the early 20th century, denies shop floor responsibility almost entirely, relying instead on experts to keep the machinery going.

Today, most large American industrial companies have large departments filled with experts—quality experts, durability experts, reliability experts—all taking scattershot approaches to solving product problems without, in some cases, even conferring with each other. Can a more schizophrenic system exist? Problems become departmentalized, and many of these experts spend most of their time solving problems by putting out fires. As everyone from Red Adair to your local smoke eater knows, putting out fires never stops new fires from starting.

The Quality Circle Pill

At the beginning of this decade, companies across the United States began instituting quality circles of employees, based on the Japanese system championed by Kaoru Ishikawa. Quality circles consist of workers in a given department engaged in thought-gathering activities to solve production or quality problems. Due to lack of focus—read poor managerial leadership—U.S. quality circles often degenerate into carping sessions between management and workers, and in some cases have been abandoned. It's not too hard to find an American executive who's grown wary of quality circles for that very reason. For such executives, quality circles' real value—namely, tapping into the vast brainpower the manufacturer has on its shop floor, yet seldom uses—is never recognized or exploited.

The SPC Pill

At about the same time, many American automotive suppliers began instituting Statistical Process Control (SPC). As discussed in Chapter 3, SPC helps keep production systems in control and thus improves quality.

American managers were amazed at the results they achieved with SPC in reducing scrap and lowering reject rates. It's recently been discovered that a portion of this isn't the result of SPC at all. It's something much more basic. In some cases, the simple act of focusing management attention on a process has inspired workers to perform more effectively. For whichever reason, SPC has produced significant quality gains. For SPC to be effective, however, it has to be consistently applied and should be charted by machine or process operators themselves.

In many SPC programs first instituted in the United States, quality-control experts, not workers, filled out SPC charts. Workers weren't involved and eventually lost any interest they might have had in SPC. Eventually, programs would drift because of lack of discipline. This is also where major problems in communication between workers and management began. The quality-control expert plotting SPC charts and the like became a "straw boss" for the operation. Workers weren't given the opportunity to measure the effectiveness of their own output and began to resent these intrusions, considering them an extension of that time-honored American manufacturing enhancer: taking names and kicking butts.

The whiz-bang improvements created by SPC also faded, and, in many cases, quality levels reverted to pre-SPC levels. This happened because most companies didn't and still don't have a company-wide quality ethic. Instead, quality is approached in a piecemeal fashion, and outside of small enclaves of quality experts scattered throughout the organization, there's little appreciation or acknowledgment of quality-oriented programs.

For SPC to be effective in the long run, machine or process operators must chart their own progress in keeping their machines under control. Operators must also be the ones responsible for continuously reducing process variation, and their ultimate goal must be 100% perfect products. Perfection, of course, is unattainable, but working toward it generates unbelievable efficiencies.

The Automation Pill

Among auto companies, GM, Ford Motor Co., and Chrysler Corp. all have their own horror stories regarding technology pills. Since 1980, GM has spent billions of dollars on high technology. Instead of "leapfrogging the Japanese" with high technology as it bannered it would, GM has lost market share and profits. Even within GM, there seems to be a divergence of opinion on the best route to take to increase productivity and quality. GM's Chevrolet-Pontiac-Canada Group (C-P-C) spent more than $2 billion on state-of-the-art, fully automated, tri-axis transfer stamping presses. These are used to stamp automotive body panels—fenders, doors, hoods—out of sheet steel. If you've ever seen a modern transfer press in action, it's an experience you'll probably never forget. They're huge, battleship-like machines capable of tremendous output with very little direct labor involved.

GM's Buick-Oldsmobile-Cadillac Group (B-O-C), on the other hand, hasn't been spending money on new stamping presses. Rather, it's been working with press operators to reduce die-change times on conventional presses, thereby making them more flexible and productive. B-O-C's results have been impressive. Within one year's time and with minimal investment, die-change time at a press line at B-O-C's Lordstown, Ohio, assembly plant was reduced from 12 hours to 23 minutes. And the press was 17 years old! At another B-O-C press line, this one in Lansing, Michigan, die-change time was reduced from four hours to 10:36 minutes. Compare that to a press at Honda's Marysville, Ohio, plant, which performs a die change in 4:38 minutes, and you can see just how dramatic B-O-C's achievement is.[3]

One of C-P-C's fully automated transfer presses will automatically change dies and begin producing good stampings in about nine minutes. Initial GM reports indicate that B-O-C's conventional presses aren't too far behind C-P-C's transfer presses in terms of productivity. In this case, C-P-C bought a technology pill, while B-O-C invested in its people and fine-tuned the productivity of its existing presses. B-O-C's method for productivity is very similar to the traditional methods Toyota uses.

The Just-in-Time Pill

The Japanese have perfected JIT production (also called "just-on-time" production), which is a pull-through system driven by the immediate needs of the final assembly line: Upstream operations build only as much product as downstream operations request.

The system demands that all parts and components be produced, ideally, at the very moment they're needed ("just in time"). Thus, no inventories are on hand, and only very small buffer stocks are kept between work stations. Production is forced to remain in tight control. If not, the assembly line will stop, and the Japanese don't like to stop assembly lines any more than Americans do.

The advantages of such a system are subtle, but very real. Very little money is tied up in inventories; scrap and rework must be kept to a bare minimum, which requires optimized processes, or the assembly line will stop; and ordering schedules must be consistent and well-organized. JIT production requires a very high level of worker involvement, so a manufacturer gets the added benefit of a highly motivated work force.

To quote a top American automotive executive, who in 1982 had observed the Japanese JIT system and obviously liked what he saw, "They have no in-system inventory to speak of. This means that if something happens to a tool or a conveyer or something else, there's no in-system inventory to put in the unit, so the line stops.

"The benefit is that all of the top management attention in the plant is focused on the problem. If something happens in the plant with the in-system inventory, the line keeps going and that sort of hides what's wrong with the system."[4]

The classic Japanese approach to JIT production stretches from the assembly line out through subassembly procedures, through stamping or molding processes, moving out from the assembly plant itself to a web of nearby supplier plants. They in turn receive products from their suppliers "just in time," and so on, right back to the raw material supplier.

JIT production helps ensure quality production because defective parts and components can't hide within the bulging inventories of a warehouse. They usually become evident as soon as they're sent to the final assembly line—and that's immediately after production. Quick and cost-effective corrective action is taken at once, before a large pile of defective parts is produced. JIT production is yet another low-cost, high-quality idea.

By the 1980s, many consumer goods manufacturers were beginning to understand the cost-effective, quality-enhancing philosophy behind JIT production, and were trying to implement it not only in-house, but among their supplier companies as well.

The resulting systems usually weren't remotely like JIT production. Rather, they more closely resembled JIT inventory control: Instead of shipping large orders of parts to final assembly plants, the suppliers would simply send the order piecemeal, little by little, without changing their traditional ways of doing business.

The supplier would continue to produce parts and components in large batches, just as it always had. The only difference, from the supplier's viewpoint at least, was that it had to spend more money to inventory parts the final assemblers would normally have carried. A supplier-company manager once said, with a conspiratorial look, that if the manufacturer wanted him to carry some extra inventory, he would do it, just to keep the peace.

In many cases, however, bad feelings erupted on all sides: The suppliers felt the final assemblers were saving money at their expense, and the final assemblers were frustrated because the expected increases in quality weren't forthcoming. The manufacturers thus had to continue incoming inspection, with its attendant costs and negative effects on quality.

The only real benefits were derived by middleman-warehousing firms, which made (and continue to make) quite a bit of money warehousing what were supposed to be JIT parts and components. This system of JIT inventory control, which is still prevalent in some sectors of industry, unwittingly combines the worst of both the Japanese and American production systems.

Manufacturers could not approach anything remotely similar to JIT production, since their outside sources of supply were delivering such inconsistent quality. Thus, manufacturers would slyly hide buffer stocks of parts and components throughout their plants, just in case their "just-in-time" system really wasn't. Instead of enforcing manufacturing discipline, it caused mad scrambles that happened time and again.

Manufacturers couldn't trust their supply, and they didn't have enough product on hand just in case something didn't work out quite as planned.

For many companies, the JIT technology pill was quite a waste of time *and* money.*

---

*Some U.S. companies are catching on rapidly. Leading suppliers in the automotive seat-making industry, for example, often ship "just in time," in sequence, to domestic automakers. Certain other suppliers are doing equally as well, and the Big Three automakers point to impressive inventory reductions in the past few years. Some of their suppliers, however, are simply warehousing products for them, not building to a full-fledged JIT production schedule.

The CIM Pill

Computer-Integrated Manufacturing (CIM) has been a buzzword in the manufacturing industry for some years, although an exact definition of the term has never really been formalized. Most define CIM as an integrated, highly automated factory controlled by a Computer-Aided Design/Computer-Aided Manufacturing (CAD/CAM) system. In a CIM system, all production planning and scheduling, as well as accounting, shipping, and factory-floor operations, would access the same database that design, engineering, and management uses.

CIM represents what people usually mean when they talk about the factory of the future. It could incorporate flexible manufacturing systems (FMS) or other automation technology. However, the ideal behind CIM is to get the entire management/manufacturing enterprise on the same wavelength, speaking the same language, and reacting quickly when action is needed. CIM allows a company to make tactical product and marketing changes with lightning speed. It also brings about tremendous gains in manufacturing and management efficiencies. Some visionaries see CIM integrating entire multinational corporations, wherein the CIM system would enable a manufacturer to design a component at any one of its worldwide operations, and instantly ensure that the components will work with other components made at other facilities, thus lowering manufacturing complexity and increasing volume-generated profits.

To date, few U.S. companies are using real CIM technology. The reason? For one, it's very expensive to implement (more on this in Chapter 11). But even among companies that have tried, pulling off a successful CIM implementation has been a frustratingly rare occurrence.

Once again, the problem can be traced to management's naivete in regard to the real cultural changes the company must undertake to realize CIM.

In reality, CIM is the exact opposite of what a technology pill represents. CIM is a long-range, strategic plan of action, and it requires vigilance on management's part to refrain from chasing quarterly profits and short-term return on investments. Perhaps most importantly, the free flow of ideas and information must drench the entire factory or company, which is a philosophy typically at odds with the entrenched, departmentalized cultures many U.S. companies operate within.

Japanese companies, while at a disadvantage to U.S. manufacturers in terms of software, are making advances in CIM implementation, even to the point of adding artificial intelligence to create "smart," flexible automation.

Two notable exceptions to the currently stalled CIM situation in the United States have occurred in the agricultural-equipment market. Deere and Co. and Tenneco's Case IH subsidiary were faced with "do or die" situations, in which they had to become more competitive or lose market share, and maybe even lose their businesses. The willingness and courage to change management approaches was found at these two companies, and their managements have continued to keenly focus on long-range implementation.[5]*

---

*GM, Ford, and Chrysler all have active programs for the implementation of company-wide CIM systems, and in early 1988, all three were selecting hardware and software vendors for CAD/CAM equipment.[6]

The Pill-less Society

During a visit to Japan in 1984, a journalist colleague was surprised to find 20-year-old American-made machinery in Toyota's—and probably the world's—most efficient engine plant. While touring the Toyota Kamigo #9 engine plant, he asked why Toyota used ancient American machinery and was told that when the plant was built, it was the best machinery in the world—another example of the technology pill's transferability.

On touring the plant, he soon discovered that the machinery was working more efficiently than much more modern machinery operating in American engine plants. The plant produced 250,000 four-cylinder engines a year and employed only 180 men working two shifts. The Kamigo plant produced engines just 30 minutes ahead of scheduled installation in cars on the final assembly line. He later discovered that Toyota, without using scads of high technology, was outproducing two comparable but more modern Big Three four-cylinder operations by almost six to one. Additionally, he learned that fully 99.5% of the finished engines were produced without the need for repairs at the end of the line.[7]

This is the point that baffles most American managers—how can a company achieve such incredible productivity while simultaneously achieving such seemingly impossible quality levels? You can't just go out and buy what Toyota has accomplished at Kamigo—it's not in the machinery. The quality and productivity advantages are generated almost entirely by management practices.

The Japanese are also in a better position to use high technology—and are very rapidly beginning to do so. Why? Because they're not looking for high technology to solve problems—they're using it solely to enhance productivity.

Notes

1. The speaker is Max Jurosek, Ford VP of North American Car Product Development. See Joseph Callahan, "Ford Bets on Pragmatic Production," *Automotive Industries*, April 1987, p. 58.

2. "American Blue Collars Get Down to Business," *US News & World Report*, Feb. 1988, p. 52, a slightly biased but readable article on the resurgence of U.S. industrial productivity.

3. John McElroy, "The Best Damn Die Change Team in America," *AI*, Nov. 1987, p. 32.

4. Callahan, "Chrysler Takes Aim at Stat Control," *AI*, April 1982, p. 8.

5. William Kalb, "Automation's Myth," *AI*, Dec. 1987, p. 12.

6. "Making Way for CIM," *AI*, Dec. 1987, p. 12.

7. McElroy, "Inside Japan," *AI* reprint of collected articles, May 1985, p. 20.

3

The High Cost of Low Quality

Until recently, American industry was unable to recognize that cost and quality aren't mutually exclusive goals, but are linked at the most fundamental level. Much of American industry, in fact, still can't see this link. A Gallup survey commissioned by the American Society for Quality Control that explored the quality-related attitudes, experiences, and practices of top American management reported the following: 70% of the executives put the cost of poor quality at 10% or less of gross sales (experts put it at 25% or more) and 16% didn't know the costs associated with producing quality. The executives also picked "increase employee motivation" two to one over "improvements in quality" as the best way to cut costs and overwhelmingly cited customer complaints as drivers of quality improvement.

Confusion about quality isn't unusual. In fact, quality has become something of a dead word in American usage. Few people can agree on what it actually means, beyond the dramatic but hazy slogans companies are painting on their marketing battle crests these days.

Try skimming through corporate advertisements in automotive trade journals from some 30 years ago. You'll rarely find the word quality in ad copy. Back then, the "hot buttons" were increased productivity, lower cost, new ideas and new techniques—all designed to help companies make larger profits. Few advertisers bothered mentioning their commitment to quality.

By the early 1970s, however, quality began to show up more and more often in ads of companies that had touted cost or productivity above all else. Today, quality is one of the nouns an advertising copywriter just can't do without when hyping a company's capabilities.

To paraphrase one automaker's slogan, quality is one job a company can't ignore. But what is quality really? For many companies, it's merely window dressing, a designer word that labels the company "up to date" and "in touch" with the marketplace. It sounds great in a speech given by the president, but it's not really tied to anything that matters in the business world. What matters to managers is cost, cost, cost—and the lower the better.

Besides that, quality is a difficult word to understand. Ask a nontechnical person how he defines quality and he'll probably mention a shirt that fits well or a car that starts every morning. Press him further and he'll probably mumble something to the effect that "you get what you pay for."

That's the phrase that leads to trouble—you get what you pay for. You're talking cost now, and, unfortunately, that phrase probably marks the widest gap between the traditional Western concept of quality and the Japanese definition of the word.

Instead of saying you get what you pay for, try thinking

about quality in these terms: Paying for quality is something only a very rich nation can afford to do.

Japan couldn't pay for quality in the years following World War II, so it shipped low-cost, low-quality products. Japan shipped junk for years, until it discovered the unseen link between low cost and high quality. The United States, on the other hand, had those wonderful margins that allowed a company to weed out substandard products at the end of the assembly line, before they were shipped to the customer. Productivity was king in America, and generating ever-increasing volumes of products was the key to success. Why? Because American managers never wanted to stop the line to fix a problem. Such an act could effectively end a career. It was thought better to overproduce and "inspect out" defective products before shipment than to stop the line, which could cost literally thousands of dollars an hour in labor and capital expense.

Not stopping the line generated costs in other areas, however: employing cadres of inspectors, warehousing inventories "just in case" something went wrong, and throwing away or reworking poor products. These costs all impact a manufacturer's productivity in negative ways: More people are needed per output, and more gross output is needed to reach target net productivity. This is one reason why Japanese automakers can outproduce their American counterparts so dramatically. It's all driven by quality, which, in turn, is driven by cost.

Japan, a starving nation compared to the United States in the 1950s, couldn't afford the luxury of sorting out junk. It had to make every washer, every casting, every drill bit count. The U.S. didn't, and because of this, the U.S. concept of quality got mixed up with salesmanship and high cost.

In a country with the seemingly limitless wherewithal

of the United States, high-quality/high-cost manufacturing was inconvenient but survivable. It was survivable, of course, because, as noted in Chapter 1, America was a market unto itself, with no significant offshore competition. We sometimes even touted the high cost of quality as something desirable.

In 1970, a division of a large U.S. automaker was besieged by warranty claims. The division's manufacturing quality was abysmal. The solution the division's executives came up with could be considered a benchmark in wrongheadedness concerning quality.

The division built a brand-new, 45,000-square-foot facility next to its manufacturing plant and hired two 60-person shifts of workers. Their job? Unbelievable as it may seem, their job was to *reinspect* every car the division built! When cars emerged from final assembly, they were routed through the redundant inspection facility and subjected to a mechanical, electrical, and visual recheck.

Quipped a spokesman at the time, "As a result of this further inspection program, we feel that our cars are reaching our dealers with the highest degree of built-in quality in the industry." Built-in quality (a trendy buzzword) it wasn't—rather, a tacked-on quality bandage.

The division's program was in reality an unwitting admission that its manufacturing processes were out of control. The division spent thousands of dollars on a program that could, at best, discover only superficial quality problems. There's no way, for example, to fix major defects like poor frame welds or bad paint application at this point without literally tearing cars apart piece by piece.

The division was attempting to solve quality problems *after the fact* by inspecting them out of the product. By this time, in contrast, the Japanese had learned that the cheapest way to solve quality problems was to eliminate them at the source. In other words, *quality begins in product and process design.*

How could such systems as the one described above evolve? One reason was those built-in margins automakers relied on to ensure a continual flow of products, no matter how many defects were being discovered. In essence, American automakers were being crippled by their ample budgets. Budgets tend to become self-fulfilling devices: If a manager is given a budget to improve quality, and he's able to perform that task using only half of that budget, will he gleefully show his boss the great savings he's been able to achieve? Many times, yes.

But many other times, the manager will believe that if he uses only half his budget this year, next year's budget for that particular program will be cut. He'll also be called upon to explain to his boss why he overbudgeted for the program in the first place. Because of this, the manager ultimately loses track of the real cost of doing business, focusing instead on using up his budget.

Quality Nightmares

The high cost of low quality adds up in a lot of different ways, and can turn into a manager's nastiest nightmare. First, you're constantly checking parts and components received from suppliers, because they've been known to ship batches of defective parts—in other words, you don't trust them. Even though you check for defects, a certain percentage always seems to sneak through into your system. So you stockpile large inventories of the supplied product, just in case a batch or two aren't up to specification.

After you've manufactured your products, you inspect

them, and scrap or send back to rework all of those that, sure enough, aren't up to specification. Because inspectors aren't 100% efficient, and because you can't check *every* product—unless you're really serious about spending money—defective products slip through and make it to the market, where they fail, causing much grumbling among customers and high warranty or replacement costs for you.

While all this is going on, you're spending money to maintain holding inventories, rework defective products that can be fixed, employ inspectors, and, finally, fulfill warranties. Additionally, you're losing money because of scrap. On top of that morass, consider what the above-mentioned automotive division had done: *It added a completely new inspection process to reinspect everything that had already been inspected!* The company was actually performing a 200% inspection on each car it shipped.

Our "Quality Costs" Mentality

Deep down inside, it's possible that most American managers think their quality programs can't be any good unless they hurt—in the pocketbook. Some companies have been known to "fix" quality programs in unusual ways.

The following story about one large American company's quality-assurance program illustrates just how much salesmanship can be involved in our concept of quality.

A young man (who told the story) was hired by a large American automotive-supplier company as a quality-assurance specialist. His first day on the job, so he says, he was introduced to several key people in the office who had been told to give him a handful of baseball tickets and $200, because they had a quality problem at one of their customers' plants. After handing out the tickets and buying lunches for key people, our friend had "solved" the plant's quality problem.

"I worked there for a year and I must have gained ten pounds," he says in retrospect. Eventually, though, he remembers, the customers would say, "We like the baseball tickets and everything, but we've got to solve this problem." And all sorts of unpleasantness would erupt.

Upper management was out to lunch, literally and figuratively, at this company. In the final summing up, this company's "quality-assurance" program only added more cost to the company's balance sheet without affecting real quality levels at all.

Another problem with the "quality costs" mentality is that during inevitable downturns in the market, "nonessential" programs such as advertising and quality control are usually the first to feel the axe.

Quality's Theory of Relativity

The confusing thing about quality is that it tends to be relative. High quality has traditionally been called high quality because, well, because no one has yet developed anything better for the price.

American automakers noticed a worrisome blip in the market in 1971. That year, Japan almost doubled its passenger-car imports to the United States, shipping 703,672 vehicles. It was the first time Japan had sent more than half a million vehicles stateside, and executives at the four domestic auto companies began to take notice. This was two years before the 1973 oil crisis, meaning sales of small Japanese cars weren't yet increasing because of higher fuel prices.

In 1972, still a year before that first oil crisis, Japan passed Germany for the first time as the nation that sent the largest share of auto imports to the United States. By offering lower prices and higher quality, Japan had become a force to be reckoned with in the U.S. market.

By the mid-to-late 1970s, a large number of American consumers began to notice the higher level of quality introduced by Japanese automakers. The amazing thing about this higher quality was that it was being produced at the bottom of the market. In expensive luxury cars, quality is usually excellent: It's ensured by exhaustive checking and rechecking of every important panel fit, hood alignment, and so forth. Cars are practically inspected to perfection. The idea of a cheap car that featured uniform fit in the various external panels and trim, with an interior that didn't have attendant rattles or ill-fitting pieces and—from certain Japanese automakers at least—a car that was incredibly reliable, was something else entirely. It was recognized as a higher order of quality: inexpensive quality.

At the same time, the first studies began to surface that the Japanese enjoyed a significant cost advantage over their American rivals that couldn't be attributed to currency rates alone. In 1980, Harbour and Associates, Inc., a Michigan-based consulting firm, released a report to the U.S. Department of Transportation that compared Japanese and American automakers' manufacturing efficiencies. The report stood the domestic automotive industry on its ear.[1]

The Japanese, said Harbour and Associates, were producing comparable subcompact and compact cars in 68% of the time it took an American automaker. Furthermore, the firm stated, the Japanese enjoyed a $1,300 advantage per car over American manufacturers. This estimate had grown to more than $1,600 by 1982, by Harbour and Associates' own accounting. Two years later, American automakers were claiming that the Japanese held a more than $2,000 advantage. (Much of this increase was attributed to the weakness of the yen in relationship to the dollar.)

American automakers began to realize that the Japanese had pulled off a manufacturing miracle. It seemed that they had found a way to knot high quality and low cost with ever-increasing productivity—an unbelievable achievement. Many American manufacturers refused to believe it for years, crediting the Japanese advantage to cheaper labor rates, a homogeneous labor force, and currency differences. Some of the explanations were truly ludicrous. One executive told a journalist that the Japanese were better at building tiny cars and components because they had smaller hands!

Some in the industry, however, did take notice—and quickly. To find out how the Japanese could produce cars so effectively and efficiently, U.S. automakers began buying Japanese vehicles and pulling them apart, looking for advances in technology. While they noted the precision with which many of the cars were built, they couldn't find many clues as to how this was accomplished—there were no laser welds, no special materials, no major breakthroughs in power-train technology. They did notice certain design features: The Japanese, for example, used only two or three pieces in a fender design—American engineers would use six or seven—without sacrificing structural integrity. When such points were made to management, responses typically were negative: One top American automaker executive allegedly told his engineers, "Nobody's going to tell this company how to build cars!"

American hubris concerning its abilities was high in the 1960s and early 1970s, especially in the automotive industry. Opposition to and abhorrence of adopting anything not invented in the United States remained a stumbling block until the early 1980s, when even the staunchest "not-invented-here" supporters had to recognize the gap separating Japanese and American quality and productivity. American car companies were able to buy shares in several Japanese auto companies in the early 1970s as the result of a restructuring in Japanese industry. General Motors Corp. tied up with Suzuki and Isuzu, Chrysler Corp. with Mitsubishi, and Ford Motor Co. with Mazda. Because of these liaisons, representatives of the Big Three could closely inspect Japanese techniques.

Once again, they were disappointed: U.S. companies were using more high technology than the Japanese. Many American observers were amazed to see a large percentage of U.S.-built machinery in the plants, including the older stamping presses and machine tools mentioned in Chapter 2. These 20-year-old stamping presses were significantly outperforming modern U.S.-built presses used by U.S. manufacturers, and they required fewer operators to boot. Ultimately, American observers had less than the desired result in locating the technological advances American executives were looking for. Americans weren't taking a comprehensive view of Japanese quality and productivity, and were often sidetracked by the most obvious differences between U.S. and Japanese organizations.

One reason U.S. companies never got a comprehensive view is that they never really looked for one. They would send experts on separate trips to tour separate facilities (stamping, machining, etc.), but they never tied it all together—they never figured out that quick die-change times on stamping presses were necessary to achieve Just-in-Time (JIT) production, that high inventories had an adverse effect on quality. Americans typically came back with a variety of different explanations for Japan's high-quality, low-cost capabilities. These ranged from widespread use of quality circles to lower labor rates to going back to basics. The most basic Japanese quality-control tools were embraced in the United States, including quality circles and Statistical Process Control (SPC). The more sophisticated techniques such as JIT production were acknowledged but initially deemed unusable in America.

Control, SPC-Style

Uniform quality is an American idea, although we don't acknowledge it as one anymore. Walter A. Shewhart designed a method for statistically tracking normal and abnormal variation in manufacturing processes back in the 1920s. Shewhart developed his methodology, which became known as Statistical Quality Control (SQC) or SPC, while working at AT&T Bell Laboratories. He subsequently published a book on the subject, which became the bible for quality-control managers at Western Electric.

In its most basic form, Shewhart's method was a chart that allowed a supervisor or machine operator to track a machine's performance by measuring critical dimensions of samples of parts being made and then plotting average measurements of the samples, thus providing a visual history of both normal and accidental variation. SPC made it possible to gauge a machine's standard deviation—a measure of how close to the target value the majority of parts were being produced.

The Japanese embraced SPC and other statistical methods in the early 1950s, due in large part to a series of lectures given in Japan by an American statistician, W. Edwards Deming. (Shewhart's and Deming's contributions to Japanese productivity are more fully covered in Chapter 5.)

The methodology and the discipline behind SPC allowed Japanese manufacturers to bring their machines and processes into control, which significantly improved quality at first. Quality went up and scrap went down, mainly because machines and processes began turning out products that were closer to target specifications on a consistent basis. This was no small feat in itself, as any manufacturing manager can tell you.

Japanese manufacturers have long since progressed beyond the notion that SPC affects quality improvement after a process is brought under control. Rather, they recognize the need for quality tools that go beyond SPC. Today, Japanese manufacturers see SPC as a first step in quality control. In many Japanese plants, very few SPC charts are seen except where a new line or process is starting up. The reason for this, aside from the use of the Taguchi system of on-line quality control (discussed in Appendix D), is that the products made by most processes are extremely uniform around target values. It's only when a new product line is begun or when new tooling is installed that SPC techniques are necessary to bring the process under control.

Why? Because SPC is expensive to implement and maintain. Instead, the Japanese looked to product and process design and more cost-effective ways to prevent defects. Toyota Motor Corp., for example, uses almost no SPC. Instead, the company uses what it calls *autonomation*—automatic measuring devices built into the line to automatically gauge 100% of critical part tolerances and stop the line if parts aren't within specification. While there's no doubt that Toyota's system is cost- and quality-effective, some observers in Japan still question the need for and wisdom of 100% inspection since it wears out measuring gauges so quickly. The difference between Toyota's 100% inspection system and systems used at U.S. companies, however, is profound: Inspection takes place automatically, without human assistance.

SPC Adopted, Taguchi Discovered

As American automotive companies and their suppliers embraced SPC in the early 1980s, the success stories seemed almost endless. Costs went down and quality went up dramatically. The need to inspect, inspect, inspect at the end of the line dropped. The scrap that results when end-of-the-line inspection is the sole method of quality control also dropped significantly. The reason results were so dramatic is fairly obvious—most manufacturing processes were out of control at this point, so merely imposing a watchdog device such as SPC generated improved uniformity.

There are a number of shortcomings to the SPC-only approach. First, SPC can't improve product-design quality. Manufacturers often talk of the need to have product designs that can be built "perfectly." A product has to be consistently buildable within the context of its process. If it's not, if the machinery can't hold the required tolerances because the product wasn't correctly designed, no amount of SPC will improve the target nominal quality. Problems like this may occur when substituting cheaper or lighter materials on an old design without compensating for the effects the new materials will have on the product's process, or when upgrading process equipment and not taking into account the effect this will have on the design. And, as many engineers will tell you, there are lots of old product designs floating around that were bad from the start.

In reality, SPC doesn't improve quality—it simply puts a process in control. SPC helps achieve and maintain designed quality levels by indicating where you need to improve the control of your processes. If it does improve quality, your processes were out of control in the first place. SPC can be used to reduce output variability, and it can indirectly show where a design should be improved. It cannot, however, improve quality beyond that point.

SPC is a first step in what appears to be a never-ending effort to achieve perfect quality. Concurrent with their adoption of SPC, Americans became aware of one of Japan's best-kept and most powerful high-quality/low-cost secrets. The Japanese had been using Dr. Genichi Taguchi's Quality Engineering methodology, known as Taguchi Methods in the United States, for more than 30 years. Taguchi Methods are a combination of engineering and statistical methods that achieve rapid improvements in costs and quality by optimizing product design and manufacturing processes. They result in products with minimal variation around target values. Taguchi Methods are based on two tools, the Signal-to-Noise (S/N) Ratio and the Quality Loss Function (explained in Chapter 4 and Appendices B and C). The Japanese use Taguchi Methods to produce high-quality/low-cost products that are insensitive to variability-causing factors found on the factory floor and in the field. This contrasts with the American convention of producing products within specification limits.

The "In-Spec" Dilemma

Quality, according to the traditional American manufacturing interpretation, is an inexact thing. Let's say you're making axle shafts. Your engineers come up with two specification limits, one upper and one lower, for a critical seal fit. If you're making axle shafts that fall within those specification limits, all of your axles are thought to be of equally good quality. This is what's known as conformance to specification (see **Figure 3-1**). Theoretically, if you're conforming to specification, you're building perfect axles, each and every one. Conformance to specification has been characterized as a "go/no go" or "pass/fail" type of control: If the part is in specification, it's a "go" or good part; if it doesn't fall within specification limits, it's a "no go" or defective part. When all your axles are "in spec," you have zero defects, and all is right with the world. But is it really? Let's take a look at a nontechnical example that illustrates why this isn't so.

Suppose there are two quarterbacks vying for a position on the same team. The coach, a hopeless technocrat, has plotted the accuracy of the two quarterbacks' passes to the team's star receiver. Both quarterbacks are usually able to place the ball within the receiver's catching range, as shown in **Figures 3-2** and **3-3**—both quarterbacks are conforming to specification. In examining the charts, the coach notices that the quarterback named Burt places the ball within the receiver's reach each and every time, but tends to vary widely in how close he gets the ball to the receiver's hands. The quarterback named Bubba, on the other hand, throws a few passes outside the receiver's reach, but otherwise all his passes drop right in the receiver's hands.

Based on experience, the coach realizes that there's another factor to take into account—the receiver's balance after he catches the ball. If the ball lands toward the outer limits of his reach, he'll be more off-balance and likely to fall, fumble the ball, or be intercepted. Which quarterback

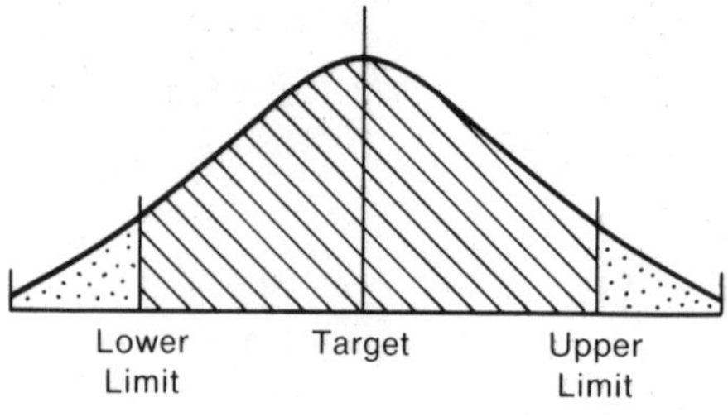

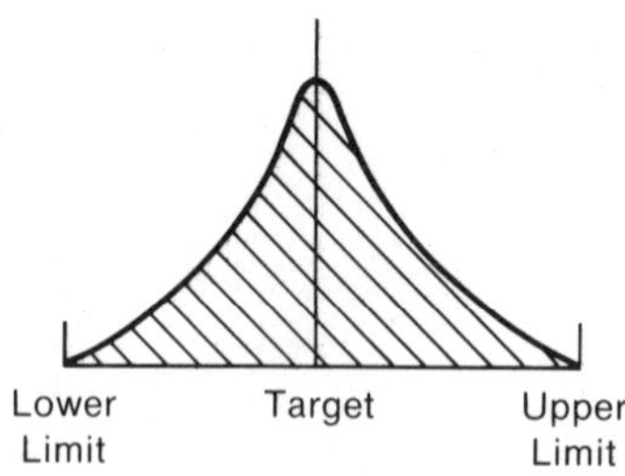

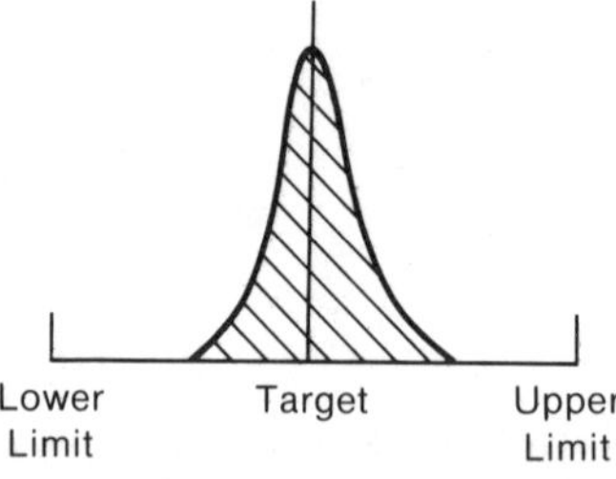

Figure 3-1. Under conformance to specification, the products represented by the striped area in the top illustration would be considered equally good, while the products represented by the dotted area outside of the tolerance limits would be considered defectives. The products measured in the middle illustration would all be considered good products, because there are no products falling outside the tolerance limits. The bottom illustration, however, follows the philosophy of uniformity at the target value. These products will consistently be of higher quality than the average products from the top and bottom illustrations.

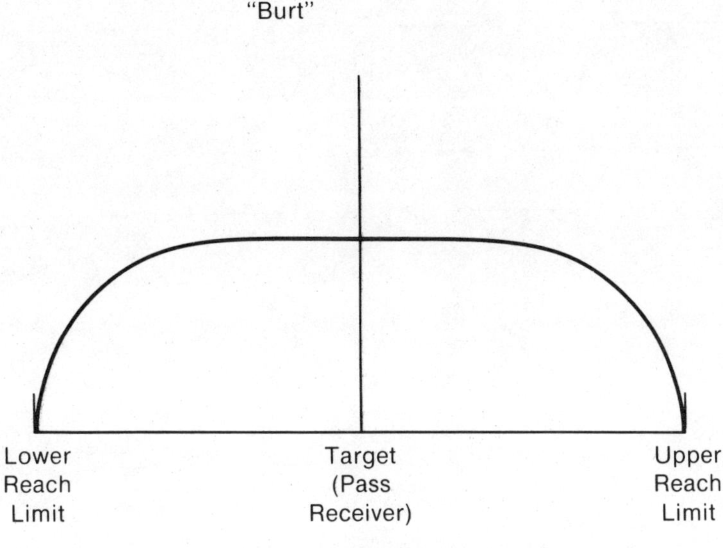

Figure 3-2. Although both Burt and Bubba (see Figure 3-3) are conforming to specification, Burt places the ball within the receiver's reach limit each and every time, but tends to vary widely in how close he gets the ball to the receiver's hands.

do you think should get the job? The coach chose Bubba. His delivery was much more consistent and uniform than Burt's, even though his passes occasionally fell outside the receiver's reach limits. The receiver stayed in balance much more often when Bubba was throwing, so his chances of falling, fumbling, or having the ball intercepted were reduced.

Now, let's substitute axle shafts for quarterbacks' passes. The axles grouped around the chart's center, the "receiver's hands," will be much closer to the target than those at the chart's edges. Why is this uniformity so impor-

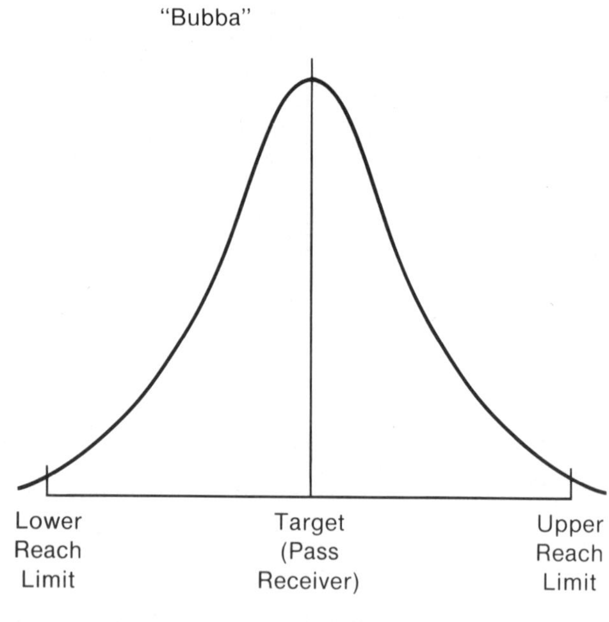

Figure 3-3. Unlike Burt (see Figure 3-2), Bubba throws a few passes outside the receiver's reach limit, but otherwise all his passes drop right in the receiver's hands. His delivery is much more consistent than Burt's —he is uniformly closer to the target.

tant, if you're within specification limits, anyway? As we noticed with the two quarterbacks, the more uniform your axles (or passes) are, the more balanced or controllable the next event or process on the assembly line (or football field) will be.

Suppose all your axle shafts conform to specification, but they are grouped around the specification's lower limit —your axle shafts are consistently thinner in diameter than what would be considered target. The oil-seal manufacturer also builds parts that conform to specification, but they tend to conform on the high side, consistently wider in diameter than target. Notice that everybody's still in the ball game as far as conformance to specification goes. The problem begins when the final assembler fits the wide-diameter seals on the narrow-diameter axle shafts. The possibility of leaks occurring in the field is much higher, because the seals have a looser-than-target fit on the shaft. This is what's known as tolerance stackup.

Tolerance Stackup Affects Quality

Tolerance stackup may not be a critical reliability problem when only two variables—the axle shaft and the seal—are involved; nonetheless, it's what produces variability in final product quality.

Tolerance stackup is the reason one car's transmission shifts so smoothly, while that of the next works like a stick twirling in a bucket of bolts. In areas where many critical tolerances meet, tolerance stackup can be disastrous. Door-closing effort is a famous example of the way tolerance stackup can affect a customer's perception of product quality (see **Figure 3-4**). An automobile door closes over a virtual crossroads of tolerances. The complexity of this stackup is so great that, even if all door-system components are assembled within specification but not to target, it's sometimes impossible to build a door system that meets all closing effort and weather-sealing specifications. Typically, doors on American cars require a greater effort to close than doors on a car built by Honda Motor Co. or Toyota because of tolerance stackup.

Customers apparently want a door that closes at a certain number of lbs. of pressure because it "feels" right to close the door at that level of force. When American engineers pulled apart Hondas and Toyotas to see how the cars

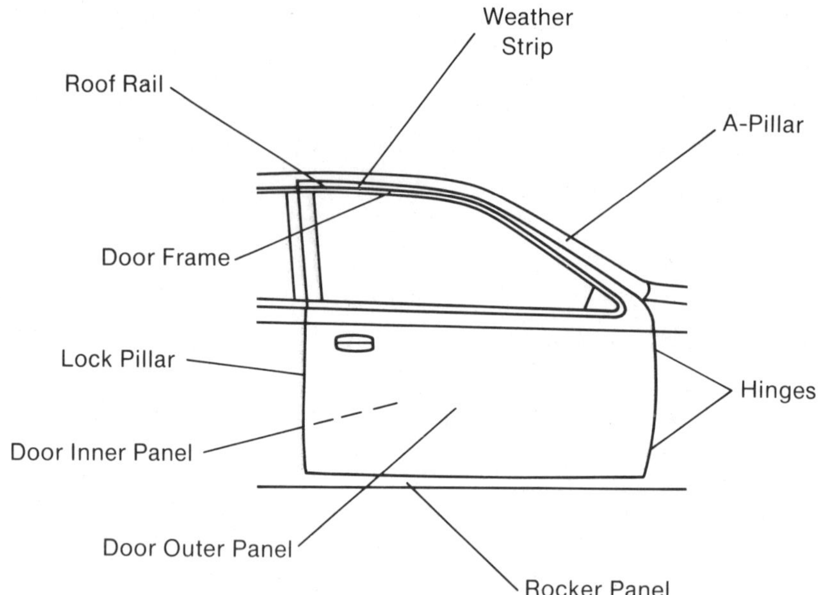

Figure 3-4. Even if parts are produced within specification limits, variation can produce tolerance stackup, which requires companies to rework parts to achieve proper fit. Door-closing effort is a famous example of tolerance stackup. Even if all door system components are assembled within specification but not to target, it's sometimes impossible to build a door system that meets all closing-effort and weather-sealing specifications.

were built, they discovered that, virtually without fail, doors on these cars closed at or around that ideal pressure, about 8 lbs. of force. The typical closing pressure for an American car was higher, about 12-16 lbs. of force, or would vary from car to car.

Why? Because all of the tolerances that meet at the door wouldn't be at or near the target, but would instead range from the specification limits' high to low ends. The result is a door that closes too lightly and thus doesn't have a watertight fit, or a door that has to be slammed shut. On just about every domestic automobile assembly line, there are door-fit "specialists" who shim hinges and seals or bend metal or make sure the recently attached doors have a watertight and nonbinding fit. As a rule, Toyota and Honda don't have door-fit repair personnel on their assembly lines.[2]

A well-known case pitting conformance to specification against target specification involved Ford and Mazda Motor Corp. (then known as Toyo Koygo) several years ago. Ford owns about 25% of Mazda and asked the Japanese company to build transmissions for a car Ford was selling in the United States. Ford was building identical transmissions for the same car at a U.S. plant. Both Ford and Mazda were supposed to build the transmissions to identical specifications. Ford, however, was using conformance to specification as its quality standard, while Mazda was building every transmission as close to the target as it possibly could.

After the transmissions had been on the road for awhile, it became apparent that the Ford-built transmissions were generating far higher warranty costs and customer complaints about noise than the Mazda gearboxes. So, Ford disassembled and measured samples of transmissions made by both companies. At first, the company thought its gauges were malfunctioning—it couldn't find any variability from transmission to transmission among the Mazda gearboxes. Then Ford discovered that instead of using the go/no go conformance to specification approach, Mazda had consistently built its transmissions to the target.

Ford also made another discovery—by working to continuously reduce variability around targets, Mazda incurred lower production costs. Ford, on the other hand, was paying for inspection, scrap, rework, and ultimately, warranty costs. Ford has since begun a very successful policy of continuous improvement around target values as its company-wide goal, and in recent years this goal has even spread to Ford's suppliers.

American racing-engine builders have always considered uniformity around the target a higher level of quality than simply being within specification limits. The whole notion of the desirability of a "blueprinted" engine supports this claim. An engine builder will meticulously measure every critical dimension of an engine—bearing clearance, piston fit, and so forth—and remove those parts that aren't at the target. The builder then substitutes parts that are built exactly to the target and rebuilds the engine. Why? To ensure optimum performance and reliability—that's quality, isn't it? Yes, that's quality, but that's expensive quality—inspecting every part and effectively scrapping those that don't measure up.

To a lesser degree, this inspection method is the way American companies have traditionally ensured quality, because they haven't attached a cost to quality. The Japanese quality surge was keyed to cost reduction, and thus the two terms became interchangeable. This interchangeability is the reason the Japanese are fanatical about quality: not because they care more about their customers than American manufacturers do, but because they care more about cutting costs. This idea is the driving force behind the concept of uniformity around the target.

The On-Target Key

Uniformity in and of itself isn't the entire answer to having the same quality level from the first part you produce to the 10 millionth. The tolerances of those 10 million products must be grouped close to the target to fulfill the designer's intent, which must be based on customer requirements.

There's a famous case in Japan regarding vinyl sheeting that supports this claim. If you tour the Japanese countryside, you'll see neat rows of vinyl sheeting positioned umbrella-like over certain easily damaged crops. They're a low-cost type of greenhouse. The vinyl is used by farmers to protect crops from the elements, thus extending the growing season. Typically, the thickness of the vinyl sheeting is, say, 1.0 mm, and acceptable tolerance limits for the thickness are +/− 0.2 mm. In other words, sheet that ranges in thickness from 0.8 mm (1.0 − 0.2 mm) to 1.2 mm (1.0 + 0.2 mm) is considered acceptable for use by farmers, according to the Japanese Vinyl Sheet Manufacturing Association.

One vinyl-sheet manufacturer, through a series of quality improvement efforts, was able to reduce the variation in its processes to a remarkable degree. This manufacturer could hold tolerances not of +/− 0.2 mm, but of +/− 0.02 mm—quite an achievement.

This new ability to create vinyl sheeting of extremely uniform thickness got the company managers thinking along these lines: If the company could make all its sheeting on the target specification's thin side, say 0.82 mm +/− 0.02 mm, it could save a considerable amount of money by using less material per square meter of vinyl sheeting, and it would still be within the association's tolerance limits. Once in the field, however, the uniformly thin sheet vinyl tore easily, and farmers had to constantly repair or replace it. Sheeting that had a manufactured thickness that was uniform around the target thickness of 1.0 mm was thick enough by design to withstand the elements.

Because of the increased number of complaints from

the field, the association specified that the average thickness of the sheet must be 1.0 mm and that thickness variation could range from +/− 0.2 mm.

As you can see, the company's sheeting was incredibly uniform in thickness. The technology that made that uniformity possible, however, wasn't used to gain a quality-driven market advantage. Such an advantage—a sales point—would be increased toughness due to fewer thin areas in the sheeting, and a resulting gain in reputation among consumers as a maker of durable vinyl. Instead, the company used its technology to uniformly reduce the quality of the sheeting, with subsequent unfortunate results for crops, farmers, and ultimately, consumers.[3]

Notes

1. Harbour and Associates, Inc., "Comparison of Japanese Car Assembly Plant Located in Japan and U.S. Car Assembly Plant Located in the U.S.," 1980 report prepared for the U.S. Department of Transportation. Also see Alan Altshuler et al, *The Future of the Automobile,* 1984, p. 161.
2. L. P. Sullivan, "Reducing Variation: A New Approach to Quality," *Quality Progress,* July 1984, p. 15.
3. Genichi Taguchi and Yuin Wu, *Introduction to Off-Line Quality Control,* 1979, p. 7.

4

Taguchi Methods

Just who suffers when product quality isn't what it should be? By reducing the average thickness of its vinyl sheeting, the manufacturer in Chapter 3 saved money. This action, however, resulted in several losses. When the sheeting tore, farmers would have to run from field to field repairing or replacing it, thus losing time and money. In situations where farmers couldn't repair or replace the sheeting, crops were destroyed. In both cases, the thin vinyl meant higher-cost produce for consumers. Farmers spent time and money when they could have been productive elsewhere, and their overhead expenses went up. Because crops perished, farmers had less to take to market. In some areas, this resulted in food shortages that drove consumer prices up. The vinyl manufacturer also suffered a loss in goodwill. Consequently, fewer stores were willing to purchase its sheeting, which resulted in loss of market share and lower profits.

In this case, no one—not even the vinyl manufacturer—came out a winner. When quality is low, somebody always loses. And the lower the quality, the higher the loss. For manufacturers, this loss is usually measured in warranty costs or returns, but it goes further than that. It can be loss of consumer trust, or loss due to consumer inconvenience when products are returned for refunds.

Sound a bit altruistic? Think back to the last time you bought something, got it home, and discovered that it wouldn't work properly or that all of the pieces weren't in the box. The word "betrayed" probably wouldn't be too strong to describe your feelings at that point. Such moments are easily forgotten by managers, however, when they're standing on the shop floor with production bottlenecks plugging up their entire assembly line.

A Honda Motor Co. executive puts it this way: "If you succeed in reducing manufacturing defects from two in 100 to one in 100, you may be tempted to think you did a good job. But Mr. Honda (founder of Honda Motor Co.) would always remind us that the customer is only buying one product. If the customer gets that one bad product, for that customer 100% of the product will be bad."[1]

A Philosophy of Loss

The concept of tying quality to degrees of loss is an important one. Dr. Genichi Taguchi defines quality in just those terms. Quality, Taguchi says, is the loss a product imposes on society after it's shipped. The philosophy behind that statement is elegantly subtle.

All products ultimately cause loss—they wear out or break and need to be repaired or replaced. The sign of quality is how much service they provide before wearing out or breaking: A high-quality product causes little loss because it fulfills its intended function for a period consumers consider adequate. A low-quality product, on the other hand, causes loss at every turn. The amount of service a product gives before creating loss has to at least equal the consumer's dollar-value expectation. Ideally, it should exceed this expectation.

The only way a manufacturer can ensure this type of quality is by producing products that closely match the original design's blueprint. The manufacturer does so by designing buildable products and then producing them to target values, rather than using specification limits and inspection to sort out defective products (which adds cost). This idea represents a dramatic departure from traditional quality/cost thinking, in which quality and cost are thought to be in conflict (the higher the quality, the higher the cost). Taguchi argues that lower cost is the driving force behind higher quality. Not only that, Taguchi bluntly states that cost is more important than quality. He notes, "American industry is amazed that Japan can produce high-quality products at such low costs; they're not amazed at Japanese quality. If Japanese automobiles cost two times more, most Americans would stop buying them."[2]

The Quality Loss Function

The Quality Loss Function (QLF) allows an engineer to put a dollar value on quality. It provides an evaluation of quality in financial terms—i.e., *quality loss* due to deviation from the target as well as *quality improvement.* It's an excellent tool that can be used to both evaluate loss at the earliest stage of product/process development and incorporate improvements in quality into management planning. It provides a common language understood by both managers and engineers.

Sony's "In-Spec" Problem

In 1979 the Japanese newspaper *Asahi* ran a story comparing two Sony Co. color television plants, one in Japan and the other in San Diego, California. Dr. Genichi Taguchi's Quality Loss Function (QLF) indicated that the U.S. plant was generating losses per unit sold that were $.89 higher than the plant in Japan, even though the American plant, on investigation, was found to be producing every television within specification, while the Japanese plant was not (see **Figure S4-1**).

However, the goal of the American plant was conformance to tolerance limits, while the goal of the Japanese plant was to build every television as close to target value as possible.

It was discovered that the American plant was adjusting TV sets that were out of specification at the end of assembly, thereby nudging them back into conformance. The Japanese plant, on the other hand, did not perform end-of-the-line adjustments, because they added expense. In addition, experience had shown that consumers who bought adjusted TVs were more likely to be unhappy with the color density of their units. A few of the Japanese sets actually fell outside of the target, but, overall, their quality was much more uniform than those produced by the American plant.

Without the QLF, Sony would have had a difficult time assigning costs to the quality levels at the two plants, or even identifying why one plant's quality levels were so much higher than the other's.[3]

The QLF curve is quadratic in nature: Loss increases by the square of the distance from the target value. Thus, if a deviation of 0.02 mm from the target value generates a $.20 loss, then a deviation of 0.04 mm would cost $.80 and a deviation of 0.06 mm, $1.80 and so forth. In other words, if deviation is doubled, the loss is quadrupled. If it's tripled, the loss increases nine times.

Uniformity and Production Quality in
Japan and the U.S.

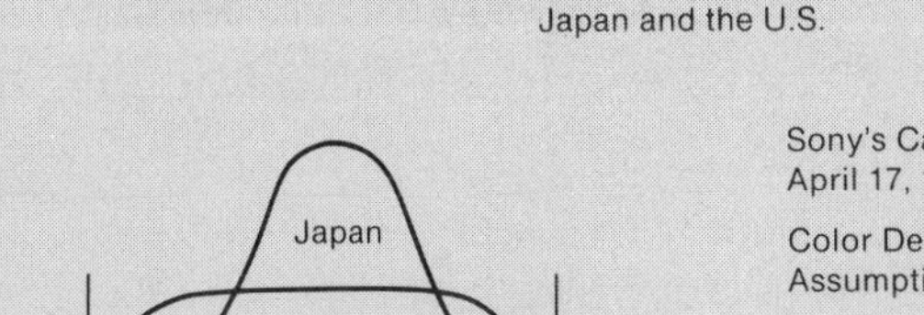

Types of Distribution in the *Asahi*

Sony's Case (Cited from the Asahi, April 17, 1979)

Color Density of TV Set
Assumption: Repairing Cost A = 4 ($)

Loss Function

$$L = \frac{4}{5^2}\sigma^2 = 0.16\sigma^2$$

$$\text{San Diego: } L = 0.16 \times \left(\frac{10}{\sqrt{12}}\right)^2 = 1.33$$

$$\text{Japan: } L = 0.16 \times \left(\frac{10}{6}\right)^2 \doteq 0.44$$

Factory Location	Type of Distribution (approx.)	Percent Out of Spec.	Standard Deviation	Loss per Unit	Difference in Quality
San Diego Japan	Uniform Normal	Almost Nil 0.3%	$\frac{10}{\sqrt{12}}$ $\frac{10}{6}$	L = $1.33 L = $0.44	$ − 0.89

Figure S4-1. The Quality Loss Function indicated that a U.S. Sony Co. TV plant was generating losses per unit sold that were $.89 higher than a Japanese Sony Co. plant. The U.S. plant was producing every TV within specification; the Japanese plant was building every TV as close to the target value as possible. (Source: The *Asahi*, April 17, 1979)

The QLF allows a manufacturer to economically justify a practice that's long been a black art in American engineering: the setting of product tolerances. Traditional tolerancing is done mainly on the basis of engineering experience—after designing a product and assigning targets for all dimensions, the engineer checks the specifications on the last product his company designed and sets his tolerances accordingly. This method of setting tolerances is usually expensive, because the conscientious engineer will typically set tolerances tighter than necessary to reduce the risk of premature failure in the field. Traditionally, tight tolerance limits are more expensive to maintain than looser limits, because they usually require better materials or high-quality manufacturing equipment.

But do these engineering specifications realistically relate to the way customers see quality? Once again, we've come back to the notion of paying for quality. The problem here is that *engineers really have no meaningful system for pinning tolerance limits to real-world requirements.* The only real-world feedback comes when warranty costs skyrocket. When this happens, the engineer then knows that his tolerances weren't correct, but the damage has already been done.

By using the QLF, the engineer can set tolerances according to customer sensitivity to loss. Ideally, the manufacturer should set tolerance limits at the break-even point between the cost to rework a product and the cost of the consumer-absorbed loss.

The following example will explain the point. An automatic transmission is manufactured with a shift pressure of 75 lbs. The engineer knows that the product won't function at a deviation of +/− 40 lbs. from this target. If the shift pressure remains at 75 lbs., the consumer experiences very little loss; if it drops to 35 lbs. or less, or climbs to 115 lbs. or more, the average driver will be dissatisfied enough to demand repair or replacement of the transmission at an average cost of $500. This is an absolute limit of functional performance—many consumers become dissatisfied long before this limit is reached. Obviously, a manufacturer wouldn't set production limits this wide.

This limit of +/− 40 lbs. is called the functional tolerance, or LD-50 (50% of the consumers are unhappy) in Taguchi terminology. It is not a specification limit; rather, it's a functional limit. Taguchi uses this information and the QLF to develop actual production tolerance limits for the product. Loss projections can be developed for any other deviation from the target pressure if the cost of the LD-50 has been established (in this case $500 at +/− 40 lbs.).

Suppose that the manufacturer can rework this transmission at the plant to bring the shift pressure to within limits at a cost of $20. The QLF can be used to discover at what shift pressure the loss to the consumer will be equal to the manufacturer's cost for fixing the transmission at the factory. In this case, the production tolerance happens to be +/− 8 lbs. If the shift pressure is less than 67 lbs. or greater than 83 lbs., the manufacturer should spend $20 to fix the transmission. Otherwise he should not.

Now the engineer has economically justified his specification limits. If the engineer had set his specification limits tighter than +/− 8 lbs., the manufacturer would be spending more money than is justifiable to meet the customer's quality needs. If, on the other hand, the engineer had set the tolerance wider than +/− 8 lbs., the manufacturer would save money in rework costs, but the cost to the consumer would be a great deal more, due to the nature of the QLF's quadratic curve. For this reason, Taguchi says that a manufacturer who betrays his customers in such a fashion is worse than a thief—he's saved $20 but robbed his customers of much more.

In figuring the loss caused by variation, a company can use concrete dollar items such as warranty or scrap costs or include intangibles such as goodwill or customer inconvenience.

Justifying Costs

The QLF, aside from pegging tolerance limits to real-world economics, also helps a manufacturer in another way. The go/no go approach of conformance to specification makes it impossible for a manager to justify spending money to improve a process if that process is already producing parts that conform to specification. The manager can't economically justify spending money to reduce the variability of a process that's conforming to specification because, under his company's definition of quality, every part that conforms to specification is perfect.

On the other hand, the manager whose company is striving for continuous process improvement realizes that while perfect production—e.g., products that are built exactly at the target—is impossible to achieve, the philosophy behind the concept provides benefits long after production quality has reached world-class levels. Why? Because workers and management have a common goal: continuous improvement. The manager at such a company can easily justify the expense if he can show that output isn't uniformly grouped close to the target and is scattered widely across the specification's range.

The concept of conformance to specification was an important first step in bringing a manufacturing operation into control. But, as noted in Chapter 3, quality is relative. So while traditional American companies continue to measure quality performance in terms of defects per 100 products, Japanese companies long ago began thinking in terms of *defects per million products.* The enlightened manager will realize that his competitors have moved their manufacturing performance far beyond conformance to specification, and that he must join them if he wishes to survive and thrive in today's competitive marketplace.

There comes a point of diminishing returns in the quest to build all parts exactly to target specification: Quality eventually becomes so uniformly high that you can't justify spending additional capital to improve it further. Under the concept of continuous improvement, however, workers can continue to strive to improve quality through low-cost methods—by developing foolproof tools, refining parts-bin positionings, and so forth.

The problem many American managers have with the idea of continuous improvement is how to determine when the point of diminished returns is met. In other words, how do you know when to stop spending cash to improve quality? For the answer to that question, we turn once again to the QLF.

As we've seen, the QLF can be used to set tolerance limits for a product. It is an extremely flexible planning tool that assigns cost to any deviation from the target specification. It can also tell a manager when to stop investing in process quality improvement.

Knowing the product or process deviation, and the loss due to scrap and rework and current tolerances, the manufacturer can determine the loss per unit for a given performance level of a process. He can then calculate the loss due to variation annually, and decide whether further expenditures for improvements in quality are justified.

It's important to remember that according to the QLF, loss is quadratic, not linear, depending on how far the product is from the target. Loss increases dramatically the further the product strays from the target specification. This loss can include consumer inconvenience caused by products that must be returned for repair, or it can be rooted in strictly accountable costs such as warranty and rework. The beauty of the QLF is that it can be custom-

(Text continued on p. 80)

Breaking Engineering Conventions—A Hypothetical Case

Traditionally, when an American automotive engineer had a problem with a product or process, he would approach the problem with one goal in mind. If his problem was a process that was producing a high percentage of rejects, his goal was to bring the process back to within its specification limits. If he could return the process to conformance with specification, he would feel satisfied—and believe he had successfully solved the problem.

To accomplish this, he would study the various factors—heat, speed, force, and so forth—that he knew through experience could have an effect on the problem. After identifying these, he would hold all of the factors being considered at their present levels or settings, except for one. This he would change to another likely setting, and then measure the effectiveness of this change.

If the result wasn't enough of an improvement, the engineer would begin again, changing one factor at a time, until he had nudged the process back into reasonable conformance to specification.

Let's say this continued through many half-smoked cigarettes and cups of coffee until, finally, he hit upon the correct settings. It could be tricky, because the effect of a factor might be different when the levels of the other factors are changed. This is what's known as an interaction, and it could throw the process even further out of kilter.

This "one-factor-at-a-time" approach was pure "seat-of-the-pants" engineering. It was how reputations were made, and troubleshooters were born, because a lucky guess could right the process, making a troubleshooting engineer a hero. His merely mortal colleagues would think that his access to higher knowledge—or so it seemed—had allowed him to nudge the process back to within specification.

However, in this case there was a nagging problem. Intelligence from the field indicated a foreign competitor was achieving less variability, higher productivity, and lower costs, using the same machinery the U.S. company was using.

Our engineer/hero would scratch his head in disbelief. How could this be? Our machines are producing within specification limits, he would muse. What else could they be doing?

As it turned out, the "what else" that his competition was doing could be tracked back to the design stage. For the sake of realism, let's use a transmission gear-cutting operation as our example. When the gear was designed, the engineer who designed it usually gave a target value for each critical diameter of the gear—the width, shaft-bore diameter, tooth width, and so forth—and then bracketed that target specification by the limits within which the gear could function. For example, a gear's shaft-bore diameter could be 1.0 inch, +/− 0.005 inch.

In the days when everyone was satisfied if the gears were simply within specification, all hands held an equal number of aces. The gears of competing companies were judged equally as good (really equally as bad), and a certain level of rejects and customer complaints about noisy transmissions and premature gear failure was expected. Nobody really got too excited about it. Quality was as relative as +/− 0.005 inch.

Then a new group of competitors arrived with a startling new concept of low-cost quality, changing the card game forever. This new concept is expressed best in the philosophy behind the work of Dr. Genichi Taguchi.

In the gear example, Taguchi's system focused on reducing the variation of the gear's shaft-bore diameter—and here was the radical part as far as U.S. auto engineers were concerned—*even if the gear's bore diameter was already being produced within specification.*

(*continued*)

In other words, Taguchi said that keeping the diameters within specification was a start, but it wasn't good enough. When you've been given a target, you should try to be as close as possible to that target, not just within a certain distance to it.

This idea seemed ridiculous to the American engineer—he had no economic justification for trying to keep production not just within specification limits, but smack on top of the target. After all, why do they give limits to begin with?

Taguchi, however, did have economic justification. Taguchi's rationale for adhering closely to the target is profoundly simple. So simple, in fact, that no one else ever thought to apply it to industrial mass-production techniques.

The rationale is a set of formulas known individually as the Quality Loss Function (QLF). The QLF proposes that the cost of deviating from the target increases quadratically (by squares) the further you get away from the target.

With the gear bore, for example, each fraction of an inch further away from 1.0 inch caused a quadratically proportional rise in cost. The increases, if plotted, formed a predictable curve, and this was the key to assigning cost. In our example, the target for the gear-shaft diameter was 1.0 inch. If the design engineer did his homework, all gears produced at 1.0 inch would carry a quality-liability cost that is very low, or even nonexistent. They are perfect, in other words. They mate with their shafts perfectly (if the shafts are made perfectly!), they're not noisy, and they don't wear out prematurely due to an excessively tight or loose fit. In other words, they don't cause warranty costs, customer inconvenience, or loss of goodwill for the company.

However, let's say the gear-bore diameters are 1.020 inch—still within specification, but a bit on the loose side. The gears ride loosely on the shafts; they vibrate, causing noise, increasing the possibility of customer complaints, and possibly causing eventual structural fatigue and failure. Granted, if the gear is built within specification, the noise and chance of early failure won't be great, but they will be present, and possibly noticeable to the customer.

According to the QLF, we've just increased the quality liability of the product we are making by an easily trackable amount. If we assign a maximum-loss cost to some point on the quadratic loss-function curve, we can mathematically pinpoint the cost associated with every other point on the curve, and thus arrive at the loss each deviation from the target generates. By basing the cost on something tangible—say, warranty cost to replace the entire transmission—we can follow the quadratic loss-function curve back up to 1.020 inch and assign a cost figure to that amount of deviation.

Thus, the logic behind Taguchi's QLF becomes readily apparent: Every time a product is produced to its target, it reduces the quality liability of the company, the possible costs involved with warranty claims, and the company's future likelihood of lost goodwill. Producing products consistently to their targets isn't fanaticism—it's just good business.

The QLF also allows the engineer to set cost-justified specification tolerances and to figure out how much money he can justify spending to reduce variation in a process or product. Before the QLF, engineers had little but dead reckoning with which to figure either value.

The QLF is the philosophy that underlies Taguchi's goal: If you're given a target, try to hit it every time. The means to that goal is Taguchi's parameter-design system, which incorporates Taguchi's other great contribution, the Signal-to-Noise (S/N) Ratio.

The S/N Ratio is used to project field quality performance from experimental results. It's actually an umbrella name for any of a large group of special equations that can be used during experi-

(*continued*)

mental analysis to find the optimum factor-level settings that will create a robust product or process. The term is taken directly from communications technology. In its communications sense, the S/N Ratio is the ratio of the power of a radio or telephone signal to the power of the background static (noise). In its simplest Taguchi Methods form, the S/N Ratio is the ratio of the mean (signal) to the standard deviation (noise). (The formula used to compute the S/N Ratio depends on the type of quality characteristic, as does the formula for the QLF.) In both Taguchi Methods and communications applications, the higher the ratio, the more robust the product is against noise—which is one of the main goals of parameter design.

Instead of working on "one factor at a time" as the engineer at the beginning of this article did, the engineer using parameter design can unholster an entire arsenal of engineering-modified statistical tools to cost-effectively find that combination of factor settings that offers robust performance under as many tested conditions as possible. The engineer will also call all relevant people in on the problem very early on for brainstorming sessions to identify factors and chart a course of action. This "meeting of the minds" isn't a formal part of what are known as Taguchi Methods: It's just good engineering. Also different is the goal of the engineer using parameter design. He's not just trying to nudge the gear-cutting operation back to within its specification range. Instead, he uses the S/N Ratio to evaluate the combination of factors that produces the lowest variation, and he then manipulates other factors to move the process as close to the target as possible (see **Figure S4-2**).

In our gear-cutting example, the engineer is seeking the combination of factor levels that allows the operation to repeatedly cut gears with as little variation as possible. These factors are called *control factors.* Once he has identified the optimum levels for these variation-reducing factors, he will use certain factors—

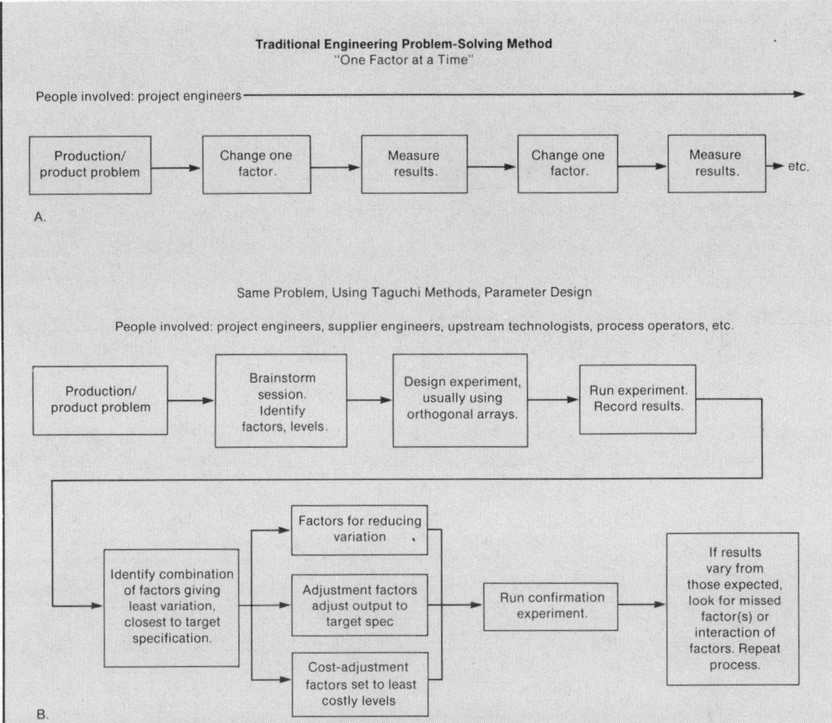

Figure S4-2. A. The goal of this "one-factor-at-a-time" experimentation is to adjust the system so that output consistently falls within specification limits. B. The goal of parameter design experimentation is to adjust the system so that output is consistently grouped tightly at a specific target specification. (Source: *Automotive Industries*)

called *adjustment factors*—to guide the process as close to its target (1.0 inch) as possible.

The beauty of parameter design is that it helps make plain which factors are important in reducing variation (control factors), which factors are important to peg output to the target (adjustment factors), and which factors aren't really that impor-

(*continued*)

tant for either task. *The latter can be set at their most cost-effective levels, thereby reducing cost without compromising quality*. Thus, they're called *cost-adjustment factors.*

The important aspect of Taguchi's philosophy is one that is often lost on American manufacturers. *One doesn't attempt to control every factor involved in a process or in making a product.* Instead, the idea is to tweak those factors that can be cost-effectively tweaked *in an organized, thorough manner* and simply ignore those factors that cannot be cost-effectively controlled.

The typical approach in the United States is to control every aspect of the process—even to the point, for example, of air-conditioning the factory if that is thought to help. This tends to increase costs. Instead, Taguchi says to look to the process or product itself—its makeup and components—and find those factors that have hidden potential in the fight to control variation. Develop those factors that make the process resistant to variation in all forms, and you will develop a superior product from the technology being used.

Parts of this sidebar first appeared in *Automotive Industries,* February 1988, p. 68.

tailored to individual company needs or philosophies. It's an extremely pragmatic, economic solution to assigning cost to variation, and thus to quality, that grew out of the work in experimental design Taguchi began in the early 1950s.

Taguchi's System

Taguchi has developed a systematic off-line quality control methodology through which an engineer with relatively little statistical training can optimize both product and process design. The core of the system is an approach to industrial experimentation that allows an engineer to develop large amounts of usable data quickly and with minimum cost. The methodology is unique in that its primary goal isn't simply to improve quality; rather, it seeks to improve quality while reducing cost. This is accomplished by cost-effectively reducing the performance variation of a product or process so it remains as close to the target value as possible, even in the face of uncontrollable environmental and usage factors. This minimizes consumer dissatisfaction and loss (see **Figure 4-1**).

Taguchi defines the development of a product or process as a three-stage operation: system design, parameter design, and tolerance design (see **Figure 4-2**).

System Design

System design is the primary development stage in which the basic architecture of a product or process is determined. During system design, the design engineer applies his knowledge and experience in his area of specialization to create a product or process with distinct capabilities that will later serve as sales points. The system designer calls upon his expertise in the design of similar systems to generate a new system that's superior in some way to previous designs.

It's estimated that U.S. engineers focus 70% of their efforts on system design (compared to Japanese engineers' 40%), and only 2% on parameter design. Japanese engineers, on the other hand, apply 40% of their efforts to parameter design, the stage where costs can be most efficiently controlled (see **Figure 4-3**).

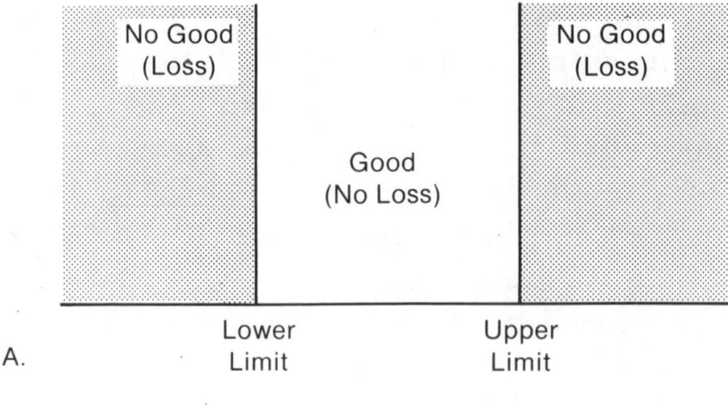

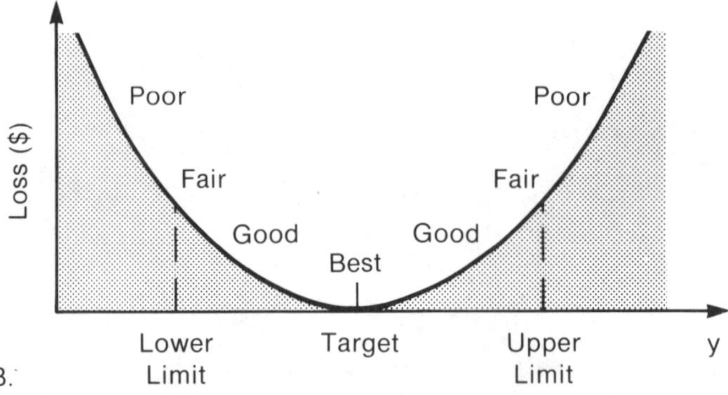

Figure 4-1. A. Under conformance to specification, quality is judged to be acceptable or unacceptable on a "good/no good" (or "go/no go") basis. Taguchi likens this thinking to two students, one of whom received a just-passing grade of 60 and the other a failing grade of 59. Is there really any difference between the two? Taguchi says no. B. Quality decreases as a product deviates from the desired target value and consumer dissatisfaction (loss to society and the company) increases. This is the philosophy behind Taguchi's quadratic Quality Loss Function curve: Loss increases by squares the further it goes from the target.

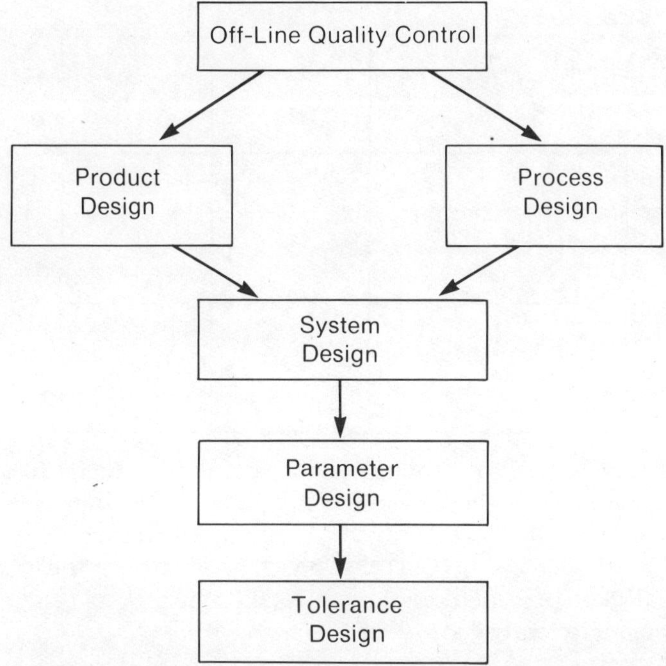

Figure 4-2. Taguchi defines the development of a product or process as a three-stage operation: system design, parameter design, and tolerance design.

Parameter Design

During *parameter design,* the design or process engineer seeks to optimize the system design through experimentation in order to minimize performance variation in the face of uncontrollable user and environmental factors. He begins by identifying those quality characteristics that most reflect the performance of the system, especially as it affects the customer.

For example, a quality characteristic for a car might be that it starts easily and quickly every time, no matter what

	U.S.	Japan
System Design	70%	40%
Parameter Design	2%	40%
Tolerance Design	28%	20%

Figure 4-3. It's estimated that U.S. engineers focus 70% of their efforts on system design (compared to Japanese engineers' 40%), and only 2% on parameter design. Japanese engineers, on the other hand, apply 40% of their efforts to parameter design, the stage where costs can be most efficiently controlled.

the external conditions are (e.g., a temperature range of -30 °F to +100 °F). Most products will have more than one quality characteristic, and it's important for the engineer to discover which quality characteristics consumers value most highly.

During parameter design, the engineer selects the quality characteristic most suitable for experimentation and seeks out all factors that will have an effect on it. He then separates those factors that he can control, in the experiment and in manufacture, from those he can't control.

In the case of the starting car, his list of factors would include outside temperature, humidity levels, the altitude range at which the car may operate during its lifetime, the fuel grades available in the regions the car may be used in, and so forth. Notice that the engineer really has no control over these factors. For example, the car company can't tell the car buyer that he shouldn't operate his vehicle when the temperature dips below or climbs above a certain point. So the engineer's goal must be to make the car resistant to these uncontrollable factors or, in Taguchi's words, "robust against noise."

Taguchi calls these uncontrollable factors *noise factors. Noise* is anything that causes a quality characteristic to deviate from its target, and which subsequently causes quality loss. Temperature, altitude, and fuel grade are considered *external* noise factors because they occur outside the product. Two other types of noise factors also exist: *internal* (e.g., deterioration over time as the car's battery wears down or as critical engine parts wear out) and *product-to-product* (e.g., piece-to-piece variability in the manufactured components of the car [see **Figure 4-4**]).

Once the engineer has identified the various sources of noise that affect the quality characteristic, he conducts an experiment that will allow the product or process to operate consistently over time regardless of noise. The engineer doesn't attempt to control the noise factors. Rather, he designs around them: Attempts to control noise usually prove impossible or add considerable cost.

The engineer identifies those design elements that can be controlled and thus can be used to make the system robust against the various noise factors. In the case of the car, these might include the primary ignition voltage, starter speed settings, and fuel- and air-delivery systems. These factors are called *parameters* or *control factors*—factors that will be optimized to create a robust product (in this case, a car that starts easily, quickly, and consistently under all conditions).

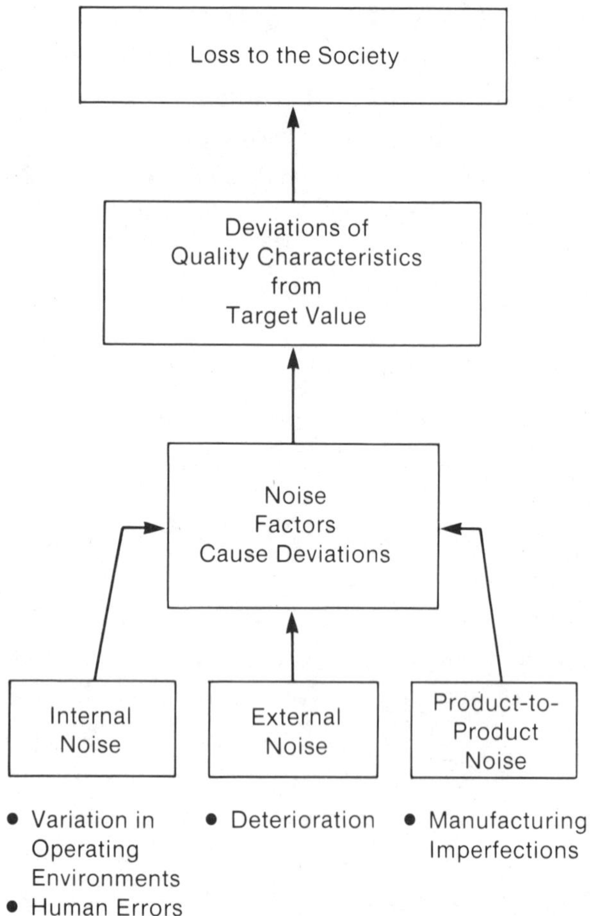

Figure 4-4. Loss occurs as quality characteristics deviate from target values due to noise factors. Taguchi has defined three types of noise factors: internal, external, and product-to-product.

Once control factors and noise factors have been identified, the engineer—in conjunction with others who have special knowledge about the various factors—determines multiple settings (levels of operation) for each factor. For example, starter settings might include tuning the engine at three different speeds (i.e., the current speed and two alternatives that might produce better results). Once the various settings or levels of operation for each factor have been determined, the engineer begins to design a series of experiments that will ultimately reveal each factor's optimum level. With Taguchi's approach to experimental design, the engineer typically need run only a portion of the total experiments possible for the various factors at their various levels. Rather than focus on the "trivial many," Taguchi Methods focus on the "vital few": A large number of factors with different settings can be easily assigned with a small number of experiments. However, the objective isn't simply to minimize the number of experiments, but to find *reproducible* results.

The engineer always begins his experimentation using the lowest-cost parts and components, with the goal of optimizing them so that the product or process is on target, has reduced variation, and provides the most stable and reliable performance at the lowest manufacturing cost. At this point, the engineer may use a *linear graph* to assign the control factors to an *orthogonal array* (see **Figure 4-5**). (A linear graph is a line/dot figure that corresponds to a particular orthogonal array. An orthogonal array is a matrix of numbers arranged in rows and columns—each row represents the state of the factors; each column, a specific factor that can be changed from experiment to experiment. Some orthogonal arrays are used in classical experimental design. Taguchi developed some orthogonal arrays, as well as linear graphs, which simplify the use of orthogonal arrays in laying out experiments.)

The orthogonal array for the control factors is called the *inner array* (see **Figure 4-6**). The inner array varies the combinations of the control factors in a systematic fashion: Each factor setting or level of operation is exposed to the other factor levels under experimentation the same number

No.	Column 1	2	3	4	5	6	7
1	1	1	1	1	1	1	1
2	1	1	1	2	2	2	2
3	1	2	2	1	1	2	2
4	1	2	2	2	2	1	1
5	2	1	2	1	2	1	2
6	2	1	2	2	1	2	1
7	2	2	1	1	2	2	1
8	2	2	1	2	1	1	2

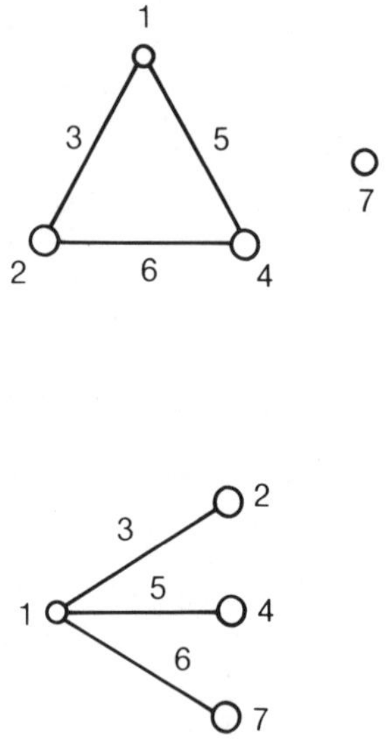

Figure 4-5. Taguchi developed linear graphs—graphical representations of the assignment of factors to the columns of an orthogonal array—to simplify the use of orthogonal arrays.

of times. This allows the engineer to make a balanced comparison between factor levels under a variety of conditions. A factor that exhibits a consistent effect with various conditions of the other factors will more than likely reproduce this effect in the field.

Once the inner array is established, the engineer creates an array for the noise factors. This is called the *outer array.* Each noise factor is also assigned settings or levels. The engineer is now ready to begin his series of experiments. Each experiment in the inner array is run several times against the combination of noise factors in the outer array. Thus, the engineer exposes the control factor settings to the effects of various combinations of noise fac-

No.	*A* *1*	*B* *2*	*C* *3*	*D* *4*	*E* *5*	*F* *6*	*G* *7*	*MNO*	Outer Array: 111	122	221	212
1	1	1	1	1	1	1	1					
2	1	1	1	2	2	2	2					
3	1	2	2	1	1	2	2					
4	1	2	2	2	2	1	1		Data			
5	2	1	2	1	2	1	2					
6	2	1	2	2	1	2	1					
7	2	2	1	1	2	2	1					
8	2	2	1	2	1	1	2					

Column (A–G); Inner Array

Figure 4-6. Control factors are placed in an inner array; noise factors in an outer array. The purpose of including the noise factors in the experiment is to deliberately create noise, so that the levels of control factors least sensitive to noise can be identified. In this example, an L_8 is used for the inner array, an L_4 for the outer array. Eight experiments featuring seven different factors at two different factor levels ("1" and "2") are run with the L_8 orthogonal array.

tors, which allows him to evaluate the product or process with respect to robustness against noise and the related costs.

Factor levels that are repeatedly stable, no matter how many different factors are changed around them, will be significant in reducing variability. These factors will increase the robustness of the system. Other factors will be used to adjust deviation from the target.

The engineer can then begin to analyze the generated data. Because each experiment was run several times, the engineer has a performance range that shows the experiment's average result and the starting performance variation around that average. The engineer should also verify the predicted results of his experimentation by performing a confirmatory experiment. If the predicted results aren't confirmed, he should redevelop the experiment.

The Signal-to-Noise Ratio

In parameter design, the engineer uses a data transformation that expresses the variability and ideal function of the quality characteristic better than the actual data would. This is the Signal-to-Noise (S/N) Ratio. A S/N Ratio is calculated for each experiment. This ratio indicates how much variation around the average or mean performance each experiment generated. The S/N Ratio is the operational way of incorporating Taguchi's Quality Loss Function (QLF) into experimental design (see **Figure 4-7**). S/N formulas are directly related to the QLF (a formula exists for each type of quality characteristic—see Appendix B). The larger the S/N Ratio, the less variability—and the smaller the quality loss.

The S/N Ratio shows the engineer exactly how robust the product developed from each experiment will be when exposed to a wide range of noise factors. For example, an engine may start well under cold temperatures and at high altitudes but suffer from vapor lock at high temperatures and low altitudes. The engineer is seeking the combination of factor settings that allows the engine to start easily no matter what the altitude, temperature, and other conditions.

At this point, the engineer could simply choose the experiment that produced the highest S/N Ratio as his optimum engine-starting condition. However, the result would probably be far from optimum. Because he ran his experi-

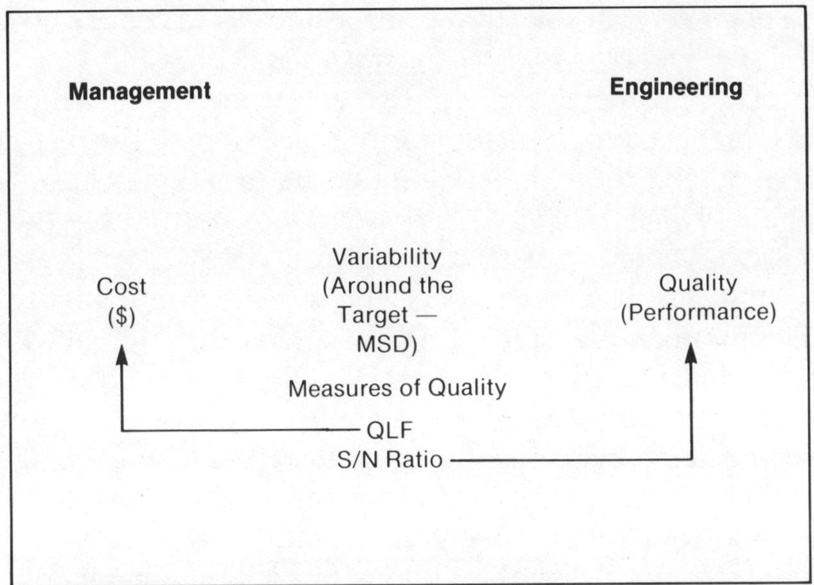

Figure 4-7. The Signal-to-Noise Ratio is the operational way of incorporating Taguchi's Quality Loss Function into experimental design. The S/N Ratio measures quality in terms of performance; the QLF, in terms of cost.

ments using orthogonal arrays, he can go one step further. He can conduct other analyses to find the effect of each factor on the average or mean performance of the quality characteristic in the experiment. The engineer is now ready to sort out his control factors into 1) those that have a strong effect on reducing variability, 2) those that have a strong effect on mean performance, and 3) those that have little effect on either.

Those factors that affect the S/N Ratio are used to reduce variability. Those with a strong effect on the mean but little effect on variability are used to adjust the mean performance to the target. They are called *adjustment* factors. Those with little effect on either are also important. Here the engineer can select the cheapest levels to reduce cost. They are referred to as *cost-adjustment* factors.

The engineer is thus able to create a product with those factors that can give, in the starting car example, the fastest starting time, those that can reduce the variation in starting time, and those that allow him to minimize cost. He has thus improved quality while reducing cost.

Finally, the engineer must check the reproducibility of his experimental results. He runs one final experiment with the optimum settings determined in the analysis. If the results of this experiment don't come close to yielding the performance level specified by his data predictions, the engineer must rethink the experiment. He has either missed an important factor that directly or indirectly affects starting performance, or the various factors may have combined to create an interaction that cancels out their combined effect, which results when a poor quality characteristic is picked for experimentation. In any case, the engineer will have to redesign the experiments.

If the results of the confirmation experiments do confirm an optimum combination that allows consistently fast starts, the engineer can then compare the predicted performance at the optimum settings with the original performance of the quality characteristic. If the performance of the optimum combination shows enough improvement in starting-speed consistency, the engineer has successfully completed his experimental-design work. He can then pursue even more improvement by performing additional experimentation.

But what if the improvements in quality and cost still aren't great enough to meet the competition? Suppose, for example, that the starting-speed consistency still doesn't meet the quality-characteristic specification. The engineer could try another experiment, or he might proceed to tolerance design. Improvements made during tolerance design usually require more expensive materials or components and therefore add cost.

Tolerance Design

During *tolerance design*, the engineer will systematically specify how much he'll have to increase the performance levels of certain factors to meet the requirements for the quality characteristic.

In tolerance design, the engineer determines the percentage that each of the noises contributes toward achieving the required performance for the quality characteristic. From this information, he can decide how much he must tighten the tolerance limits of each factor in order to achieve his objective. Tightening the tolerances of the factors almost always involves upgrading with higher-cost parts or components. The QLF is applied during tolerance design to find the most cost-effective way of determining which tolerances must be tightened, and which can be left in place or opened up, in order to reduce cost.

For example, if the starter is drawing too much power from the battery, the engineer will upgrade it with a more efficient and expensive unit. By using the QLF, the engineer can evaluate the cost increase due to tighter tolerances versus the quality improvement due to reduced variation. Hence, he won't upgrade a factor beyond actual need, which would be more costly than necessary.

At this point, the experimenter can perform another experimental-design run to select the most appropriate upgrades for the various factors. The engineer has now completed his optimization and can be assured that the starter will perform as intended and under all foreseen conditions.

As a final step, he calculates a QLF to determine the savings generated by the optimization.

The philosophy of the QLF is the foundation of Taguchi's entire Quality Engineering system. It is also used at the end of the design system to measure the quality improvement achieved by the experiment. Again, this improvement is calculated according to the quadratic loss curve, which gives the experimenter a pinpoint reading of the effectiveness of his efforts in achieving the target and reducing variation.

Uniformity at a target has become a hallmark of a competitive manufacturer. Amazingly, this revolutionary realization came very early in Taguchi's career.

Notes

1. Jeffrey Leestma, Honda Motor Co. Public Relations Spokesman, telephone interview with Lindsay Brooke, June 1986.
2. Genichi Taguchi, "Evaluation of Quality Level: In Reference to the Desired Target Characteristic," lecture printed in *Collection of Publications on Taguchi Methods*, 1984, Section VII.
3. L. P. Sullivan, "Reducing Variation: A New Approach to Quality," *Quality Progress*, July 1984, p. 15.

5

Genichi Taguchi: Beginnings

In the years following World War II, Japan was a cracked shell of a country. For the first time in its history, Japan had lost a war—and it had lost much else in the process as well. The country's war losses equaled 25% of the value of its national wealth. Almost 25% of all buildings and structures had been destroyed; almost 35% of all industrial equipment was lost. All of Japan's major cities except ancient and non-strategic Kyoto (which was spared to provide a base for reconstruction) had been demolished; the average income had dropped to less than $30 a year at the beginning of the Allied Occupation.[1]

Americans stationed in Japan during the Occupation recall the coal-burning taxis that chuffed through the streets of Tokyo trailing clouds of black smoke. The country was literally starving for want of resources. Shortages of every kind, from materials to basic foodstuffs, were rampant. On top of this, severe inflation and high unemployment hampered Japan's ability to finance its way out of trouble.

Japan, and its people and economy, had been humbled, and Americans in charge of bringing it back to economic life faced a formidable task. One American engineering executive who now works for a large, multinational firm recalls an episode that occurred while he was stationed in Japan during the Occupation. American engineers requested help from the Japanese on a project. They needed some very close-tolerance measuring and several engineers to do it. They were assigned several Japanese engineers who, having nothing else to use, showed up for work with a seamstress' tape measure! "But their determination was amazing," he adds, and tells a second story that proves his point.

He was assigned the job of training the Japanese engineers in electronics. A translator introduced him to a small group of engineers and then left, never to be seen again. The American couldn't speak Japanese, nor the Japanese English, so most communication was accomplished by crude hand signals. The American was at a loss as to what to do. He gave the Japanese engineers basic busywork—sweeping floors and tinkering with old tube radio sets. This went on for several months. Finally, at the end of four months, the Japanese engineers approached the American, and their leader proudly said, "We speak English now."

The American was dumbstruck—was this some kind of bad joke? He soon learned that it wasn't. Shortly after they realized that they'd learn nothing because of the language barrier, the Japanese engineers decided to meet in the evenings to listen to a Japanese/English tutorial program on the radio and teach themselves English. Their English was imperfect, as one would expect, but it was a start, and the American could begin teaching them electronics.

As it turned out, Japan had a lot to learn from the United States, and the tremendous economic pressures the country faced made the job as urgent as any wartime mobilization.

The GHQ

The job of rebuilding Japan was given to the General Headquarters of the Supreme Commander for the Allied Powers, known in Japan as the GHQ. The GHQ and the Occupation itself were run by the Americans with little regard for the desires of the 11-nation Far Eastern Commission, whose member countries, including the Soviet Union, protested in vain.[2]

Since it was an American ballgame, the Americans naturally brought American ideas in technology with them. For example, they introduced statistical sampling plans and Statistical Process Control (SPC) to Japanese scientists and engineers, hoping to improve Japan's communications network and the country's ability to build trucks and other equipment needed by the U.S. Army Forces stationed in Japan and Korea.

During World War II, the U.S. government had required many defense contractors to adopt statistical methods in the manufacture of ordnance to reduce the number of dud bombs and torpedoes finding their way into battle. The sampling methods allowed inspectors to check just a few samples from each lot and then statistically determine whether the lot was good or bad without instituting 100% inspection techniques.[3] Some defense contractors also instituted simple forms of SPC with the help of AT&T Bell Laboratories.

The inspection sampling plans and SPC were based on

the work pioneered at Bell Labs and Western Electric by people like Walter A. Shewhart, Harold Dodge, and Harry G. Romig before the war. Shewhart, of course, developed SPC control charts and made significant contributions in the area of sampling, while Dodge and Romig created the sampling inspection plans actually used during the war effort.[4]

Bell Labs, in fact, was recruited by the War Department to teach simple quality-control techniques to the fledgling wartime American work force, which lacked skilled workers for obvious reasons.

Bell Labs seems to surface at some point in most conversations regarding quality-control methods in America. Bell Labs' contributions to shaping the thinking of the world in terms of Statistical Quality Control (SQC) are fairly well-documented. The work done by Dodge and Romig formed the basis of the U.S. military's quality standard, MIL-STD-105A, developed in 1950, and now known as MIL-STD-105D. This standard, in its many forms, remains the most widely used quality standard in the world today.[5]

The concepts behind Shewhart's SQC work ultimately had a profound effect on Japanese thought about quality control. As a renowned Japanese quality expert, Kaoru Ishikawa, wrote in 1967, "About 1950, when I began to study quality-control concepts, I developed a great respect for Dr. Shewhart through the study of his deep thoughts in quality control. . . . It was when I visited the Bell Telephone Laboratories as a member of the QC study team in 1958 that I first met Dr. Shewhart. Again in 1959, I had the opportunity to hear his talks here in Japan and again I was greatly impressed with the depth of his philosophy."[6]

Shewhart, however, wasn't the one who introduced the Japanese to SQC. That task went to an admirer and eventual friend of Shewhart's, an American statistician who worked at the War Department during World War II. W. Edwards Deming, who held a doctoral degree from Yale University and had followed Shewhart's work at Bell Labs, had served with the U.S. Department of Agriculture and the Census Bureau as an expert in population and sampling statistics.

Deming later wrote in a tribute to Shewhart, "Quality control meant to him use of statistical methods all the way from raw materials to the consumer and back again, through redesign of product, reworking of specifications of raw materials, in a continuous cycle as results come in from consumer research and from other tests.

"He was quick to see that quality must mean not necessarily high quality, but dependable and economic quality, which in turn meant quality suited to the purpose."[7]

Deming went to Japan in the late 1940s to teach statistics at the request of the GHQ, and later gave a series of lectures on statistical methods that were attended by a diverse cross section of Japanese scientists, engineers, and manufacturing people. Deming's lectures, and his address to the Industry Club of Japan on July 26, 1950, have been called the bedrock on which Japan's new quality ethic was built. Writing of his experiences some years later, Deming stated, "Seeing their serious determination, I predicted at an assembly of Japanese manufacturers in Tokyo in July 1950 that in five years, manufacturers in other industrial nations would be on the defensive and that in ten years, the reputation for top quality in Japanese products would be firmly established the world over."[8]

Deming's seemingly miraculous influence on the Japanese was actually aided by a number of people and factors. The Japanese, facing tremendous manufacturing-quality problems, were eager to discover any methodology that could produce products to the exacting specifications of the U.S. Army, which sourced trucks and other equipment from Japan for the Korean War effort. Additionally, Japan had a large population of motivated and skilled technicians, engineers, and scientists, as well as top managers who immediately became involved with the concepts of quality control.

At about the same time, Kaoru Ishikawa began studying and eventually translating American statistical methodology into language Japanese machine operators and shop-floor workers could easily understand. Another aid was the Japanese Union of Scientists and Engineers (JUSE), which promoted SPC techniques to the point of broadcasting SPC classes over the radio.

Ironically, many American companies in the postwar era stopped using SPC and didn't again seriously embrace it until almost 35 years later. The reason they did so wasn't simply cavalier disregard for quality control. Rather, as Ishikawa and others have noted, it was the degree of difficulty inherent in the understanding of Shewhart's work that relegated it to specialist circles in the United States.

As Joseph M. Juran, another American quality expert who brought American quality-control ideas to postwar Japan, writes, "(Shewhart) had no reticence about speaking or writing, so that he was increasingly in demand. However, the invitations, and they were international, came from the world of the intelligentsia rather than from the world of managers. In dealing with managers he had neither the operating experience nor the vocabulary to communicate effectively. This same lack of communication necessarily limited the dissemination of his concepts."[9]

Thus, from the very start of SQC techniques in the United States, we see a quality ethic that is rooted among specialists, but not generalists or management.

Tokyo's Telephones

The GHQ faced a reconstruction effort of Herculean proportions in the years immediately following World War II, and one of its first challenges was the systematic improvement of Japan's existing communications network. Tokyo's phone system operated in such an erratic fashion that some Americans—only half in jest—suggested that smoke signals or carrier pigeons might prove more effective. It seemed as though every time the weather turned rough most of the phones in Tokyo went dead. Waiting for as many as ten hours to make a connection was commonplace, and once a connection was made, businesses would often be forced to hang on the line for hours for fear of not being able to get through later.[10]

Smooth and predictable communication was vital to the success and security of the relatively small Occupation forces, so the GHQ planned to totally revamp Japan's communications network. To that end, the GHQ gave special funding and assistance to Japanese electrical equipment firms. The Civil Communications Section (CCS) of the GHQ was organized and given responsibility for the job. The CCS subsequently enlisted the help of Western Electric and Bell Labs engineers, who taught a course on quality fundamentals, including SQC methods.[11]

GHQ staff members soon discovered, however, that effective communications required more than the simple transfer of American technology. To that end, the GHQ ordered the creation of a Japanese equivalent to Bell Labs, a research-and-development facility capable of contributing to Japanese growth instead of just borrowing American technology. In 1949, the Nippon Telephone and Telegraph Co.'s Electrical Communications Laboratories (ECL) began operations. The ECL, which was attached to the Nippon

Dr. Genichi Taguchi
Key Dates

1924	Born January 1, Tokamichi, Niigata-ken
1936–41	Middle School, Tokamichi
1942	Kiryu Technical College (textile engineering)
1942–45	Imperial Japanese Navy Astronomical Dept., Navigation Institute
1947–48	Ministry of Public Health and Welfare

Dr. Genichi Taguchi

1947–49	Consultant, Morinaga Seika
1948–50	Institute of Statistical Mathematics, Ministry of Education
1950–62	Electrical Communications Laboratory, Nippon Telephone & Telegraph
	Teaching experimental design to ECL engineers; industrial consulting

1951	*Experimental Design and Life Test Analysis* (book is out of print and considered out of date by Taguchi)
1954–55	Visiting Professor, Indian Statistical Institute; met R. A. Fisher; conducted 20 experimental-design applications in Indian industry
1956–57	Wrote first version of *Design of Experiments* (*Jikken Keikakuho*), in which he introduced the use of orthogonal arrays and analysis of categorical data
1960	Awarded Deming Prize
	Met W. Edwards Deming at international statistics conference
1962	Published second version of *Design of Experiments*, in which he introduced Signal-to-Noise Ratio
	Visiting Research Associate, Princeton University; interested in ideas of Dr. John Tukey, including the "jackknife" method, although not specifically for Quality Engineering
	Awarded Ph.D. in Science degree by Kyushu University
1963–64	Asked to be Professor at Aoyama Gakuin University, the College of Science and Engineering then under construction
1964-82	Professor, Aoyama Gakuin and consultant in industry.

(*continued*)

Dr. Genichi Taguchi Key Dates (*continued*)	
1976	Published third (and current) edition of *Design of Experiments* and changed the mathematical base of his methodology from statistics to the quadratic system
1982	Retired from Aoyama Gakuin, and became Advisor at the Japanese Standards Assn.
1983	Executive Director, American Supplier Institute, Inc.
1986	Awarded the Willard F. Rockwell Medal by the International Technology Institute

Telephone and Telegraph Co. much the way Bell Labs is to AT&T, cost Japan as much as 2% of the total government budget—a sign of the importance placed on developing a reliable communications network.[12]

Still, the ECL employed only 1,400 people—one-fifth of Bell Labs' payroll at the time—and its budget, although huge in terms of Japanese resources, was less than 1/50 that of Bell Labs'.[13]

A young Japanese engineering consultant named Genichi Taguchi was recruited by the ECL for the purpose of increasing the productivity of its research-and-development activities. Taguchi, who was 25 years old at this point, had already established a reputation in Japan as an expert in advanced statistical methods.

Taguchi joined the ECL in 1950. His job assignment was to train engineers in effective research-and-development techniques. He worked under the direction of a Mr. Kayano as head of experimental-design instruction. Taguchi would work at the ECL for more than 12 years. During that time, a great deal of the groundwork would be laid concerning his revolutionary ideas about quality.[14]

Taguchi had a natural aptitude for mathematics, although he had received little formal training in that subject or in statistical analysis. He attended middle school in Tokamachi, Japan, graduating in March 1941. From there, Taguchi attended Kiryu Technical College for one year, although he received no degree. He primarily studied courses concerning textile engineering, with the goal of helping his mother at the family's small kimono factory. His father had died when Taguchi was ten years old.

The kimono factory was forced to produce other products because of the war effort, and Taguchi had to join the Armed Forces. He was assigned to the Astronomical Department of the Navy Navigation Institute in 1942. Here, he was charged with tabulating astronavigational data. His intent was to live quietly through a war he did not like.

He spent his free time during the war poring over statistical texts in the local library, including one by an M. Masuyama entitled "Statistics With Small Sample Sizes."[15] He also read every publication of the Japan Mathematical Physics Society.

After the war, Taguchi joined the Japanese Ministry of Public Health and Welfare. Here, he initiated the nation's first nutrition-planning survey, which plotted the general health and well-being of the Japanese people—it has been noted that the average life span of the Japanese increased by ten years during the time U.S. General Douglas MacArthur was in command in Japan. The surveys covered areas as varied as typical food consumption (since many people were undernourished because of the pervasive shortages of food), prevalent disease levels, and rates of infection.

To perform the surveys, Taguchi realized the need for and implemented a statistical sampling plan, because of the difficulty in collecting relevant data in areas as individualized as food intake or disease. This type of survey is still conducted to this day in Japan, and remains one of the most extensive such studies performed in the world.[16]

While working at the Ministry of Public Health and Welfare, Taguchi met Motosaburo Masuyama, the man whose book he had studied during the war. Masuyama was doing consulting work for Morinaga Pharmaceutical Co. regarding the production of penicillin, and he would have a large influence on Taguchi's career direction in the coming years.[17]

The race to manufacture penicillin in Japan actually began during the war. Japan learned of the wonder drug that had been developed in Britain from its Axis partner, Germany, which shipped German medical journals describing penicillin's importance to Japan via submarine. The Japanese daily newspaper *Asahi* published a long article detailing penicillin manufacture on January 27, 1944.

Shortly thereafter, Japanese pharmaceutical companies began penicillin production, and claims have been made that more than 16,000 strains of the drug had been tested by the war's end.[18]

Masuyama was using British experimental-design techniques in his work to develop penicillin, work that was driven by intense competitive rivalry among Japanese companies. At that time, there were as many as 64 different companies working on penicillin production. Success depended on producing high-quality/high-volume amounts of the drug quickly and efficiently.

After the war, Masuyama won the *Asahi* Prize for a study on the effects of the atomic bombing of Hiroshima. He is also cited as the first person to introduce an effective new penicillin-potency test method using diffusion theory.

He continued to work at Morinaga Pharmaceuticals, and persuaded the young Taguchi to join him there.[19]

Taguchi learned a great deal about statistical methods and experimental design from Masuyama, which is typically the way young Japanese scientists and engineers are exposed to the craft of statistics. Taguchi had very little formal education in statistics—it's still not taught as a separate discipline in Japanese universities with any regularity. Most statisticians come from other fields. Engineers, physicists, chemists, and the like learn statistics as they apply to their work, and usually in the course of their work. Most of Taguchi's statistical training had been undertaken on the job. From the very beginning, his thinking had been shaped by the real-world necessities of industry, not the theoretical niceties of statistical academia. However, Taguchi's understanding of classical design-of-experiments techniques was extensive. He later translated *Experimental Designs*—a book by two leading statisticians, W. G. Cochran, an Englishman, and Gertrude Cox, an American—into Japanese.

Masuyama actually published a small manual on experimental design during the war. Masuyama himself learned about statistical methods through his training in physics. He's an interesting individual who also studied medicine and meteorology in order to study the relationship between climate and health.

It was Masuyama who taught Taguchi experimental-design techniques and introduced him to the use of orthogonal arrays, simple examples of which Masuyama used very effectively in the development of medicine. Taguchi ultimately replaced Masuyama at Morinaga Pharmaceuticals as a consultant, and was soon doing consulting work for Morinaga Seika, the parent company of Morinaga

Pharmaceuticals, which made candy and other products. His success was evidenced by the annual tenfold increase in productivity the company experienced for several years.[20] In 1948, Taguchi became a member of the Institute of Statistical Mathematics, a Ministry of Education organization. Here, he authored a paper that related to the work done by S. D. Rice of Bell Labs regarding the theory of random noises.[21]

Taguchi's respect for the scientific excellence that Bell Labs was known for seems to have taken hold very early in his career. Indeed, in the mid-1940s there were few industrial labs in the world that could match the brainpower in Bell's East Coast facilities.

Experimental Design in Japan

The Japanese, as mentioned earlier, have taken a much less academic approach to statistical training than some countries. It's not possible to receive a degree in statistics in Japan, although most universities offer training that ranges from six months to two years in statistics as it impacts other courses of study. For example, a person pursuing science and engineering studies would be exposed to mathematical statistics, stochastic processes, sample survey theory, statistical mechanics, and statistical inference. A certain amount of Taguchi's experimental-design techniques are covered in university courses, but most engineers receive their primary instruction in the form of work-related training and education after entering industry. A very large number of Japanese students, however, do take courses in statistics. Travelers to Japan are sometimes surprised to see statistical results of various national surveys displayed in public areas. Such is the mania for statistical methods in Japan.

Design of Experiments

An English mathematician, Sir Ronald Aylmer Fisher, better known as R. A. Fisher, first developed design-of-experiments techniques (also called experimental design) in the mid-1920s—about the same time Walter A. Shewhart developed his Statistical Quality Control charts.

Fisher was a man of wide-ranging genius who made significant contributions in an incredibly diverse cross section of scientific disciplines, from botany to economics to genetics.[22]

Fisher's goal in experimental design was to create a statistically valid method to effectively generate and analyze data for agricultural experiments at the Rothamsted Experimental Station, an agricultural research center located in the countryside just north of London. Here Fisher, working alone, would bring sublimely elegant order to the application of statistics.

Fisher began using statistical analysis on wheat-yield results that had been collected over a period of 67 years. His early work proved frustrating, as the data-collection methods used in yearly crop "experiments" had significant holes in them. Data had been generated over the years in a nonsystematic fashion, and statistical analysis of the data was hampered because of this inconsistency.

Before Fisher, researchers didn't have a statistically valid method for determining which factors had a significant influence on the growth and fecundity of plants: Most experimentation was done on a hit-or-miss basis.

With experimental design, the statistician became the one who influenced how experiments were laid out and conducted—he "designed" them, in other words—and he decided what types of data collection would be required.

Fisher organized the collection of data into logical patterns and used randomization to prevent unwanted factors from influencing the results of the experiment.

(*continued*)

Design of Experiments (*continued*)

For example, in laying out an experiment that would measure the effectiveness of four different kinds of fertilizer, a presumably logical method would be to plant the four quarters of a field with the different types of fertilizer and then monitor the results. To generate a statistically valid database, however, it would be necessary to plant the field using one uniform type of fertilizer for several years before experimenting to measure the uniformity of fertility. In other words, the statistician would want to generate an estimate of error for his results that would remove the effect of unwanted variation in crop yield from his analysis. Such variation could be caused by any number of factors, including drainage, fertility, nutrient levels, and so forth, which are known to vary considerably from area to area in the same field.

Instead of going through this time-consuming process, Fisher exploited the idea of using experiment replication to generate a valid estimate of error while the experiment was being run. The experimenter would section the field into blocks, and would then usually grow separate plots in each block using each of the four types of fertilizer. The experiment was then replicated in other blocks randomly arranged in the field, and the results from all of the blocks were combined. Thus, the possible effects of unwanted variables were reduced.

By blocking, Fisher greatly reduced the possibility of variation that would have otherwise been present. The plots in the blocks were physically close to each other, and thus could be assumed to face relatively similar growth environments. Fisher arranged the blocks in the field so that they wouldn't unintentionally conform to such unknown variations as fertility and drainage that could crisscross the field.

Fisher arranged his experiment-replication blocks according to either a randomized block design or another, more balanced design known as a randomized Latin square. The Latin square is an orthogonal array, meaning it's made up of a series of rows which, when viewed from top to bottom or from side to side, contain every different element of the experiment. The Latin square allowed for double-blocking—each column of plots was in effect a block, as was each row of plots. An orthogonal array is considered to be a "balanced" layout for this reason. In the randomized Latin square, while each column and row still contains one plot of each set of factors, the arrangement of the rows and columns adjacent to each other is purely random.

A famous experiment featuring Fisher's randomized Latin square concerned the effects altitude has on different types of trees. The trees were arranged on a hillside in Wales that rose in elevation from 1,250 to 1,800 feet. The random orthogonal nature of the Latin square was dramatically visible in a photograph taken 16 years later, when it was possible to see blocks of thriving trees next to blocks of trees stunted by the conditions.

Fisher spent a considerable amount of time working out the possible random arrangements a four-by-four and five-by-five Latin square contained. This work led him to the layout possibilities contained in the Greco-Latin square, which allows the experimenter to add an extra series of orthogonal variables to the experiment.

One of the problems Fisher came up against in more complex experimental designs was how to identify the effects of interactions between factors in an experiment. The traditional method of running experiments was to change only one factor at a time while keeping all other factors constant, and then recording the results.

This "one-factor-at-a-time" methodology didn't take into account interactions between factors, and tended to assume that all other factors would remain constant, which is seldom the case in real life.

Fisher's solution was the full-factorial design. For example, say the experimenter wished to test the effects four different fertilizer

(*continued*)

Design of Experiments (*continued*)

elements had on plant growth—both independent of each other and in combination with each other, and under two different levels of experimentation, say under light and heavy moisture conditions. He would run two to the fourth power tests, or 2×2×2× 2 = 16 experiments in total. To remove the effect of unwanted variation, the experiments would be replicated several times in a randomized block layout, for the reason noted above.

This design would give the experimenter every possible combination of factors and interaction of factors. The full factorial delivers a maximum amount of data concerning an experiment. It "dots every i and crosses every t" for the statistician, and generates a tremendous amount of usable data, not only concerning the effects of factors but also, to an extent, the effects of the interactions of those factors. It's capable of almost pinpoint accuracy in the generation and analysis of data.

However, the full factorial can easily become overwhelmingly complex, as you can well imagine. Suppose, for instance, the experimenter wanted to test the effects of ten factors, each at three different levels. The experiment would thus consist of three to the tenth power or 3×3×3×3×3×3×3×3×3×3 = 59,049 experiments! Add to that several replications of the experiment and things get out of hand rather quickly.

Fisher later attempted to streamline his factorial experimental designs, statistically weeding out those interactions that were of

Pursuit of Less Complicated Techniques

Shortly after assuming Masuyama's position at Morinaga Pharmaceuticals, Taguchi began to use several more practical versions of the orthogonal Latin square. Taguchi credits Masuyama for beginning to use orthogonal arrays in a more dynamic manner than is found in classical experi-

little significance and thus simplifying his system somewhat. Nevertheless, his experimental-design techniques have remained in the realm of statisticians.

Fisher published his findings in 1935 in a volume titled *The Design of Experiments.*

Experimental Design Spreads

Fisher traveled to various countries during the late 1930s, notably India. He was invited to India by P. C. Mahalanobis, a physics and meteorology professor at Presidency College in Calcutta. Mahalanobis used statistical methodology in the course of his meteorological studies. This later led to his involvement in applications of statistical analysis in other fields, including agriculture. It was from an agricultural case study of Mahalanobis' that Fisher first learned of the Indian statistician and made contact with him. This led Mahalanobis to England, where he sought out Fisher and later invited him to visit India.

It's interesting to note the Indian link that connects Fisher and Dr. Genichi Taguchi. It was Mahalanobis who some 17 years later would invite Taguchi to share his experimental-design techniques with India's research engineers. And, by and large, it was the sustained interest of an Indian-born engineer-cum-statistician that helped make Taguchi's work known in America in 1980 (see Chapter 7).

mental-design techniques, although it was Taguchi himself who greatly expanded the work in this area.[23]

Orthogonal arrays allow an experimenter to reduce the number of experimental trials he would normally have to perform in a full-factorial experimental design. While R. A. Fisher (see sidebar, "Design of Experiments") originally used the orthogonal Latin square to control error in an experiment, Taguchi uses the orthogonal array to find the individual impact of each factor on the mean result and on the variation from that mean result. Rather than expend effort trying to remove the cause of a problem—which may be impossible or extremely costly to do—Taguchi seeks to find a countermeasure to reduce the influence of the cause.

An orthogonal array allows an experimenter to analyze the average change in factor levels under different sets of experimental conditions. This helps ensure repeatable results. With an orthogonal array, the experimenter can isolate the effects each factor has on the experimentation. He doesn't have to complete all of the experimental trials required for a full factorial. He can thus extract large amounts of useful information from small-scale experiments and attain reliable results. For example, using an L_{27} orthogonal array, he need run only 27 experiments, rather than the more than 1,594,323 required when using a full factorial (see **Figure 5-1**).

Taguchi saw the orthogonal array as a sophisticated switching system into which as many different factors and factor levels as possible could be plugged. Because the switching system was designed to allow an experimenter to extract the average effect each of the factors had on the experimental results, the experimenter could reach reliable conclusions during his analysis despite the large number of changing variables. The experimenter would then select all the optimum levels of the factors and use them to run a confirmatory experiment, which should yield the predicted result. Taguchi uses orthogonal arrays to find *optimum combinations of factors,* not simply to reduce the unwanted bias in experiments.

Factor Levels

Column

Experiments

No.	*A* *1*	*B* *2*	*C* *3*	*D* *4*	*E* *5*	*F* *6*	*G* *7*	*H* *8*	*I* *9*	*J* *10*	*K* *11*	*L* *12*	*M* *13*	
1	1	1	1	1	1	1	1	1	1	1	1	1	1	Factor Levels
2	1	1	1	1	2	2	2	2	2	2	2	2	2	for First
3	1	1	1	1	3	3	3	3	3	3	3	3	3	Experiment
4	1	2	2	2	1	1	1	2	2	2	3	3	3	
5	1	2	2	2	2	2	2	3	3	3	1	1	1	
6	1	2	2	2	3	3	3	1	1	1	2	2	2	
7	1	3	3	3	1	1	1	3	3	3	2	2	2	
8	1	3	3	3	2	2	2	1	1	1	3	3	3	
9	1	3	3	3	3	3	3	2	2	2	1	1	1	
10	2	1	2	3	1	2	3	1	2	3	1	2	3	
11	2	1	2	3	2	3	1	2	3	1	2	3	1	
12	2	1	2	3	3	1	2	3	1	2	3	1	2	
13	2	2	3	1	1	2	3	2	3	1	3	1	2	
14	2	2	3	1	2	3	1	3	1	2	1	2	3	
15	2	2	3	1	3	1	2	1	2	3	2	3	1	
16	2	3	1	2	1	2	3	3	1	2	2	3	1	
17	2	3	1	2	2	3	1	1	2	3	3	1	2	
18	2	3	1	2	3	1	2	2	3	1	1	2	3	
19	3	1	3	2	1	3	2	1	3	2	1	3	2	
20	3	1	3	2	2	1	3	2	1	3	2	1	3	
21	3	1	3	2	3	2	1	3	2	1	3	2	1	
22	3	2	1	3	1	3	2	2	1	3	3	2	1	
23	3	2	1	3	2	1	3	3	2	1	1	3	2	
24	3	2	1	3	3	2	1	1	3	2	2	1	3	
25	3	3	2	1	1	3	2	3	2	1	2	1	3	Factor Levels
26	3	3	2	1	2	1	3	1	3	2	3	2	1	for 27th
27	3	3	2	1	3	2	1	2	1	3	1	3	2	Experiment

Figure 5-1. With the L_{27} orthogonal array, 27 experiments featuring 13 different factors are run at three different factor levels ("1," "2," and "3"). Each factor is exposed to all other factors an equal number of times for each level.

From Caramels to Telephones

Soon after beginning work at Morinaga Pharmaceuticals, Taguchi became involved in experiments done by the firm's parent company on the formulation of caramel candy. The goal was to develop caramels that wouldn't melt under extremes of room temperature.[24]

An experiment was set up to test the effectiveness of several different mixing formulas. The resulting candy from each formula was then tested at three different room temperatures. Taguchi used his orthogonal arrays to lay out the controllable mixing factors and the uncontrollable temperature factors. While he later insisted that the experiment wasn't a complete success, the plasticity of the caramels across the range of temperatures (32 to 104 °F) was dramatically reduced. Taguchi also hit upon another element of what would become known as his experimental-design methodology: the idea of inner error and the variation it causes. (Taguchi later labeled error by a communications-industry-inspired name tag, noise.)

Fisher had already identified outer error (e.g., external noise), but Taguchi discovered that noise also occurs *within* a product or process, and can manifest itself either as variation due to deterioration over time or as variation between products.

Even at this early stage, Taguchi recognized the two criteria for a superior product: high stability of performance over an extended time period and uniformity from product to product, which only comes when a manufacturer is concentrating on designing and producing products that are grouped tightly at a target specification.

Taguchi thought that these variation-causing inner and outer factors were so important that he developed what has become known as an outer orthogonal array, which is used in conjunction with a standard (or inner) orthogonal array. An experimenter would lay out his experiments, assigning the various control factors at their various levels of composition, according to the inner array. The outer array is an orthogonal design used in conjunction with the inner array to expose the experiments to various sources of error. The idea is to expose the experiments to as many error-causing factors as possible, with the aim of finding the combination of control factors least affected by them.

To understand Taguchi's thinking, let's look at a nontechnical example of variation around the mean. Let's say you're running an experiment designed to find the quickest way to get to work. You have several choices of routes and several time windows you can juggle for each route to avoid the heaviest rush-hour traffic.

You design your experiment, assigning the variables of your trip to an orthogonal array. After running the experiment, you analyze your data and identify the combination of routes and time windows that allows the quickest mean traveling time. This route happens to take you right through the heart of the city. So far, so good. But you haven't checked the day-to-day variation around that mean traveling time. Ideally, you would want the smallest amount of variation in travel time possible so that you could confidently predict when you'd arrive for work. This is where the outer array comes in.

Using Taguchi's methodology, you would also assign the error-producing factors—those factors that are impossible or too expensive to control—to an outer array. The error or noise factors in this case would include bad weather, gridlocks, unsynchronized traffic signals, and so forth—anything beyond your control that would create variation in the time it takes you to get to work.

Let's say that you discover that the route that allows your quickest mean traveling time (the route through town) actually has quite a bit of day-to-day variation—because of local congestion, your luck with traffic signals, and so forth. After checking the day-to-day variation of the other possible routes, you find one that has a longer mean traveling time but a much tighter grouping in day-to-day variation around the mean (this route, an expressway, bypasses the "iffy" traffic lights but takes you slightly out of your way, which takes more time).

Your goal is to leave the house at a predetermined time and make it to work exactly on time. Which route would you choose? You'd be better off taking the expressway route—although it will take you slightly longer, it will take the same time to drive to work, day in, day out.

Ideally, in a Taguchi Methods experiment, you would take a further step. After finding the route with the least amount of variation, you would manipulate one of the factors that had a significant effect on the mean time it took you to drive to work. By adjusting this factor—by slightly increasing your average speed, for example—you would bring your driving time as close as possible to your target time. In this case, you'd probably come to the same conclusion without experimental-design techniques, using nothing more complicated than gut instinct. Taguchi Methods are intended for much less obvious situations.

Taguchi's Work at the ECL

Taguchi brought the idea of using orthogonal arrays and noise factors with him when he was placed in charge of research-and-development efficiency at the ECL.

While allowing the experimenter to dramatically reduce the number of experiments needed, the orthogonal array made it easy to set up an experimental design, compared with the traditional methods. Taguchi was also interested in finding ways to simplify the statistical barrage an experimenter subjects his data to after an experimental design is run, thereby allowing a nonexpert to confidently analyze data and predict results.

The GHQ wanted the ECL to use traditional, Western experimental-design techniques. Although Taguchi appreciated the breadth of assistance the GHQ (and America) was offering, he doubted the efficiency of Fisher's system when it was used in dynamic, fast-paced industrial environments. Whereas Fisher's experiments could literally take a lifetime to complete, for statistics to work in industry, experiments had to be quick, relatively small, and verifiable. Performing a full-factorial experiment typically took more time and money than most industrial managers were willing to spend.

In postwar Japan, expensive experimentation was a luxury industry couldn't afford, so Taguchi introduced the experimental-design techniques he'd used at Morinaga Pharmaceuticals. While at the ECL, Taguchi made frequent lecture appearances at leading Japanese companies, including the Nippon Electric Co., Hitachi, OKI, Fujitsu, and Nippondenso Co., Ltd. By the early 1950s, the effectiveness of Taguchi's system was already becoming well-known in Japanese industry.

Simultaneously, Taguchi was becoming interested in the possibilities his techniques held in theoretical experimentation. In the communications industry, for example, where theoretical equations had already been established, Taguchi realized that an experimenter could actually optimize his product or process without any physical experimentation, relying solely on mathematics. At this point, however, the creation and availability of computers able to carry out such number-crunching was limited. Even so, Taguchi was able to perform several theoretical case studies, using unwieldy relay-type computers.[25]

Taguchi's work at the ECL produced some fairly dramatic results. A famous example of the power of his system in product design was the development of a crossbar-switching system for use by Japan's telephone industry. The crossbar switch contained tiny wire-spring relays whose individual cost was nominal. The relays were so important to the functioning of the system, however, that the ECL was prepared to invest several million dollars in their design. It was an ambitious series of experiments, involving more than 2,000 factors and several hundred experiments.

An interesting irony is the fact that Bell Labs was concurrently designing its own crossbar-switching system. The crossbar systems developed by both companies took seven years to complete. When both systems were finished, the ECL's wire-spring relay was tested against Bell Labs'. Both relays were subjected to one billion make-or-break cycles of durability testing, and despite the use of inferior-quality materials and the fact that most of the system's parts were of poor quality, the ECL's relay was judged to be better than Bell Labs'. The ECL's system was successful to the point that Western Electric, Bell Labs' parent company, stopped manufacturing the systems and began importing them from Japan. The crossbar system ultimately earned the Japanese company billions of dollars in sales.[26]

At the heart of Taguchi's techniques is the *strong reliance on the knowledge of a product or process that an engineer or a technician brings with him to an experiment.* This is the real key to why significant results can be achieved when performing a limited number of experiments instead of a full factorial. Unlike the full factorial, Taguchi Methods can't "dot every i or cross every t." They're much quicker than the full factorial, however. And by relying on a working engineer's experience and knowledge, important factors (the "vital few"), and levels of operation can be identified and nonessentials (the "trivial many") ignored.

It's been said that Taguchi Methods are valuable because they typically get you 70% of the way to your goal quickly and inexpensively. The final 30% can be swept up in subsequent experimentation. It's this compounding of results—following the idea of continuous improvement—that makes Taguchi Methods so successful and attractive to industry.

Taguchi originally described this methodology as the optimization of factors using the response characteristics given by engineers. It was the first component of what is now known as parameter design.

Notes

1. Shotaro Kamiya, *My Life With Toyota,* 1976, p. 112, chart listing Japan's war losses. Source given: Economic Planning Agency, Postwar Editing Section, "Postwar Economic History," 1957, p. 11. Also see Noel Busch, *The Horizon Concise History of Japan,* 1972, p. 176.
2. K. Hopper, "Creating Japan's New Industrial Management: the Americans as Teachers," *Human Resources Quarterly,* Summer/Fall 1982, pp. 13–34.
3. Michael A. Cusumano, *The Japanese Automobile Industry,* 1985, p. 321.
4. A. Blanton Godfrey, "The History and Evolution of Quality in AT&T," *AT&T Technical Journal,* March–April 1986, p. 11.
5. *Ibid.,* p. 15.

6. Kaoru Ishikawa, tribute to Walter A. Shewhart upon his death, *Industrial Quality Control* (hereafter known as *IQC*), Aug. 1967, p. 115.

7. W. Edwards Deming, tribute to Shewhart, *IQC,* Aug. 1967, pp. 112–113.

8. Deming, "What Happened in Japan," *IQC,* Aug. 1967, pp. 88–90.

9. Joseph M. Juran, tribute to Shewhart, *IQC,* Aug. 1967, p. 116.

10. Description taken from various sources, including interviews with Genichi Taguchi and others.

11. Edward Fuchs, "Quality: Theory and Practice," *AT&T Technical Journal,* March–April 1986, p. 7.

12. Genichi Taguchi and Yuin Wu, *Introduction to Off-Line Quality Control,* 1979, p. 1.

13. *Ibid.,* p. 1.

14. Letter from Taguchi to John Kennedy of the American Supplier Institute, Inc., Jan. 1988.

15. *Ibid.*

16. Interview with Taguchi, May 1987, Belleville, Michigan.

17. Letter from Taguchi to Kennedy, interview with Taguchi.

18. Ronald W. Clark, *The Life of Ernst Chain,* 1985, p. 68, and Gladys I. Hobby, *Penicillin: Meeting the Challenge,* 1985, pp. 209–210.

19. Letter from Taguchi to Kennedy, interview with Taguchi.

20. Letter from Taguchi to Kennedy.

21. *Ibid.*

22. Various sources, including Joan Fisher Box's biography of her father, *R. A. Fisher: The Life of a Scientist,* 1978.

23. Interview with Taguchi. Also, Taguchi ms., "The Development of Quality Engineering," *Hinshitsu,* April 1986, ms. pp. 3–4.

24. Taguchi, "The Development of Quality Engineering," p. 4.

25. *Ibid.,* p. 9.

26. Taguchi and Wu, *Introduction to Off-Line Quality Control,* p. 11.

6

Japanese Acceptance Grows

Dr. Genichi Taguchi worked at the Nippon Telephone and Telegraph Co.'s Electrical Communications Laboratories (ECL) from 1949 to 1961. Because of the dramatic results achieved at the ECL during this time and through his widespread industrial consulting activities, many Japanese engineers quickly accepted Taguchi's methodology. However, Quality Engineering was not always easily implemented in Japan. As is discussed in Chapter 11, many of the same stumbling blocks that American companies face—such as fear, disbelief, and unwillingness to try new ideas—were present in varying degrees. The Japanese companies were spurred on to accept Taguchi Methods because Japan was far behind the United States and Europe in the design and production of quality products. The need to catch up fostered an acceptance of new ideas in Japan in the 1950s. (This same force is subtly felt in America today, as U.S. companies seek competitive parity.)[1]

In light of some of the results engineers were achieving with the methods, however, it's not too surprising that Taguchi's techniques quickly became standard operating tools.

Nippondenso Co., Ltd., today Japan's leading automotive-component supplier and a leading practitioner of Taguchi Methods in Japan, first introduced the methodology in 1951. Nippondenso was established in 1949 and is a 21.5% subsidiary of Toyota Motor Corp. The company has actively promoted Taguchi Methods internally since 1951, developing its own experimental-design manual for in-plant use in 1962 and inviting Taguchi for consultation the following year. Nippondenso earned the prestigious Deming Prize in 1961 and has been credited with serving as the model from which Toyota developed its own quality-control program.[2]

Toyota itself embraced Taguchi Methods early on, and today mandates that all its engineers complete experimental-design training. Toyota is also requiring its supplier companies to do the same.[3]

Taguchi's first book, introducing orthogonal arrays and entitled *Experimental Design and Analysis for Life Test,* was published in 1951.[4] Two years later, the Japanese tile company Ina Seito, now called INAX Corp., performed a classic Taguchi Methods case study involving tile shrinkage.

The company had purchased a $2 million kiln from West Germany that was used for baking tiles. The tiles were typically stacked on skids and moved into the kiln for baking. After the kiln was stoked up and put into operation, managers and workers at Ina Seito noticed a strange phenomenon: The tiles stacked around the outside of the pile weren't baking uniformly and thus came out of the kiln in a wide variety of sizes. The tiles stacked toward the inside of the pile, however, were much more uniform in size.

Company technicians quickly deduced that the problem was caused by uneven temperature levels inside the kiln. Correcting the problem by redesigning the kiln was prohibitively expensive for the company. The problem couldn't be ignored, however, because it, too, was costing Ina Seito tremendous amounts in scrap and resulting in low productivity. Company managers consulted with Taguchi and decided to use his techniques to address the problem.

At the beginning of the experiment, and this is typical of any Taguchi Methods application, all of the people who were experts in tile manufacture and baking were brought together for a brainstorming session. These included engineers, chemists, and floor managers—anyone with special knowledge about the procedure.*

These brainstorming sessions typically generate benefits far beyond simply completing the task at hand. They increase communication flow between departments and cause people within those departments to begin thinking in terms that follow the actual manufacturing sequence: from concept to design to manufacture, even to packaging and shipping. Some American engineers have been surprised to find the actual solution to their problem during

---

*While technically not a part of Taguchi's Quality Engineering process, brainstorming techniques have been associated with it from the beginning. During a 1959 round-table discussion in Japan, brainstorming was alluded to as an integral component of Taguchi's system. Brainstorming is simply good engineering; some American companies have used the technique for years.

these sessions, without having to undertake a Quality Engineering study at all. Typically, they say, someone from another department will suddenly clarify a technique or correct an assumption concerning a mixing process or mold cycle that had been misinterpreted from the start!

Because Ina Seito couldn't afford to control the uneven temperature in the kiln, they labeled it an error (noise) factor—an uncontrollable factor that causes variation in the product.

During the brainstorming session, seven major control factors were identified that the group thought would have an effect on the tile shrinkage or productivity. The group then assigned two different performance levels to each factor: 1) the existing level of the factor and 2) a new level that the brainstorming team thought would have a positive effect on the process. The factors were assigned to an orthogonal array with either a "1" or "2" to indicate at which level the factor would be tested in that particular experiment.

This is thought by many to be one of the most important aspects of the entire process. The quality of all subsequent experimentation and analysis depends on choosing the correct control factors and the performance levels of those factors.

Ina Seito engineers ran eight experiments using an appropriate orthogonal array. If they had performed a full-factorial experiment, they would have had to run 128 experiments.

The noise factors were the various positions on the stack at which tiles could be placed to measure the variation caused by uneven temperature levels in the kiln.

One hundred tiles were sampled from each of the

eight experimental runs and checked for defects. By checking the number of defective tiles with the factor levels used in each experiment, the engineers discovered that limestone content had the largest consistent effect on shrinkage. The engineers also discovered that by increasing the amount of limestone in the tiles from its original level of 1% to the suggested level of 5%, and by using optimum levels of certain other materials, the kiln's defect rate dropped from 30% to less than 1%. A confirmation experiment—a must when using Taguchi Methods—proved the results to be correct.

In this case, the experimenters were lucky as well as accurate—limestone was the cheapest material in the tiles. They also discovered that they could reduce the amount of the most expensive ingredient, agalmatolite, without affecting tile size or quality and increase productivity 10% by adopting a new level of a certain factor.

Ina Seito simultaneously increased both productivity and quality while cutting costs by reducing both the defect rate and the amount of the most expensive material used in the tiles. Right here, in miniature, is the entire Japanese philosophy of reducing costs while increasing quality.[5]

Ina Seito never solved the problem of the kiln's uneven temperature: Instead, it developed a product robust enough to withstand uneven baking temperatures without shrinkage.

Moving Beyond Japan

In 1954, the year after the Ina Seito experiments, Taguchi was invited to introduce his methodology to Indian engineers by P. C. Mahalanobis, the same professor who invited

R. A. Fisher to visit India in the late 1930s. At about this time, Mahalanobis was finishing an ambitious study of world-wide statistics training capabilities for the United Nations. Mahalanobis first extended an invitation to Motosaburo Masuyama to visit India several years earlier. Masuyama subsequently suggested Taguchi to Mahalanobis, as Taguchi was more experienced in industrial statistics applications.[6] Taguchi remembers the year he spent in India in 1954 and 1955 as ultimately unsuccessful. While he helped conduct 20 experimental-design applications involving orthogonal arrays, Taguchi felt that his efforts weren't fruitful for several reasons.

India was using statistical methods in such traditional areas as agriculture and population surveys. At the same time, much of India's manufacturing technology had been imported from other countries, most notably Great Britain. Few Indian statisticians were engaged in research and development or production engineering. Because of this, India actually had few manufacturing problems. Most important parts and materials were imported. Products were simply assembled in Indian shops according to procedures established by engineers from the exporting companies. There was little need for Taguchi's techniques for creating robust products and processes.[7]

From a historical perspective, this trip was interesting, as Taguchi met Fisher and Walter A. Shewhart. Taguchi recalls having his picture taken with Shewhart and Prime Minister Nehru, a friend of Mahalanobis'.[8]

As a footnote to this visit, Taguchi had much better success in promoting his methods when he returned to India in the early 1970s. By then, India was developing its own manufacturing industries and was in great need of techniques that offered low cost and high quality. Typically,

Taguchi returns to India once every four years to help Indian engineers carry out Quality Engineering experiments.[9]

Taiwan's Involvement

In 1953, a young engineer named Yuin Wu and two associates began Taiwan's first foray into Statistical Process Control (SPC) at the Taiwan Fertilizer Co. One of the vice presidents of this national company had learned of Japan's progress with quality control and took steps to implement the system.[10]

Wu and his two colleagues pored over texts from America and Japan on SPC and gradually taught themselves how to set up and run an SPC program. Their successes over the years with SPC emboldened them to try other statistical methodology they had run across in their studies, namely experimental-design techniques. Wu soon realized that here was a system that offered much greater benefits than were possible with control charts and SPC.

So, once again, Wu sent away for texts from the United States on the subject. As Wu tells the story, he had tremendous difficulty even grasping the fundamentals of the American approach to Fisher's experimental-design techniques.

In 1957 and 1958, a large, two-volume book on experimental design written by Taguchi was published. Wu read about Taguchi's methodology and noted how much easier his approach was for an engineer to understand and use. "From that time on, I became a believer of Dr. Taguchi's methods," says Wu.

Wu studied Taguchi's methodology and ran several experiments based on his techniques in the early 1960s. It soon became evident to him that to gain a full understanding of Taguchi's Quality Engineering system, he would need a more active, give-and-take type of learning than was possible from reading books alone. He thus decided to travel to Japan and contact Taguchi.

A Trip to America

Taguchi, meanwhile, had embarked on his first trip to the United States. In 1962, Taguchi visited AT&T Bell Laboratories while on an eight-month research visit to Princeton University. At Princeton, Taguchi was hosted by John Tukey, a renowned statistician who then held a joint appointment between Princeton and Bell Labs. Tukey was department head of statistics research at Bell Labs, and he mentioned Taguchi's visit to one of his subordinates, a statistician named Ram Gnanadesikan. Tukey suggested that it might be valuable for Taguchi to work with the industrial statisticians at Bell Labs. Gnanadesikan agreed to host Taguchi for the six months he visited Bell Labs. Taguchi apparently never returned to Princeton after his introduction to Bell Labs, and Tukey's role during the visit diminished from this point on.

Gnanadesikan remembers Taguchi's lack of fluency in English as a major stumbling block during this first visit.[11] Taguchi recalls this trip primarily for the work he was able to do in studying the relationship of experimental design to communications theory developed at Bell Labs by C. Shannon. He indicates that he made significant progress in developing the Signal-to-Noise (S/N) Ratio for dynamic characteristics, notably digital or binary data.[12]

As their name implies, dynamic characteristics involve both a target and a signal that aren't statically fixed by the designer. In the case of a bathroom scale, for instance, the output of the system depends on the input, which is the weight of the person using the scale. Thus, the output is variable in proportion to the input, and the system must deviate as little as possible from accepted measuring standards across an infinitely variable range.[13] Dynamic characteristics are categorized in several different ways, including continuous signal and response, digital (on/off) signal and response, and various combinations of the two.

Static characteristics, on the other hand, will generally be included in one of three different response groups: "nominal the best," where the engineer wants the product or process to react in exactly the same way each time (e.g., engine assembly process); "smaller the better," where the engineer strives to generate the smallest result possible (e.g., engine exhaust emissions, tire wear, etc.); and "larger the better," where the engineer wants to obtain the largest result possible (e.g., engine-fuel efficiency, weld strength, etc.).

According to Gnanadesikan, Taguchi also developed an approach to analyzing categorical data using an engineering S/N Ratio while at Bell Labs.[14] "It turned out that the analysis was very much a standard statistical one, except that he was deriving it from the S/N Ratio point of view," says Gnanadesikan. Toward the end of his visit, Taguchi wrote a monograph on his findings regarding the S/N Ratio.

Taguchi also expressed an interest in the sampling techniques being used in quality control, and Gnanadesikan recalls attempts to link Taguchi up with members of Bell Labs' Quality Assurance Department, although little apparently came of it.[15]

Gnanadesikan, now an Assistant Vice President at Bell Communications Research (Bellcore), notes that during

Taguchi's 1962 visit there was no discussion on quality-control topics. "His total interest at that point was in analyzing so-called contingency tables and categorical data; in my view, he was rediscovering what are called chi-squares," he says. Taguchi recalls making a report at the end of his visit. However, he adds, "I think they didn't quite understand what I was doing." During this visit, no experimentation was done, although Taguchi began to apply the methods he discovered at Bell Labs once he returned to Japan.[16]

Gnanadesikan stayed in touch with Taguchi after the visit and remembers the tremendous hospitality Taguchi and his peers showed Gnanadesikan and his family during their 1968 visit to Japan. During this visit, Gnanadesikan first learned that Taguchi was consulting with Japanese automobile manufacturers on quality issues.

Gnanadesikan and Taguchi wrote to each other in the ensuing years, and when Taguchi wanted to return to Bell Labs in 1980, he turned to Gnanadesikan. Taguchi also came to the United States in 1978 with a group of Japanese automobile engineers and toured Bell Labs with Gnanadesikan's help. Tukey and Gnanadesikan joined the group for lunch, and Gnanadesikan recalls there being quite a bit of discussion regarding the extreme importance of quality control in Japan.[17]

Meeting the Master

After returning to Japan from his trip to America in 1962, Taguchi resumed work at the ECL until becoming a professor at Aoyama Gakuin University in Tokyo in 1964, a position he held until 1982. Taguchi also received a doctorate in science from Kyushu University in 1962.[18]

In the meantime, Wu had decided it was time to meet

this Dr. Taguchi and ask him questions concerning his techniques face to face. Wu applied through the China Productivity Center to the Japanese Standards Association (JSA), specifically requesting a consultation with Taguchi. Wu visited Taguchi in Japan in 1967 and stayed for four months. By this time, Taguchi was consulting, teaching, and giving seminars on his methodology on a frequent basis. He invited Wu to audit his classes, and in between Wu traveled with Taguchi to such Japanese companies as Toyota, where Taguchi was a consultant.[19]

On his return to Taiwan, Wu began to actively promote the use of Taguchi's methodology in his company and enjoyed some significant successes.

Taguchi and several co-authors wrote a book on management techniques that was published in 1966. The book, *Management by Total Results,* was published by the JSA and became a bestseller.[20] Wu translated it into Chinese.[21] In the book, Taguchi clearly defines the responsibilities of each department within a corporation. Even today, parts of the book seem fairly revolutionary to American managers. For example, Taguchi wrote that the sales department was responsible for setting the design-quality standards for the product. Sales, not engineering, decided at what level the product must be in terms of price, innovation, and quality to compete successfully in the marketplace. The design, engineering, and manufacturing departments were responsible for meeting that standard with as little deviation as possible.

An index was then developed for each department that, when compared with past indexes, showed the rate of improvement each department exhibited in reaching its various goals.

The book appealed to managers because of Taguchi's

brass-tacks approach to cutting costs while improving quality. Also in 1966, Taguchi published *Statistical Analysis*, which further developed his statistical techniques.

Wu invited Taguchi to visit Taiwan often, and the link between the two men grew into friendship. With every visit, Taguchi brought with him texts of new techniques he had developed. Wu translated these into Chinese. Through this effort, Wu gradually became an expert in Taguchi's methodology.[22]

Wu enjoyed a variety of career positions during this time, from plant manager to president of a small chemical company. Whenever his work took him to Japan, he always made it a point to look up Taguchi because, as he recalls, "I always had new questions for him."[23]

At this point, in the late 1960s and the early 1970s, the only two countries outside of Japan with knowledge of Taguchi's methodology were Taiwan and India.[24] The results achieved in Japan through Taguchi's techniques were incredible, to say the least. During this time period and throughout the 1970s, most of the work using Taguchi's techniques involved improvements in process capabilities, such as the tile experiment at Ina Seito. The Japanese have switched their emphasis to product design in the past decade. At Nippondenso, for instance, 48% of the Taguchi Methods case studies performed yearly deal with product design.[25]

Taguchi Methods can be very dramatic in solving process problems, and results tend to be quick. Taguchi himself has maintained, however, that cost benefits increase greatly as his methods are put to work in design areas. If an optimum product is designed in the first place, all of the possible downstream redesign and process costs are never even incurred.

Notes

1. Transcript of round-table meeting, "Plant Experiments Using Orthogonal Array," June 29, 1959, Japan. Provided by Genichi Taguchi.
2. "The History of Nippondenso's Activities of Application of the Taguchi Method," April 1987. Provided by Nippondenso Co., Ltd.
3. Yuin Wu, "Off-Line Quality Control—Japanese Quality Engineering," reprinted in *Collection of Publications on Taguchi Methods,* 1984, Section III.
4. Letter from Taguchi to John Kennedy of the American Supplier Institute, Inc., Jan. 1988.
5. Taguchi and Wu, *Introduction to Off-Line Quality Control,* 1979, p. 49, and Diane M. Byrne and Shin Taguchi, "The Taguchi Approach to Parameter Design," *ASQC Quality Congress Transactions,* 1986.
6. Letter from Taguchi to Kennedy.
7. Taguchi and Wu, *Introduction to Off-Line Quality Control,* p. 11.
8. Letter from Taguchi to Kennedy.
9. Interview with Shin Taguchi, April 1987, Nagoya, Japan.
10. Interview with Wu, June 1987, Dearborn, Michigan.
11. Telephone interview with Ram Gnanadesikan, Aug. 1987.
12. Letter from Taguchi to Kennedy.
13. Ramon V. Leon et al., "Performance Measures Independent of Adjustment: An Explanation and Extension of Taguchi's Signal-to-Noise Ratios," Bell Laboratories, 1986.
14. Telephone interview with Gnanadesikan.
15. *Ibid.*
16. Interview with Taguchi, May 1987, Belleville, Michigan.
17. Telephone interview with Gnanadesikan.
18. Letter from Taguchi to Kennedy.
19. Interview with Wu.
20. Letter from Taguchi to Kennedy.
21. Interview with Wu.
22. *Ibid.*
23. *Ibid.*

24. Wu, "An Unknown Key to Japanese Productivity," reprinted in *Collection of Publications on Taguchi Methods,* 1984, Section IV.

25. "The History of Nippondenso's Activities of Application of the Taguchi Method."

7

Consolidating the System

Over the years, Dr. Genichi Taguchi polished and added to his experimental-design techniques, finally naming them "parameter design." He developed the concept of the Quality Loss Function (QLF) in the early 1970s.[1] The results of parameter design can be fine-tuned by determining cost-effective tolerances during tolerance design, which incorporates the QLF. Together, parameter design and tolerance design became known as a form of off-line quality control.

Taguchi also developed a form of on-line quality control that economically justified sample and testing limits for a process (see Appendix D). In the past, engineers had simply instituted Statistical Process Control (SPC) to measure the standard deviation of a process, no matter what the cost. Taguchi's methodology was based on economic consideration, again highlighting his primary concern in industry—cutting costs.

Together, Taguchi's off-line and on-line quality-control techniques represent a complete, cost-based system of quality control that has few equals. In fact, a mid-1980 report from Ford Motor Co. credited Taguchi's system as a significant reason for Japan's cost and quality advantages during the 1970s and 1980s. Taguchi published two books—*Quality Evaluations* in 1972, written with several others, and *Quality and Economy*, printed in 1977—that further defined his techniques.[2]

In 1976, Yuin Wu immigrated to the United States. President Richard Nixon had reestablished contact with mainland China, and many Taiwanese were afraid that China would regain control of the tiny island nation that had separated from it following World War II.

On his way to the United States, Wu visited Taguchi in Tokyo. At the meeting, Taguchi asked Wu to promote his methods in the United States, which Wu promised to do. Wu's initial forays into the job market in California's Silicon Valley were less than successful, however. He sent out more than 200 resumes describing his expertise with Taguchi's Quality Engineering techniques. Not one company responded. "They probably thought, 'What is design of experiments, Japanese-style?' " he muses now.

For the next four years, Wu searched for a job in California, living on his savings. Finally, after continuous searching, Wu landed a job with a stereo-speaker manufacturer in Sacramento. Here, Wu applied Taguchi's techniques in some of his work and achieved very good results. These applications were the first Taguchi Methods experiments performed in the United States. While several of his colleagues saw the potential of the new system, most of Wu's co-workers continued using classical experimental-design techniques or changing one factor at a time and measuring the results.[3]

Acclaim in Japan

By the late 1970s, Taguchi's renown in Japan had become impressive. He had won the prestigious Deming Prize for quality applications, named after W. Edwards Deming and awarded by the Japanese Union of Scientists and Engineers (JUSE). In addition to the application prize, given in 1960, Taguchi won Deming awards for literature on quality in 1951, 1953, and most recently in 1984.

The Deming Prize was first instituted in 1951 by JUSE in recognition of Deming's work promoting Statistical Quality Control in Japan. Deming donated the royalties generated by a Japanese translation of one of his books and several other writings to fund the initial awardings of the prize. In more recent years, the prize has been funded by donations from JUSE.[4]

There are several categories of the Deming Prize. The one for individuals is given to the person whose work does the most to either develop or promote statistical quality methods. There are also prizes awarded to companies and specific plants within companies that have undergone rigorous examination by independent judges. Worthiness is judged on how well a company has adopted the concept of Company-Wide Quality Control and the rate of improvement in quality and market share that company has experienced. Many Japanese companies with known quality problems go after the Deming Prize not simply for the award itself, but for the overall improvement in quality and performance such a quest brings about. The Deming Prize has long been recognized as the premier award in Japan.[5]

America on the Ropes

Despite such acclaim in Japan, few people in the United States knew of Taguchi's achievements in developing economically driven and practical experimental-design methods for use in industry.

By 1980, the American auto industry had hit bottom in the eyes of many observers. It was entering a recession that came within a hair's breadth of destroying Chrysler Corp. entirely. New Chrysler head Lee Iacocca was forced to plead with the U.S. Congress for loan guarantees that would enable the company to continue borrowing money to remain afloat. Ford sustained an operating loss of more than $1.5 billion that year and was existing partially on the strength of its international operations. Ford would lose more than a billion dollars the following year and more than half a billion the year after that.[6]

The long-term debt of General Motors Corp. and Ford doubled between 1979 and 1980. In comparison, Toyota Motor Corp. had reduced its long-term debt to zero in 1977, and has funded operating projects from existing capital since that time.[7]

Between 1979 and 1980, passenger car sales fell by almost 2 million units. The drop, however, wasn't uniformly spread across the entire market—it was limited almost entirely to the domestic automakers. Imports, on the strength of Japanese sales, actually increased in the same time period, and would probably have grown even more if the Japanese Ministry of International Trade and Industry (MITI), under intense pressure from the U.S. government, hadn't set export quotas in the early 1980s, which limited the number of cars Japanese companies could ship to the United States.

American quality levels, when measured against the Japanese, had hit rock bottom. For an America searching for fuel efficiency, value, and high quality, the domestic automakers weren't even in the same league as the Japanese. The writing had been on the wall in several ways.

America was rapidly falling behind in the field of design. By the mid-1970s, the Japanese auto companies had passed the American auto industry in the number of automobile-related patents granted in the United States. That's a lead U.S. manufacturers have yet to overcome.[8]

Patent activity, which has an obvious correlation to design innovation, is one way to measure the effectiveness of an industry's research-and-development activities. While American automotive companies were outspending the Japanese significantly in total dollars in R&D, they were apparently achieving fewer design breakthroughs than their Oriental competitors. One reason was the tremendous amounts of cash the Americans were spending to downsize their products. The Americans were running hard just to slow the fall-behind rate they were experiencing.

Indeed, the American automakers lagged behind the Japanese and European makers in hardware development in many areas. Antilock brake systems, high-performance multi-valve engines, electronically controlled transmissions, four-wheel-steering systems, on-demand four-wheel-drive systems—all came to the U.S. market first on imported cars.

On the process front, it seemed as though American automakers had finally lost control of their manufacturing facilities. Work-in-process inventories ballooned to record levels. The lesson that high inventories hide quality problems and ultimately add tremendous cost at the manufacturing level was still a few years off at this point.

By 1980, these factors were taking their toll on the domestic automotive industry. This same year, Taguchi once again came to the United States.

Taguchi Comes to the U.S.

Taguchi recognized the great debt Japan owed to the United States of America, which had provided the economic and technical horsepower that drove Japan into its favored position in the world economy. A measure of the admiration he held for the United States was demonstrated when he enrolled his 15-year-old son, Shin, at Cranbrook Educational Community, located in Bloomfield Hills, Michigan, near Detroit. This decision required great conviction on Taguchi's part, because it would be very difficult for Shin to find his way in Japan's incredibly competitive secondary-school system after having been out of that environment for several years.

Taguchi wanted his son to be exposed to American culture and regarded Cranbrook as the best private school in America. As it turned out, Shin received all of his later education in Michigan, graduating from the engineering school at the University of Michigan.

In 1980, Wu invited Taguchi to give a seminar on his techniques at Wu's company in the United States.[9] Taguchi, who in addition to holding a professorship at Aoyama Gakuin University was director of the Japanese Academy of Quality by this time, accepted the invitation. Meanwhile, Taguchi wrote a letter to Ram Gnanadesikan, now the department head of statistics at AT&T Bell Laboratories' Murray Hill, New Jersey, facility.[10]

"He said that he had a really new approach to quality control," says Gnanadesikan. "He said that because the old system of quality control was born in Bell Labs with Shewhart and so on, he really wanted to come to Bell Labs to do this."

In his letter, Taguchi offered his time and services to Bell Labs for free, requesting no stipend or expense money.

Taguchi's letter indicated that he wished to address the use of experimental design in quality control and quality assurance. Gnanadesikan, while head of statistics, wasn't directly involved with quality, so he sent Taguchi's letter to Erold Hinds, a West Indian who headed up the Quality Theory and Systems Department at Bell Labs' Quality Assurance Center. Hinds agreed to Taguchi's offer, and Taguchi visited Bell Labs' West Long Branch, New Jersey, facility from August through October of 1980.[11]

At West Long Branch, Taguchi met a supervisor named Roshan Chaddha, an Indian mathematician who had been educated in classical statistical methods at Manchester University in England and received his Ph.D. in statistics from Virginia Polytechnic and State University. Chaddha had taught quality techniques at Kansas State University and was interested in Taguchi's techniques. "I got the inkling that Taguchi had a slightly different perspective on quality," he recalls. "I thoroughly enjoyed the first visit by Taguchi. He thought about the issues of quality differently than we did at the time. It struck me as a worthwhile thing for us to look at."[12]

Within a week of Taguchi's arrival, Chaddha realized that Taguchi wasn't attacking the problem of "mean" results, but instead was concentrating on reducing variance around the average. "It was a new, novel, different way of looking at things," says Chaddha. Taguchi's concept of robustness also appealed to Chaddha. "He was using the concepts of design of experiments, but he was using them in the context of building quality into the product at the design stage."

In looking for day-to-day contacts for Taguchi, Chaddha talked with several Bell Labs statisticians, whose reactions weren't enthusiastic. "The general feeling was that the United States knew all about experimental design," says

Madhav Phadke, an Indian engineer with a background in statistics who agreed to host Taguchi's visit.[13]

Phadke reviewed Taguchi's methodology and was attracted in particular by his novel approach to engineering, including the idea of designing robust products that could tolerate error-causing conditions (noise) without significantly varying a product's performance from the target value. However, even Phadke admits that his appreciation of Taguchi's experimental-design techniques was clouded by the pervasive feeling among the statisticians at Bell Labs that America knew all there was to know about design of experiments.[14]

As Hinds remembers, there were statisticians in the department who were doubtful of Taguchi's claims and proposals and thus paid little attention to the Japanese visitor. Others would argue heatedly about his methodology, but Taguchi remained unfazed by their comments.[15]

"Taguchi wanted to talk to engineers," Hinds remembers. "He consistently said that he wasn't interested in statisticians, that he was interested in helping engineers do their work. So he ignored all the complaints the statisticians had about the worthwhile nature of his work."

"We immediately sensed that he was more at ease talking to engineers. And his concepts appeared to go down faster with engineers than with statisticians," says Chaddha, himself a statistician. He described the problem: "Statisticians have a whole set of jargon, a whole set of orientations on how we approach the design of experimental problems, interactions, and so on. We always brought them out, and Taguchi always said that those weren't important issues. Because of this, some of us couldn't get off the dime as far as communication was concerned. Others of us felt that we should go past those issues."

To escape the deadlocked academic discussion on statistical issues, Phadke arranged for Taguchi to give a number of seminars, inviting many of his engineer colleagues and encouraging them to use Taguchi's methodology in their design/development efforts. Subsequent successful completion of a window lithography project (described in Chapter 8) and other projects helped establish Taguchi Methods within Bell Labs as a superior method for designing quality into products and processes.

Chaddha, Phadke, and Raghu Kackar, another Bell Labs statistician, are from India, and Hinds is a native of the West Indies. "It wasn't the easiest communication," says Chaddha. "I think the early history would show you that those of us [at Bell labs] who first associated with [Taguchi] almost all grew up outside of the United States.

"We all had, to a degree, the Oriental patience to listen to the story. I did try to involve, at that stage, some of my staff members who grew up here, but they had some difficulty communicating," Chaddha adds.

Chaddha notes the special interest Phadke had in Taguchi's methodology. "He led the way for me in particular, and Bell Labs in general, to understand what it was that Taguchi was saying."

Hinds was impressed by several managerial concepts Taguchi put forth while at Bell Labs, particularly the idea that a company had internal customers.

"Up to that point, whenever we talked about customer satisfaction, we thought of the end user," Hinds says. "He gave me the idea that you have internal customers, and if your idea is to have customer satisfaction, you'd better realize that the person you hand off your work to is your customer."

Hinds subsequently built his total-quality program

around the concept. He recalls that Taguchi also made another significant point. Hinds' department was involved in developing statistical-sampling plans—a Bell Labs specialty—for inspection and audit that were based on costs, field problems, and other hard data.

"He wasn't particularly keen about the way we were doing our sampling processes in the factory," Hinds explains. "His other point, which we took very seriously, was that while we were putting a lot of effort into inspection, it was a very costly thing to do, because that inspection was performed at the end of the assembly line. He said that we should be putting more effort into design, so that we were talking about preventing problems further down the line."

Hinds remembers Taguchi as a quiet man with a youthful look that belied his age. He was a tireless worker while at Bell Labs, says Hinds, although he never pushed his ideas on anyone. In meetings with management, Taguchi would respond to questions but wouldn't project himself into discussions.

Hinds was fascinated by Taguchi. "He'd start in a very simple manner and gradually get more and more complicated, so that you really saw the depth of the individual. He wasn't a shallow person. He could talk statistics if he wanted to talk statistics, but he didn't try to impress you with his knowledge. He was just trying to solve some fundamental problems by some tried-and-true procedures he'd adopted in Japan."

When asked why Taguchi took upon himself the expensive trip to Bell Labs, Hinds responds thoughtfully, "He gave his lectures freely, he gave his notes freely, he gave free copies of the book he'd written [which was translated into English by Yuin Wu].

"He told me that he was paying back a debt which he thought was incurred by what the United States had given to Japan after World War II. He said that he thought the United States had given Japan a lot of help in getting its quality act together. He thought that Deming and Juran had done a lot for the country, and he was doing his best to give back a little bit of what he had learned."

Hinds' story is corroborated by Gnanadesikan. "He pointed out to me that he'd been working at Nippon Telephone's Laboratories after the war, and that he felt the United States, in particular, had helped that laboratory so much that he wanted to do something in return.

"I felt he was motivated by a lot of things that weren't just technical in nature, and that he really wanted to come and do something for the United States. And I thought he really felt he wouldn't get national attention in quality control if he didn't come to its birthplace—namely, Bell Labs."

Gnanadesikan sees Taguchi's visit as a fortunate combination of the right people being in the right place at the right time. "A lot of things came together that summer. Madhav Phadke was already at Bell Labs and Raghu Kackar had just been hired from Iowa State University, and those two guys shepherded him around for the summer and were patient enough to learn his whole approach."

Notes

1. Genichi Taguchi indicated that he did not publish anything regarding the Quality Loss Function until around 1970 in an interview in Detroit in October 1987.

2. Letter from Taguchi to John Kennedy of the American Supplier Institute, Inc., Jan. 1988.

3. Interview with Yuin Wu, June 1987, Dearborn, Michigan.

4. Michael A. Cusumano, *The Japanese Automobile Industry,* 1985, pp. 322–23. Also see pamphlet outlining the goals, history, rules, and regulations of the Deming Prize, published by the Japanese Union of Scientists and Engineers.

5. *Ibid.*

6. Taken from Ford Motor Co. annual reports.

7. Alan Altshuler et al., *The Future of the Automobile,* 1984, p. 154.

8. *Ibid.,* p. 102. Also, William J. Broad, "Novel Technique Shows Japanese Outpace Americans in Innovations," *New York Times,* March 7, 1988, p. 1.

9. Interview with Wu.

10. Telephone interview with Ram Gnanadesikan, Aug. 1987.

11. Interview with Erold Hinds, July 1987, AT&T, Middletown, New Jersey.

12. Interview with Roshan L. Chaddha, July 1987, Bellcore, Red Bank, New Jersey.

13. Interview with Madhav S. Phadke, April 1987, Detroit International Airport, Detroit, Michigan.

14. *Ibid.*

15. Interview with Hinds.

8

Putting It to the Test

Roger Edwards, then working at AT&T's Integrated Circuit Design Capability Laboratory in Murray Hill, New Jersey, attended one of Dr. Genichi Taguchi's lectures and was intrigued. Edwards, an Englishman, was in charge of manufacturing wafers used in the fabrication of integrated circuits, and he was dealing with a serious problem. A large-scale integrated-circuit chip typically includes thousands of contact points, called "windows." These windows are actually microscopic holes etched through various oxide layers of the wafer that allow the interconnections between the various devices in the integrated circuit.[1]

Edwards' problem involved variability—if the windows in the wafer were too large, it greatly increased the chances of electrical shorts. If the windows were too small, some devices wouldn't be properly connected. The need to reduce variability in window size is best illustrated by the sheer number of windows each circuit contains: A typical microprocessor chip of this type has more than 250,000 windows in an area roughly half the size of a postage stamp.[2]

With the encouragement of Edwards, Erold Hinds, and Roshan Chaddha, the window-forming problem became the basis for an early and successful application of Taguchi Methods in the United States.*

Taguchi helped lay out the experiment, which was performed during his second visit to AT&T Bell Laboratories.

In fact, the eye-opening results of the experiment were achieved the day Taguchi was to catch his plane home to Japan. Madhav Phadke has been recognized as the driving force behind this first experiment. He was assisted by several colleagues, including Donald Speeney and Michael Grieco, members of the technical staff.

Speeney was assigned to actually run the experiments, and he admits the initial reaction among his colleagues at Murray Hill was one of disbelief. "Because of this, you had to dig people out and say, 'Come on, let's go, let's set up this experiment,' " Speeney recalls.[3]

Up to this point, Murray Hill engineers had already attempted certain "one-shot" fixes for the problem—changing one process factor at a time and then checking the results. None of these had proven satisfactory. "This experiment coordinated all the variables; it included the intuitive solutions of the engineers assigned to solve the problem," Speeney says. "The problem was significant, because we were going to the next-generation smaller dimension in device processing. And if we couldn't solve the problem at the

---

*As noted in Chapter 7, Yuin Wu performed the first Taguchi Methods applications in the United States while working for a California-based audio-equipment manufacturer.

larger dimension, it would be an even bigger problem at the proposed smaller dimension."

Together with Taguchi, the group came up with what they thought were the important variables for the experiment through two brainstorming sessions. The group selected nine factors, three with two different setting levels and six with three different setting levels, and assigned them to an 18-experiment (L_{18}) orthogonal array. At this point, the skeptics had a field day. How did they plan to solve a problem with 5,832 possible solutions by running only 18 of them? It seemed impossible. In this instance, only the 18-experiment inner array was used.

After running the experiment and performing statistical analysis of the results, Taguchi, Phadke, and the others discovered that if they changed the settings of three factors out of nine and used a fourth factor to adjust the mean results back to the target value, they could achieve a fourfold reduction in window variability. Before the experiment, one out of every four chips produced would have a window that wasn't "open." After the experiment, the ratio dropped to one defective window in 25 chips. Another benefit was seen after several weeks of production at the optimized settings: The reduction in defects allowed AT&T to reduce its wafer-inspection levels by a factor of two. "I think a lot of designers got sold on that one, because it worked," says Chaddha.

For Phadke, the success of that initial experiment led to a subsequent immersion in Taguchi's thinking. "The whole interaction with Dr. Taguchi at that time, planning that first experiment, analyzing the data—and thinking about it—that's where I learned tremendously. That was my best motivational experience," he says.

In the years that followed, Phadke and others at Bell

Labs continued to pursue Taguchi Methods, and Taguchi has been invited back to Bell Labs every year since 1980 to lecture and review case studies.

Recently, researchers at Bell Labs developed theoretical proofs for some forms of Taguchi's Quality Loss Function (QLF). Taguchi himself, when questioned on these activities, only smiles and indicates he has his own set of theories as to why his system works.

Today, AT&T, through Bell Labs, teaches Taguchi Methods to its design- and production-engineering staffs on a regular basis, and the methodology is an acknowledged driver behind AT&T's robust design campaign of recent years.

Taguchi's Influence Spreads to U.S. Industry

In the years that followed his 1980 visit to the United States, more and more American manufacturers learned of and implemented Taguchi Methods, even as a storm was brewing among American statisticians over Taguchi's practices.

Many statisticians were nonplussed by the "cookbook" nature of Taguchi's design-of-experiments techniques. They concentrated on attacking isolated segments of his methodology without taking into account the systematic series of checks and balances Taguchi had engineered in to prevent deceptive results. Arguments raged over whether it was more scientifically correct to use the Signal-to-Noise Ratio or to analyze mean results and variation around the mean separately.

The statisticians' objections seemed to center on the fact that Taguchi wasn't playing by the established rules, that he was disregarding aspects of the full-factorial experimental-design techniques. One thing no one could argue with, however, was the real-world effectiveness and results of Taguchi Methods.

Even as the statistical community locked ideological horns with Taguchi's system, U.S. manufacturers began reporting incredible results through its use. Taguchi, as is his habit, largely ignored this controversy, preferring instead to immerse himself in the problems engineers face in industrial situations.

Xerox Corp. and Taguchi

In 1980, a Xerox Corp. engineer named Don Clausing obtained from Bell Labs a copy of the blue workbook Taguchi had first handed out at Bell that same year. As Clausing pored over the book, he became enthusiastic over the discussion of the QLF. However, when he reached the chapters concerning parameter design, he couldn't follow the technique. He later discovered the reason for his mystification: Several of the equations in key examples contained language-translation errors. Clausing set the book aside for two years, until he met Taguchi in 1982. In discussing parameter design with Taguchi, Clausing soon recognized similarities between it and a system Xerox was developing involving stress testing and operating windows.[4]

The Xerox system measured failure rates, distinguishing between a soft failure, during which a product simply malfunctions one time, and a hard failure, after which the product will not operate.[5]

In the case of a soft failure, the goal was to locate the two control factors whose tolerances had the highest effect on the performance of the system. The performance coordinates of these factors were plotted on a two-dimensional graph, creating a "window" whose boundaries were the boundaries of system failure. As long as both control factors remained within the operating window of the graph, the system-failure rate remained below a predetermined amount. The idea was to enlarge the windows as much as possible, so that system failures occurred less and less often (and thus became robust against noise, to use Taguchi terms).

The operating window was widened by using engineering judgment in selecting mean control values for the two control factors, and through the use of stress-testing procedures. Additional improvements could also be made through the use of Failure Projection Modeling, a technique developed at Xerox.[6]

Compared with the old method of changing one factor at a time over and over until an engineer stumbled across acceptable settings, the Xerox system was highly effective, and improvements in quality had been dramatic.

Clausing realized Taguchi's approach was more highly developed and more efficient than the system Xerox was using, however, and began promoting the system within Xerox.*

Despite Clausing's interest, Xerox did not begin using Taguchi's Quality Engineering technique until 1982. That year, the company was exposed to the technique through its copier-manufacturing joint venture with Fuji Photo Film Co. of Japan. Fuji Photo Film had been a leader in the use of Taguchi Methods in Japan for decades, and Taguchi

---

*Clausing, by the way, accepts credit for coining the phrase "Taguchi Methods" to describe Taguchi's Quality Engineering techniques. The Taguchi Methods tag isn't used in Japan, although recently it has been mentioned in print.

himself had done consulting work with the company for years.

Because of this relationship, Taguchi also did work for the joint-venture company, Fuji-Xerox, Ltd.

On the strength of the successes seen at Fuji-Xerox, Taguchi was invited to come to Xerox in early 1982. During this initial visit, he worked with the Xerox Supplies Manufacturing Group, which builds photoreceptors and other copier components. This first session lasted about one week, and wasn't well received.

"Our engineers challenged his techniques, which were clearly in contention with the traditional statistical design that we had used," says Wayland Hicks, Xerox Corp. Executive Vice President and President of the Business Products and Systems Group. Hicks also mentions the communication difficulties caused by the translation of complicated ideas and concepts from Japanese into English. "That made it tougher for him to be immediately accepted."[7]

Clausing and Jean Parks, the developer of the Failure Projection Modeling system Xerox was using, were assigned to study Taguchi Methods to determine their potential impact on one of the subsystems of a copier machine.

Clausing and Parks thus became leaders in the technology for the company.* But as Hicks notes, "Having two

*Clausing has since become Bernard M. Gordon Adjunct Professor of Engineering Innovation and Practice at Massachusetts Institute of Technology in Cambridge, Massachusetts, and is recognized as one of the pioneers in the promotion and development of not only Taguchi Methods, but a broad array of other innovative industrial-research and technological-development tools as well, including Quality Function Deployment.

people in a large organization sold on something isn't particularly helpful, either. You still have a lot of inertia, a lot of resistance, and other inhibiting factors."

Hicks himself met Taguchi in 1983. He had just been made president of the Xerox copier/duplicator business, known as the Reprographics Business Group. He was responsible for the technology, design engineering, and manufacturing of the company's products. At the time, the company was facing significant cost and quality disadvantages against its Japanese competitors. Because of scheduling commitments both men had, Hicks met with Taguchi at 6:00 a.m. at a hotel in Rochester, New York.

At the meeting Hicks urged Taguchi to work closely with Xerox to gain acceptance for his methods. Taguchi accepted the challenge, and, with Hicks' help, Taguchi Methods gained acceptance in the company.

"After meeting with Taguchi in 1983, I invited him to come back and do two things. I asked him to meet with me and my senior management team and to give us a tutorial, which he did, a two-hour presentation on the cost of quality to society," Hicks explains. "We also picked opinion leaders in the organization, key people who carried the respect of their colleagues."

These people received a similar tutorial. The idea was to convince the people who were in positions of authority to "pull" Taguchi Methods into the company, rather than have Clausing and Parks try to push the technique through from department to department. The plan worked. As Hicks says now, "If the senior management team in an organization feels strongly about it, people will have a tendency to follow that authority."

Hicks himself developed a close personal relationship with Taguchi, meeting his family on trips to Japan and inviting him to dinner at his home whenever Taguchi visited Xerox in the United States.

"The people in the organization understand that I have a fairly close relationship with Dr. Taguchi. Because of that relationship, there may have been a natural inclination to take him a bit more seriously than they otherwise would have."

Hicks came to realize that many of the problems the company was having in its product-development cycle could be traced back to one key area—a lack of readiness in regard to the technology that had been put into the products being designed. Hicks defines it using Taguchi's term: a lack of robustness.

Alluding to this problem, he mentions that when Xerox developed a new copier, the company would conduct exhaustive testing procedures, simulating environmental conditions from all over the world; literally thousands of hours of testing would be undertaken before the final product was arrived at. Testing would continue throughout the design cycle, meaning it could take from two to four years—sometimes, even longer.

Once, during a conversation in Japan, Taguchi mentioned the crossbar-switching system that had been developed by the Electrical Communications Laboratories back in the late 1940s. "He basically said that the reliability of the switchboard was such that it couldn't have a failure for a 40-year period of time. He then said, 'Think about your own testing procedures, and understand how long the design-and-development cycle would have to be in order to accomplish that degree of reliability.' "

Hicks mulled the idea over during his flight back to the United States. "I concluded that it would have to be 200 to 300 years long."

Today, Taguchi Methods are used regularly throughout Xerox to test the robustness of technology in designs very early in the design/development cycle. In the early years, Taguchi would be called in as a troubleshooter for a specific problem area. Today when he visits—which is usually for two to three weeks a year—his role is more that of a teacher, lecturing to broad groups of engineers.

From America, Xerox has spread the word about Taguchi Methods to its design and engineering community in Europe, and Taguchi himself has aided in the training. Rank-Xerox, in fact, has already started an in-house Taguchi newsletter.

Notes Hicks regarding negative reactions to Taguchi's methodology, "That has changed dramatically. Taguchi's ideas are pulled into the corporation today, rather than pushed in."

Leading to the Auto Industry

An intriguing chain of events began in 1980, the same year Taguchi visited Bell Labs. In June 1980, NBC aired a white paper on Japanese manufacturing titled "If Japan Can, Why Can't We?"

The program highlighted W. Edwards Deming's contributions to Japanese quality control and caused a riot of interest in Statistical Process Control (SPC) among U.S. automakers. That same year, the U.S. Department of Transportation issued its largely negative report on the prospects for the domestic automotive industry. A study by Harbour and Associates, Inc., that contributed to the report indicated that Japanese automakers were saving nearly $400 per car by emphasizing defect prevention rather than the after-the-fact inspection systems then popular with U.S. automakers.[8]

In February 1981, Ford Motor Co. invited Deming to visit and explain the concepts of SPC. Deming ultimately handpicked a fellow statistician to implement SPC at Ford, and Ford began sending its top managers and engineers through Deming's four-day seminars. General Motors' Pontiac Division also secured a long-term commitment with Deming's organization for the implementation of SPC training.

Ford, Pontiac, and much of the rest of the automotive industry subsequently began using SPC, and most began programs to expose their outside suppliers to the technique. Ford, in particular, asked supplier-company chief executives to attend Deming's classes, following Deming's philosophy that top management must drive any quality program if it's going to be successful.

A question lingers to this day concerning the U.S. automakers' 11th-hour interest in statistical methods. Why did it take the domestic automotive industry so long to wholeheartedly embrace a quality concept as straightforward as SPC?

In the years following World War II and into the 1950s, some parts of the U.S. automotive industry were actively involved with SPC, but these efforts were largely confined to quality-control departments and never really used or understood by top management. Some within the industry feel that there's a direct correlation between the declining use of statistical methods in the early 1950s and the emergence of short-term, financially oriented professional managers. Eventually, SPC was all but forgotten.

While the Americans had seen the Japanese building in

power over the years, it took an earth-shattering event—like Ford losing $1.5 billion in 1980—to really shake company managers out of their complacency. Not many managers, no matter how professional, could put an optimistic face on an industry that was losing $10.9 million every day in 1980—a total of more than $4 billion.

Until 1980, American industry had continued to function under the impression that it remained the manufacturing overlord of the world, and that anything the Japanese or anybody else could do, America could do better. It was a classic case of the "not-invented-here" syndrome, and it infected not only the domestic automotive industry, but other industries throughout the country.

To its credit, Ford really led the way for the industry in pursuing a high-quality/low-cost ethic. Ford executives realized that there was a better way to ensure quality than to employ the 15,000 "quality-control specialists"—many of whom were inspectors—the company had in its U.S. operations in 1978.[9]

Donald Petersen, President of Ford at the time, personally endorsed the SPC effort, and Ford first instituted SPC training both in-house and among its suppliers in May 1981, opening the Ford Supplier Institute, whose primary goal was to teach Ford suppliers SPC.

In July 1981, an ITT Automotive plant initiated the first Ford-related SPC case study. One month later, Ford introduced its SPC-based Q-1 supplier quality award. Ford also began its continuous improvement program, which has since spread from manufacturing to every other segment of the company, including finance.

In March 1982, Ford sent its first study mission of in-house and supplier quality engineers to Japan on a fact-finding tour. During a visit to Nippondenso Co., Ltd., the group was first exposed to Taguchi Methods of experimental design. That same month, Petersen issued an internal document that outlined Ford's goal of reducing the variability of process output, rather than concentrating on simply meeting specifications.

Creation of the American Supplier Institute

During October 1982, Lawrence P. Sullivan, Director of Supplier Quality Assurance at Ford's Body and Assembly Division, went to Japan to meet Taguchi. Sullivan invited Taguchi to visit Ford and the Ford Supplier Institute. The following March, Ford retained Yuin Wu and Taguchi's son, Shin—still a student at the University of Michigan at the time—to teach Taguchi Methods to Ford and Ford supplier engineers at the Ford Supplier Institute. By 1984, the demand for Taguchi Methods seminars from companies throughout the United States grew so dramatically that Ford decided to spin off the Ford Supplier Institute into an independent, nonprofit organization, the American Supplier Institute (ASI), Inc. Taguchi was named Executive Director of the training facility. Two years later, Sullivan became its Chairman and Chief Executive Officer.

In July 1983, Shin Taguchi assisted in the first Taguchi Methods case study performed in the American automotive industry. The study involved a welding problem at ITT's wiring-harness-assembly plant in Cairo, Georgia. ITT was supplying wiring harnesses to Ford and using SPC to monitor their quality. The company was meeting Ford's specification requirements. Certain connections in the harnesses, however, were fracturing during assembly or subsequent handling and installation at ITT and Ford.[10]

The fracture would later separate in the field, causing

electrical failures and even fires. It was an infrequent but vexing problem, and field diagnosis could be extremely difficult. Ford proposed a method for solving the problem that involved replacing the current resistance-welding technology with new, state-of-the-art ultrasonic-welding technology that would cost the company roughly $1 million.

Instead, a small group of engineers and technicians performed a bare-bones, 27-experiment Taguchi Methods design of experiments. During the case study, which took about two days to perform and cost about $100, the participants discovered that many of the preconceived "fixes" for the problem—increasing the number of welds or upping the amount of current in the welds—could actually have a negative impact on weld strength. Some of the suggested solutions would cause brittleness, for example, and potentially make the problem worse.

"The perception or knowledge in the technology proved to be wrong," notes J.K. (Jim) Pratt, ITT's Director of Statistical Programs and an acknowledged pioneer in Taguchi Methods in the United States. "The things that we thought would increase weld strength did not increase weld strength—in fact, they often had deleterious effects."

After running the experiments, which involved 13 factors at three different levels, and laboriously analyzing the data by hand, the experimenters discovered that using straight wire, rather than wire that was twisted, was very important, as was the amount of weld area.

By selecting the optimum levels of the 13 factors, it was possible to increase the weld strength to such an extent that the wire itself would consistently break before the weld would give way. The new method also reduced the variability of the welds by 23% compared to the existing equipment-operating conditions. The division solved the problem and saved the $1 million it would have had to invest in the ultrasonic equipment. It also recommended that destructive pull testing be discontinued on the welding circuits, and estimated that the move could save the harness industry almost $1 million.

Seeing Is Believing

ITT was the pioneer automotive supplier in the implementation of Taguchi Methods in the United States and remains a leader. A number of other companies also began using Taguchi's experimental-design techniques, including AT&T, Allen-Bradley Co., Allied Corp., The Budd Co., Control Data Corp., Copeland, Dana Corp., Davidson Textron Co., Diversitech General, Eaton Corp., Flex Technologies, General Electric Co., General Tire Co., Goodyear Tire and Rubber Co., Johnson Controls Inc., Kelsey-Hayes Co., Mercury Marine, Polaroid, Sheller-Globe Corp., A.O. Smith, Texas Instruments, United Technologies Automotive, and Xerox Corp.

Taguchi has always maintained that hands-on experience is the most valuable teaching tool possible when it comes to his methods. In pursuing this philosophy, Taguchi helped Nippondenso to develop a structured review of Taguchi Methods case studies in a symposium format. Many American companies, including Ford, GM, and Chrysler Corp., have also instituted internal symposia to review and discuss their case studies—an extremely effective method for transferring techniques and procedures. It's interesting to note that many companies measure their success with Taguchi Methods in terms of dollars saved versus defects prevented. And even at this early stage, the results have been impressive.

Compared to the Japanese, however, American companies have barely scratched the surface. By 1987, it was estimated that more than 6,000 Taguchi Methods case studies had been completed in the United States. Nippondenso, on the other hand—a company with 35,000 employees of whom 6,000 are engineers—performed almost 3,000 Taguchi Methods case studies in 1986 alone.[11]*

Taguchi has written literally hundreds of articles and several books on the subject—including his definitive two-volume reference work, *Design of Experiments (Jikken Keikakuho),* which, after having gone through three editions, has sold more than 100,000 copies. The English edition, *The System of Experimental Design,* was co-published by UNIPUB/Kraus Publications and ASI in 1987.[12]

Almost all of the case studies performed in the United States so far have involved off-line process optimization, such as ITT's welding application. Process-design experimentation yields quick and dramatic results—one moment a machine or process is generating rejects, the next moment it's not. Almost 50% of the case studies Nippondenso performed in 1986, on the other hand, involved product-design optimization. As American managers discover the full range and flexibility of Taguchi's system, they, too, will focus more on design. As one American engineer put it, the Japanese have had more than 30 years to get their products and processes in order and under control using Taguchi Methods, while America has had less than a decade.

---

*By the early 1980s, more than 21,000 Japanese engineers and scientists had attended 60 hours of training in Japanese experimental design. More than 7,000 had taken a 120-hour seminar, and an additional 3,000 had studied the technique through eight-month correspondence courses.[13]

Notes

1. Interview with R. L. Chaddha, M. S. Phadke, R. N. Kackar, D. V. Speeney, and M. J. Grieco, "Off-Line Quality Control in Integrated Circuit Fabrication Using Experimental Design," *The Bell System Journal*, May-June 1983, pp. 1273-1309.

2. *Ibid.*

3. Interview with Donald V. Speeney, July 1987, AT&T Bell Laboratories, Holmdel, New Jersey.

4. Don. P. Clausing, "The Role of Specialists in the Introduction of Taguchi Methods Into the United States," transcription of speech given at the Fifth Annual Taguchi Symposium, October 1987, Detroit, Michigan.

5. Clausing, "A Comparison of Three Methods of Engineering Optimization," *Collection of Publications on Taguchi Methods*, Section IX.

6. *Ibid.*, p. 6.

7. Telephone interview with Wayland Hicks, Feb. 1988.

8. John McElroy, "Report Details Japanese Advantage," *Automotive Industries*, Jan. 1982, p. 24.

9. Information taken from Ford Motor Co. annual report.

10. Interview with J. K. (Jim) Pratt, Aug. 1987, Farmington Hills, Michigan.

11. "The History of Nippondenso's Activities of Application of the Taguchi Method," April 1987. Provided by Nippondenso Co., Ltd.

12. Yuin Wu, "An Unknown Key to Japanese Productivity," reprinted in *Collection of Publications on Taguchi Methods*, 1984, Section IV.

13. *Ibid.*

9

Taguchi Methods Among Defense Contractors

In the years following 1980, many forward-thinking American manufacturing companies adopted Dr. Genichi Taguchi's Quality Engineering techniques. Today, Taguchi Methods are beginning to have an impact on the American defense industry, an industry that's ripe for change where quality and cost improvement are concerned.

During the mid-1980s, the Pentagon began an aggressive drive to promote competition among defense contractors. The U.S. Air Force, for example, was developing a new Advanced Tactical Fighter (ATF) and awarded fixed-price contracts for the plane to two companies. Each company was to design and build a prototype version of the ATF and the two would compete in a "fly-off," the winner of which would be granted a production contract. Selection was to be based on not only technical ability, but also estimated production costs. This new toe-to-toe procurement system could become the model on which similar U.S. Army and Navy projects are based.*

The idea is to improve the efficiency of the Pentagon's procurement procedures by putting free-market forces to work among defense contractors. While the new system will force contractors to battle more ferociously for contracts, it will also mean that contractors will have to take bigger, more expensive gambles than ever before: investing company funds in prototype aircraft, modernizing facilities, building multi-million-dollar simulators, and the like. In the past, much of this cost was defrayed by government funding. The new system seeks to shift more of the financial burden to the contractors.

The program has its critics. Nevertheless, it points to an increased awareness by both the U.S. government and military of the need to manage America's enormous defense budget with a greater sense of fiscal responsibility. The added burden of such a program means that defense contractors will have to work smarter than ever, both in terms of product *and* process design.

America Led the Way

The U.S. military was the leader in adopting statistical-sampling methods for random inspection among its contractors during World War II, and it developed exhaustive documentation on inspection-qualification techniques. The

---

*The system of competing for contracts is already achieving results. A competitive program between General Dynamics Corp. and McDonnell-Douglas Corp. cut the average price of a Tomahawk cruise missile from more than $1 million to $653,000.[1]

military hasn't been a leader in adopting some of the more current quality technologies, however, including the need for continuous quality improvement. While the use of Statistical Process Control (SPC) is now being mandated in many defense contracts, the intent is almost always to conform to specifications rather than maintain uniformity at a target value within specification. Often, the target value is unknown.

In many cases, the military hasn't realized that post-production-inspection techniques don't prevent defective parts from getting to the field, and that inspection actually adds cost to most programs.

Areas of Difficulty

Among the problems many defense contractors have faced—aside from the obvious political and bureaucratic entanglements—are short production runs, enforced supply sources, uncertain year-to-year budgets, and the lack of a unified quality standard in dealings with the Armed Services' three branches.

Of major concern to some defense suppliers is the military's product-acquisition system, which bases purchasing decisions on government-generated specifications rather than product-performance requirements. According to sources within the industry, the agencies that issue contracts are not the same agencies that establish the specifications. And the agencies that establish the specifications have limited contact with military R&D laboratories, not to mention end users. Complicating this is the three-pronged structure of the Armed Services and its various bureaucracies and military/civilian infrastructures.

Additionally, defense companies face tremendous contract "buy-in" pressures based on the need to sustain operating and employment levels. Because of this, some long-term program contracts are pursued with a "win-at-all-cost" mentality, and are thus underbid. One of the contractor's options is to win the contract, fill his order schedule, and then increase prices when the government places subsequent orders (typical Congressionally funded increments span only the first few years of a program).

This system directly affects a product's critical research-and-development cycle, which is always undertaken at the very beginning of the program. Because it underbid, a company often lacks sufficient funding to generate a state-of-the-art design. Funds usually remain short during prototype testing, subsequent tooling-up activities, and even into the onset of actual production. In other words, the contractor is forced to chew through the contract's meat with wooden teeth. The result can be an inadequately developed design that's being built with less-than-optimum tooling on a make-do assembly line.

The "win-at-all-cost" scenario puts maximum effort in the political/procurement arena, while the actual product and its production system become somewhat secondary concerns. Often, subsequent attempts to solve product and production problems involve adding layer upon layer of management cross-check and inspection systems designed to catch defective products before they reach the customer (in this case, members of the Armed Forces). This is yet another example of managing problems rather than systematizing solutions.

In light of the new, more competitive contracts being proposed by the Pentagon, it's doubtful that the pressures to underbid will lessen, which means that defense contractors must learn to improve both quality and cost.

A Report to Congress

The impact of these and other factors on the quality of defense hardware has been profound. The General Accounting Office (GAO) made a study of the Department of Defense's (DOD) quality-assurance programs and reported its findings to the U.S. Senate in late 1986.[2]

The DOD began its in-house quality-assurance program in order to document whether major defense contractors were complying with the quality specifications set forth in their contracts. As the GAO describes it, the task of seeing that contract quality specifications are met belongs to Army, Navy, and Air Force Plant Representative Offices (PROs) and the Defense Contract Administration Service.

After scrutinizing the quality-assurance operations at various defense contractors, the GAO said in its report that "We believe the present in-plant quality-assurance program is not as effective as it should be in ensuring that quality products are delivered to field activities. Evidence of this ineffectiveness can be found in service and (Defense Logistics Agency) studies which document that many contractors are not adequately controlling quality and producing hardware which conforms with contract requirements."

The report goes on to state that Air Force teams began a study to assess how well Air Force contractors were fulfilling their contractual quality requirements. The teams found problems at most of the monitored plants. These problems often ranged the entire spectrum of functions that impact quality: manufacturing, material management, contract management, subcontract management, safety and fire protection, engineering, quality assurance, and product integrity. Of 24 plants studied, only three received satisfactory ratings in all of these areas.

When studying product integrity, the Air Force found that one contractor was producing 40% defective parts and that its inspection system was allowing 24% defective parts to go to the field. At another plant, 38% of the hardware examined according to the contractor's own inspection criteria was defective.

In a 1985 review of subcontractor quality, the Defense Logistics Agency gave 79% of the 224 primary defense contractors it studied unacceptable ratings because they weren't adequately controlling the quality of parts and materials sourced from subcontractors.

The GAO reports that the Navy's concern over the integrity of its missiles led it to disassemble a missile in December 1984 to check its various systems. The Navy noted what it termed "inspection escapes"—a fancy way of saying that government and contractor inspectors had allowed the missile to get through with defective or missing hardware. Other parts of the missile that *had* been inspected and reworked indicated substandard repairs, and the Navy found uninsulated wiring that endangered nearby circuits. Obviously, the Navy deemed the missile unacceptable. That the missile in question wasn't an isolated case of poor quality is substantiated by a proposal that the Navy institute a formal hardware "teardown" policy, the GAO notes.

The GAO report inadvertently emphasizes the dominant role inspection plays in defense-industry quality-assurance programs. In addition to the contractor's inspectors, the government fields its own inspectors from the PROs. Inspection, as many commercial industries have learned, in no way guarantees good quality—even 100% inspection. At two of the examined aircraft manufacturers, the GAO discovered that in a fairly large percentage of cases, the government inspectors weren't even performing the inspections mandated by the Army and Navy on certain critical aircraft functions.

The GAO notes that the secretary of the Navy at that time sent a memorandum to the secretary of defense, stating that the defect rate among hardware produced for the Naval Air Systems Command was higher than 20%, and that much of the defective hardware had nonetheless been passed by government inspectors at defense-contractor plants. The secretary of the Navy complained that the reason for the rise in defect rates could be traced to a decision that shifted emphasis from inspection of products to approval of the contractor's quality-assurance program.

On the face of it, it seems as though the secretary of the Navy was considering taking a giant step backward in quality assurance, moving away from effective process-quality management and toward line inspection. The secretary goes on to state, however, that the agency responsible for approving and reviewing contractor quality systems hadn't been provided with a staff large enough to effectively perform this duty. The agency in question notes its difficulty in hiring and retaining quality-assurance specialists.

The military's inspection system brings to mind the system used by the automaker cited in Chapter 3. After cars were assembled and inspected in the factory, they were taken to another building where other inspectors would reinspect the work the factory inspectors had already performed.

In the defense industry, the reinspection technique is similar in form but different in function—the government inspectors are there to make sure that the contractor inspectors are doing their jobs. Instead of ensuring that the product is built right the first time, the defense industry's inspection system is designed solely to catch mistakes. Even if it's 100% effective in doing that—which it can't be simply because human inspectors aren't infallible—it does little to reduce the cost of scrapped or reworked hardware.

Other Problems

Capping this highly bureaucratic quality-assurance system is the almost year-to-year uncertainty that programs will continue to be funded. The contractor typically has more at risk in investing in added research or production capabilities for long-range product- or process-improvement programs. In some cases, contractors are actually compensated for terminated contracts.

In many cases, the equipment used by U.S. defense contractors in producing state-of-the-art fighter aircraft and the like is less than state-of-the-art itself. An article in *The Wall Street Journal* outlined the problem rather dramatically.[3] Grumman Corp.—the company that created the F-14 fighter—was found to be producing the F-14 and four other aircraft on machine tools with an average age of 34 years in 1987. The article also makes it clear that Grumman is by no means alone in falling behind in capital spending.

Industry insiders defend today's quality levels with the argument that the high levels of complexity of military hardware make military suppliers look bad compared to commercial industry.

However, according to a National Academy of Sciences investigation, the defense industry has invested in new equipment and technology at only half the rate of commercial industry.

Dealing with the Problems

A complaint heard among builders of low-volume hardware in the defense industry is that inspection is the only way they can audit quality levels. The reason given is that short-run setups of SPC-measuring devices often prove to be too complicated or expensive. As previously noted, process control is ensured through the same inspection techniques that led to the automotive industry's quality and cost problems. In such cases, Taguchi's cost-driven methods of on-line quality control (reviewed in Appendix D) could be used in conjunction with off-line quality-control activities. The most reliable quality-control method is to optimize design and process parameters so that inspection and SPC aren't even necessary.

The defense industry would seem to be a ripe target for many of the established Japanese quality-control techniques, including Just-in-Time (JIT) production, Quality Function Deployment (QFD), and Taguchi Methods.

In terms of the latter, one defense contractor has already made significant strides. Thomas R. Stuelpnagel, retired President of Hughes Helicopter, Inc., now McDonnell-Douglas Helicopter, has been a defense-industry consultant for the past eight years. It was through his consulting work at Aerojet Ordnance Co., Tustin, California, that Stuelpnagel first encountered Taguchi's Quality Engineering techniques. He subsequently attended an awareness seminar on Taguchi Methods at the American Supplier Institute (ASI), Inc.

Stuelpnagel, a research-and-development engineer by background who pursued a statistics-based hardware-development strategy while at Hughes Helicopter, immediately recognized the benefits of Taguchi's system in the area of design.

"I think there is going to be an absolute groundswell in this country in what I term Total Quality Control (TQC), and Taguchi Methods will play a large part in it," Stuelpnagel predicts. "I see a definite relationship between what Deming is doing and what Taguchi is doing." In fact, Stuelpnagel has proposed an integrated approach that combines the methods of Deming, Taguchi, and Willis Willoughby—a U.S. Navy executive—to launch the defense industry into the new quality age.[4]

Stuelpnagel's concept of TQC can be best defined as a superior product with higher quality, lower cost, and satisfied users. "The basis for all of this is statistical methods," he adds.

Stuelpnagel has worked with the Army Materiel Command and its Ordnance Command (known as AMCCOM), located at the Rock Island Arsenal in Rock Island, Illinois. AMCCOM, in fact, has added the stipulation that operator-maintained SPC techniques be included in all of its contracts.

Still, the progress being made to date only scratches the surface of what needs to be done. The Army is just now in the process of qualifying suppliers in the use of SPC, even though the commercial arms of those companies have been recognized leaders in the field for many years. One of the primary problems involves the sheer number of different parts that may have to be qualified in any given plant, which can range up to the thousands.

First Successes

Aerojet Ordnance was one of the first defense contractors to use Taguchi Methods, and it's added a few wrinkles of its own to the application of the techniques. Aerojet Ordnance is part of Aerojet General, the defense arm of GenCorp. A former GenCorp subsidiary, General Tire Corp., was a pioneer in the use of statistical quality methods, as well as Taguchi Methods.

Because of General Tire's successes with SPC, GenCorp management asked various Aerojet Ordnance executives to attend SPC classes at ASI in 1985. The president did and came back highly enthusiastic about SPC's benefits.

Thus, quite a few Aerojet Ordnance employees took SPC training at ASI, including James Kowalick, director of productivity and quality improvement. While doing so, Kowalick learned about ASI's Taguchi Methods training program, which he decided to take. Kowalick had, in his own words, no extraordinary statistical background prior to his work at Aerojet Ordnance.[5]

Something Clicks

"I inherited responsibility for the engineering side of the company, which included troubleshooting on product problems, and believe me, I was throwing my hands up until I heard about Taguchi. Then bells started to ring and things started to click," Kowalick says. "It answers many, many questions which I frankly didn't think there were answers to."

Before joining Aerojet Ordnance in 1984, Kowalick had extensive experience on both sides of the fence in the defense industry. He directed a U.S. government defense laboratory and ran the Army Combat Vehicles Science and Technology program. He has also worked as a technical director at another defense contractor and as an industry consultant. Kowalick, who holds a Ph.D. in material engineering from Drexel University, said that before his exposure to Taguchi Methods, Aerojet Ordnance had seldom used the more traditional experimental-design techniques, opting instead for experimentation that involved changing one factor at a time.

"We have some very creative people at our company and they were doing a good job with what they had, but we had the normal product problems that contribute to the cost of poor quality; and our quality costs were too high in terms of their percentage of total product cost," he says.

Aerojet Ordnance is a munitions supplier whose main products are "bomblets," combined-effect munitions that are fired from aircraft. The company also produces millions of ammunition rounds a year. It was in the ammunition side of the business that Taguchi Methods were first applied.

Aerojet Ordnance initially concentrated its efforts on pyrotechnic tracer elements. If you've ever seen a war movie where a machine gunner is firing at the enemy and the bullets have comet-like tails, you've seen tracers. Tracers are used to help the machine gunner bring his gun on target quickly and accurately. Aerojet's tracer projectiles are fired from ground vehicles.

Tracers are made by filling a cavity in the rear of the projectile with a pyrotechnic charge that begins burning while the bullet is still in the gun and continues to burn the whole effective distance to the target. Each tracer round is usually spaced by several nontracer rounds. The two most important design characteristics for a tracer charge are brightness and burn time: The gunner has to be able to see the round under widely varied conditions and all the way to the target.

One Taguchi Methods application studied the wide variation in tracer burn time over a broad temperature range with a large lot of tracer-element pellets. The pellets had been supplied by an outside vendor, and they passed inspection but wouldn't function correctly in the real weapon. Typically, it's very difficult to reduce burn-time standard deviation even by as little as 10%.[6] By performing a Taguchi Methods parameter-design study on the deficient lot of tracer pellets, Aerojet Ordnance was able to reduce the standard deviation by 58%, thus making the pellets fit for use. The savings per projectile were calculated at $1.19.

Aerojet Ordnance has performed dozens of Taguchi Methods case studies, which have already saved the company millions of dollars. These have involved not only pyrotechnics, but metal-alloy development and fabrication processes for certain critical heavy-metal ammunition elements and other product- and process-design optimizations.

Aerojet Ordnance is also exposing its supplier companies to the benefits of Taguchi Methods, particularly vendors who supply solid propellants. These are similar to rocket propellants but are used in some munitions. One of the propellant elements is made from cellulose, which is obtained from many different forests. Unfortunately, cellulose from pine forests in the South and in Oregon don't behave the same way during processing. Because of this, the company is working with its propellant suppliers to reduce variation using parameter design. It's also looking into applying Taguchi Methods to the actual blending of propellants to reduce variation using parameter design.

A New Application

Kowalick has made a remarkable contribution to Taguchi's parameter-design technique, a contribution that Aerojet Ordnance conservatively estimates is already worth more than $60 million in present value to the company. Instead of using Taguchi's orthogonal arrays to perform individual case studies, Kowalick used them to develop a new product database for pyrotechnic pellets.

The way Kowalick explains it, each time Aerojet Ordnance developed a new pellet or improved an existing one, it had to undertake an extensive battery of pyrotechnic testing, development work, engineering changes, and the like. Added to this were the usual incredible amounts of paperwork. The company had faced the situation several times within a two-year span, and even when Kowalick and his engineers began applying Taguchi Methods to pellet development, it remained an expensive proposition.

The testing involves transporting an automatic gun to a rented range at night with a full test crew and a large assortment of measuring instruments and then firing the rounds and recording the results. This could cost up to $20,000 a night, and before Aerojet Ordnance used Taguchi Methods, testing could take up to six months. Such testing could total from $250,000 to $500,000 per product. Even with the help of parameter design, testing over the program's duration could still take up to three months and would have to be repeated for every new product.

Kowalick set out to conduct one Taguchi Methods design of experiments that could serve as a database for all current and future pellet-design requirements. Aerojet Ordnance's ammunition is all medium-caliber, between 20 and 30 mm. So Kowalick and his engineers worked out the span of requirements for medium-caliber tracer ammunition, including the various tracer-pellet-cavity diameters and depths, and wall thicknesses of the projectiles. These were the control factors for the parameter-design study.

Other control factors included families of pyrotechnic chemicals and compositions and items such as ignition time, and other elements Kowalick calls "consolidation-process parameters." Kowalick used an outer array to introduce noise-causing factors such as temperature, relative humidity, whether the barrel was old or new, projectile spin rates, and so forth.

The output from the experiments included tracer burn time, color, and brightness. Because Kowalick included design and compositional requirements for all of the tracers Aerojet Ordnance makes or will conceivably make in the future, the burn-time and brightness information was in effect a database. Whenever Aerojet Ordnance engineers have a new product they want to perform a parameter-design study on, they already have the experimental data. Hence, they don't have to run any experiments.

Instead, the engineers simply draw the appropriate data from the database pertaining to the product and then perform their statistical analysis, including generating Signal-to-Noise Ratios and other calculations. Once the product has been optimized, the engineers need only run the confirmation experiment.

The database experiment was completed in only three man-months, and Kowalick estimates that it would have taken the company 800 man-months—the equivalent of one man working 67 years—to acquire the same information doing full-factorial experiments.

Aerojet Ordnance has already used such a database to design tracers for three new products. Kowalick notes that U.S. Army laboratories have been working to establish this sort of a comprehensive database for more than 30 years and at a cost in excess of $50 million. Even so, Kowalick states, these programs have not successfully developed a technology database that helps a designer meet a new requirement without performing a series of experiments.[7]

Kowalick has ingeniously optimized Taguchi's Quality Engineering techniques so as to run only one series of experiments to generate data for countless new products. Patrick Norausky, Vice President of Quality Assurance and Test at Aerojet Ordnance, believes that Kowalick's work has broad applications in other industries as well.

As a testament to the power of Taguchi Methods, Norausky points to the continued problems both of Aerojet Ordnance's competitors are having in the pyrotechnic area, problems the company just doesn't have anymore. "Pyrotechnics is an area that's a black-magic kind of thing," he notes. "It's more alchemy than it is chemistry. For us, it's becoming more chemistry and less alchemy."

Spreading Through the Industry

Some observers believe that the spread of Taguchi Methods through the defense industry will follow the path of Aerojet Ordnance—a commercial arm of a corporation will introduce the defense arm to the system. Aerojet Ordnance indirectly learned of the system because GenCorp's General Tire subsidiary was actively pursuing quality and cost leadership, which includes heavy emphasis on Taguchi

Methods. In other companies, the flow of information is already beginning. Ford Aerospace and Communications Corp. is being exposed to Taguchi Methods through its ties to Ford Motor Co. It also seems likely that Hughes Electronics will hear about Taguchi Methods from General Motors Corp. Likewise, ITT's Defense Technology units will most likely be exposed to the system by the company's automotive arm.

Others believe that the methods will spread only as tremendous successes such as those experienced by Aerojet Ordnance gain wider recognition. Aerojet Ordnance, in fact, is currently training many of its supplier companies and some government customer representatives in parameter design. It's also just beginning to teach the system to engineers from another Aerojet company, Aerojet Tactical Co. of Sacramento, California, which builds propulsion systems for rockets.

The Future

It's obvious that Taguchi Methods were custom-made for an industry so involved in research and development and testing, an industry that's paying an incredibly high price for quality, an industry that the United States depends on so greatly. As a result of interest in Quality Engineering expressed by the Pentagon, some of the leaders in the defense industry have already begun training programs in Taguchi Methods.

This interest began as an inquiry to ASI by U.S. Air Force Brigadier General Frank Goodell, who was seeking new quality technology to support the USAF Reliability and Maintainability 2000 program, which is principally focused at eight airframe and electronics manufacturers. Taguchi

Methods—as well as QFD, a product-planning and implementation methodology—are now being applied to meet the program's objectives.

In the spring of 1988, ASI executives—including Taguchi, ASI Executive Director, and Lawrence P. Sullivan, ASI Chairman and Chief Executive Officer—met with Undersecretary of Defense for Acquisitions Robert Costello to discuss how Taguchi Methods could be incorporated into a broad-based DOD initiative.

Both the USAF Reliability and Maintainability 2000 program and a larger-scale Taguchi Methods DOD implementation are generating much interest within the defense industry.

As for the future, it's possible that Taguchi's system, coupled with the high-technology prowess of America's defense industry, could help raise U.S. military preparedness to hitherto unseen levels and also help cut our massive defense budget.

Notes

1. Richard W. Stevenson, "Competition for Contracts Trims Costs for Pentagon," *New York Times*, March 31, 1988, p. 1.
2. U.S. General Accounting Office, "Report to the Chairman, Committee on Governmental Affairs," U.S. Senate: "Quality Assurance, Efforts to Strengthen DOD's Program," Nov. 3, 1986.
3. Cynthia F. Mitchell and Tim Carrington, "Antique Arsenals: Many Defense Firms Make High-Tech Gear in Low-Tech Factories," *The Wall Street Journal*, Oct. 8, 1987, p. 1.
4. Telephone interview with Thomas R. Stuelpnagel, July 1987.
5. Telephone interview with James Kowalick, Aug. 1987.
6. Kowalick, "The Importance of Quality Consideration in the Ammunition Technology Stage," transcript of presentation

given at the 1987 ADPA Gun and Ammunition Technical Meeting, April 8-9, 1987, Naval Post Graduate School, Monterey, California. Published by Aerojet Ordnance Co.

7. Telephone interview with Kowalick, additional information taken from case study submitted by Kowalick and Aerojet Ordnance Co. to the American Supplier Institute, Inc.

10

Low-Cost Quality: Design Engineering

There's a legendary comment concerning Rolls-Royce that was made during the long reign of the incredibly durable and beautiful automobile that became known as the Silver Ghost, the car that first earned Rolls-Royce its "best car in the world" tag line. The remark was made by a competing luxury-car builder, and it wasn't meant as a compliment. The Rolls-Royce, he said, is a triumph of craftsmanship over design.

To discover what he meant by that, let's take a look at the man behind the machine. Sir Frederick Henry Royce was a meticulous English engineer who demanded nothing short of perfection from any mechanical device that bore his name. He first built a reputation manufacturing lighting dynamos in the early years of the 20th century. Royce (he hadn't been knighted yet) bought a French car one day, one of the finest in the world at that time, and, being totally dissatisfied with its performance, decided to design and build his own car. His efforts ultimately attracted the attention of the young, adventurous son of an English baron, Sir Charles Rolls, and thus the Rolls-Royce Motor Co. came into being.

Rolls died young and in spectacular fashion, leaving Royce in control of the company. Royce was a perfectionist whose nature wouldn't allow him to leave anything to chance—the type of man who would probably wear a belt *and* suspenders just to be safe. This approach manifested itself in his cars, which were understressed in the extreme. Where competing automakers would use four large bolts to fasten an axle housing together, Royce would "sew" the housing together with 20 smaller bolts. Such a fanatical approach gained the Silver Ghost an almost otherworldly reputation for durability and smooth, silent operation compared to the cars of other manufacturers. Royce specified only the highest-quality materials for his cars, and in any design consideration, reliability, durability, and quietness always won out over innovation. Royce's "nothing but the best" approach made the Silver Ghost not only sublimely smooth and reliable, but also prohibitively expensive.

Royce's approach to car building, then, was to "engineer" his designs to perfection, no matter what the cost. That's not to take anything away from Rolls-Royce: For the few who could afford them, Silver Ghosts were, indeed, the best cars in the world. Unfortunately, buying a Rolls-Royce just wasn't an option for most duffers of that time (or even our own).

If you substitute the word "engineering" for "craftsmanship," the disgruntled competitor's comment concerning Rolls-Royce points to one of the major differences in the way Japanese and Western automakers approach the task of designing and building cars.

One sharp young engineer recently put it this way: The Japanese use a Just-in-Time (JIT) production system, wherein parts are built and delivered to the assembly line as they are needed. This reduces temporary inventory costs and demands a low scrap and rework rate. In America, we have our own JIT system, although it's not something we planned. Instead of JIT production, we unwittingly discovered "just-in-time engineering"—and have been paying dearly for it ever since.

"Just-in-Time Engineering"

An engineer at one of the domestic automakers once told the following story about how companies traditionally judge a design's capability. If two samples of a design are tested, say a window winder for an automobile, and one passes and the other fails, the engineers would assume that the one that passed validated the design, and the one that failed was just a quality problem that could be fixed. From a Japanese viewpoint, however, the design experienced a 50% failure rate.

To see where "engineering" fits in, let's follow this story to its logical conclusion.

The American engineers would then build a prototype of the design and ultimately attach it to a prototype of the car being built. The prototype would be the first of many used during the initial phases of the new car program. In the United States, prototypes are typically used to identify problems. This is where the engineers discover whether the exhaust system is really going to fit or not, or if it's possible for anyone short of a chimpanzee to enter the car without tying himself in knots. The prototypes would be tested endlessly, through iteration after iteration, to work the bugs out.

For a new American car that's a "clean-sheet" design (not directly derived from another existing car platform), as much as 80% of the entire car will feature new design work, while the remaining 20% will be adapted from existing hardware. That means that up to 80% of the prototype is unproven. The various staffs working on different pieces will routinely be issued respecification orders concerning the part they're responsible for designing, which means they have to redesign some part of their piece—or maybe the whole piece—to accommodate some other change in the total car design. At any given time, any given prototype will have various pieces on it that aren't up to current specifications. Meanwhile, the scheduled "Job 1" (the production start date) for the car continues to loom larger on the horizon, and the pressure to sign off the prototype in design and send it through to production and manufacturing grows with each passing day. Finally, to meet schedules, the design is signed off, even though there are probably several important parts and possibly components on the protoype that aren't current in terms of the latest respecification orders.

Subsequently, the redesigned parts catch up with the project, and it's discovered that, because of the redesign, a wiring harness doesn't fit or there isn't enough underhood clearance for an air-filter flange.

The Perils of a Handoff System

Meanwhile, all sorts of trouble is erupting in the manufacturing department. The production engineers flatly state that the design can't be built—so it's thrown back to engineering to be tweaked.

Until relatively recently, the typical American car-building system has been a sequential one, in which design, engineering, and manufacturing hand off assignments, much the way relay racers hand off a baton. The designer hands the part design to engineering, which hands it to manufacturing—all with surprisingly little interdepartmental communication or cooperation.

Hence, the manufacturing and process engineers are handed a design that theoretically can be built "perfectly," but in real-world terms is going to be very difficult, if not impossible, to mass produce. If the manufacturing engineers had been consulted beforehand, the design engineer could have learned that the design, while looking good on paper, couldn't be sustained in the company's manufacturing environment.

Instead of communicating, the managers from the different departments spend their time managing problems. In the mid-1970s at Ford Motor Co., it was literally unheard of for a member of the design staff to spend time working with the manufacturing department. A Ford executive has even stated that in Ford's European operations, design and manufacturing relations deteriorated to such a degree that design engineers weren't even allowed inside the company's plants![1]

Solving Problems

So far, if you've noticed, the entire U.S. design process has centered on problem solving. Prototypes are used to find problems and correct them, and engineers playing catch-up with timetables find themselves chasing unconsolidated designs literally right down to the assembly line to make them fit or work.

Enter the concept of "just-in-time engineering." Under this system, maximum engineering effort is exerted just as Job 1 rolls off the assembly line. The important point to note is that "just-in-time engineering" is always used in a problem-rich environment. It's usually the company's last line of defense against catastrophe in the marketplace. Therefore, this final, massive engineering effort is usually totally uncoordinated and relies on a quick-fix, bandage approach. And it's not unheard-of for the fixes to be executed even as cars are rolling off the assembly line. Some American cars have been recalled several times for design changes before they've even made it to dealer showrooms.

The Problem with Problem Solving

In such a design-engineering environment, it's impossible for a manufacturer to build 100% good products, even if every worker on every line is well-trained in Statistical Process Control and every operation in the plant is 100% in control. It's easy to see why the Americans were in trouble: Serious design-management problems were being compounded by a manufacturing culture that seemed to consider being out of control as some kind of perverse natural order. Having accepted that premise, it was easy to come to the conclusion that the only way to combat being out of control was to add more and more inspectors. Additionally, the ultimate shape of the product kept changing right up to and, in many cases, beyond, Job 1.

Actually, the notion of inspecting in quality is closely followed not only during production, but also during the design phase by many traditional U.S. companies. This heavy reliance on prototype testing and retesting is really nothing more than design inspection.

Many American engineers have built impressive careers based on the ability to provide quick fixes in desperate situations. This practice is not limited to the auto industry. Problem solving has become a celebrated talent in American industry in general. Many managers start the day with a list of problems and spend their day chewing on that list until an appropriate solution for each problem is found.

No one should spend their entire day solving problems. If they do, it points to a fundamental flaw in the management infrastructure of the company. Let's put it this way: If you spend your day managing problems, you're not managing for quality. In fact, if you're not really managing anything but problems, you yourself have become a problem for the company. Your very presence means the organization has a hole in it, through which energy and money are being poured. That's what problems cost a company: energy and money. If you're solving problems all day, you've unwittingly become a "just-in-time manager," which means that instead of concentrating on the long term, you fill your adrenalin-pumped days putting the lid on things.

Paying for Design

And what about the original design, where one prototype worked and the other failed? Well, its performance didn't improve by itself—a massive reengineering effort, costing thousands of dollars, was probably needed to bring it up to spec.

Why is all of this necessary? Because American companies have unwittingly used engineering to compensate for incomplete design work. Is the traditional American automobile also a triumph of craftsmanship or engineering over design?

Let's look at the typical Japanese expenditure of engineering effort. A "clean-sheet" Japanese vehicle, say, by Toyota Motor Corp. or Mazda Motor Corp., will almost never contain 80% new design work, the way some recent American cars have. The average is closer to 40% or 50%. That means that up to half of the car is already a proven commodity, rather than only 20% of it. This is done for several reasons, *but mainly to reduce cost.* The new design work, fully optimized using Taguchi Methods of experimental design and other techniques, allows the designer to specify the least-costly parts and materials possible without affecting quality, again, with the main purpose of cutting costs.

Typically, the American method for cutting costs is to "down-dress" an existing design, using cheaper materials the engineer hopes won't adversely affect performance or durability. In other words, you whittle cost out of a design that already exists rather than use techniques that would more fully optimize the function of the design before it's put into production. Conversely, if you optimize the product before it leaves the design stage, you've created a robust design even though you're using the least-costly materials possible right from the beginning.

In the Japanese engineering example, you'll notice that *the maximum amount of engineering effort is put forth very early in the product program* (**Figure 10-1**). Instead of having the design, engineering, and manufacturing departments hand off the design from one to another in a sequential fashion, all three departments are called in at the start of the program, along with other department heads

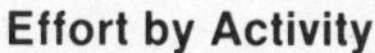

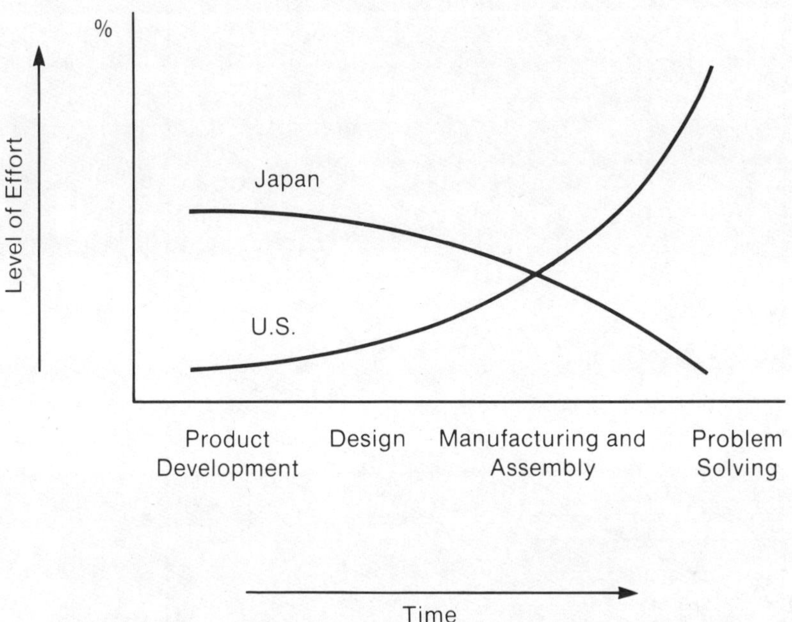

Figure 10-1. Japanese companies front-load product development, while American companies expend most effort solving problems.

who will ultimately become involved with the program. This is what's known as simultaneous engineering, and it's recently become the rage among domestic automakers as well.

The Japanese take a lot longer to sign off on a completed design than American automakers typically do, but once the design is formalized, subsequent events tend to occur swiftly and smoothly. As Job 1 approaches, there's a slight rise in engineering effort, although it comes nowhere near the leap made at American companies (see **Figure 10-2**).

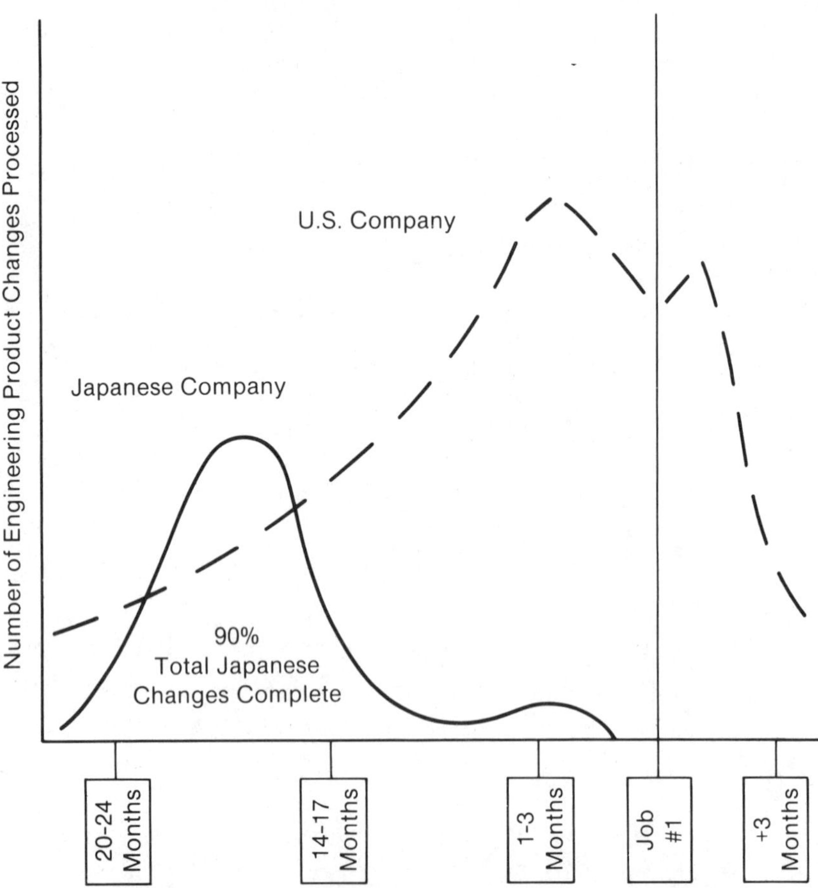

Figure 10-2. A comparison of the percentage of engineering product changes made by a good Japanese company and a good U.S. company by "Job 1" (the production start date).

When the Japanese finally get around to building a prototype of the finished product, they build it not to find problems but to validate the design. If problems *are* found, the implication is that they've failed during the design stage. There's little room here for "just-in-time engineering."

Getting Rid of Cost

The Japanese have discovered that the key to cost-efficient success in most manufacturing endeavors is ultimately found in the realm of design. That is why they front-load their engineering efforts. Paying particular attention during the design stage saves an incredible amount of problem solving later on. Redesign costs go down, prototype costs go down, and stop-gap, "just-in-time engineering" practices—which should be considered as having a negative impact on the product, no matter how heroic the effort—drop tremendously. And the savings continue to multiply right through the manufacturing stage and on to Job 1 (See **Figure 10-3**).

That's not to say that the Japanese don't have their own small "just-in-time engineering" cadres—they do. But they're usually put to work solving manufacturing and assembly-process problems, not fixing faulty design work.

The High-Cost Design Dilemma

High-cost quality usually means one of two things: The component in question is a critical, must-work part of a system, or the design of the component wasn't fully tested for close-to-optimum performance.

The analogy of the race-car builder who "blueprints" his engines is a good example of the first situation. From an entire parts counter of engine parts, he chooses only those components that are as close to specification limits as pos-

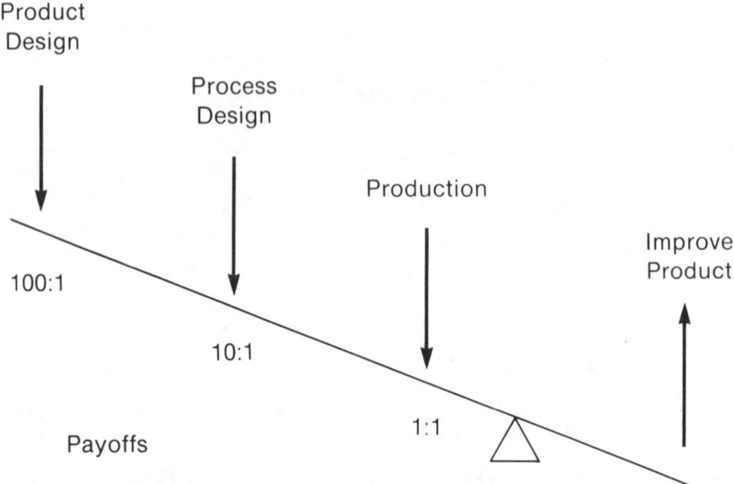

Figure 10-3. The sooner quality is improved in the product-development cycle, the higher the payoff is in terms of both effort and cost.

sible and then builds an engine that will fulfill its design requirement—to win races—with little regard for cost.

NASA and the Armed Services seek this type of expensive quality from suppliers—triple and quadruple fail-safe components made out of the finest materials available. This sort of high-cost quality will not survive in a competitive market, simply because it doesn't serve the value-driven needs of consumers (See **Figure 10-4**).

The second type of high-cost quality is fairly typical in American industry. A system is designed. In certain high-tech disciplines, Americans tend to be very good at system design—in fact, we're among the best in the world. System design is the brainstorming, get-your-creative-juices-flowing part of product design where you decide the species of

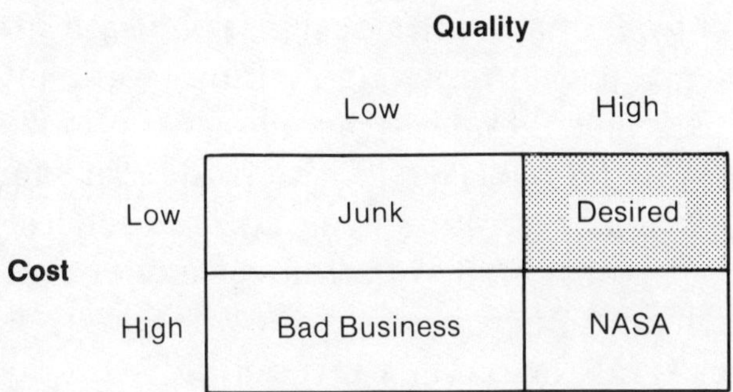

Figure 10-4. The quality/cost equation has four possible results, ranging from high cost/high quality, as exemplified by "NASA quality," to low cost/high quality, which outstanding Japanese companies attain.

the product—if it's a car, whether you're designing a luxurious Jaguar or a cost-efficient Rabbit. During system design, the designer selects those elements that will give the product its own special look, sound, feel, or level of performance. Once the system design is in place, American manufacturers will typically jump right into tolerance design. As mentioned in Chapter 4, this is where the engineer sets the various tolerance limits for the product. Tolerance design can be, and usually is, fairly expensive if a manufacturer does not economically justify his tolerances using the Quality Loss Function (QLF). Even with the QLF, however, tolerance design can add costs.

The crucial step that American engineers usually miss, but that Japanese engineers exploit to the fullest extent possible, is the step between system design and tolerance design involving product optimization: parameter design.[2] As noted in previous chapters, parameter design is the step during which an engineer can simultaneously reduce cost and improve quality.

Skipping over parameter design is one of the main reasons stop-gap "just-in-time engineering" came into being among American companies. By failing to optimize the design as fully as possible while it's on the drawing board, American designers habitually release product designs that are still green, both in terms of product function and in manufacturability. It's the reason so many designs that look so good on paper fall flat on their faces either in production or in the field.

Designs on Sale

Contrary to popular belief, manufacturers today *aren't selling products; they're selling product designs.* When you get right down to it, the real trench warfare in the marketplace is being waged in design studios, not on assembly lines or in retail markets. A good design works for the company—it's easy to build, it's cost-effective, and it performs in the marketplace. A bad design, on the other hand, is your competition's best friend—stealing downstream-engineering cost and effort, ensuring a high number of product start-up problems, and generally making life both costly and miserable for everyone from engineering to manufacturing to sales. Product design impacts every downstream operation in a company. If a company's designs aren't up to snuff—if they're not robust, if they're still green—there's little you can do to compensate for it. The company won't be able to offer the product at a competitive price and still be assured that the product will perform in the marketplace with a minimum of warranty costs or loss of goodwill. Your competitors from Japan on the other hand, are taking great pains to optimize their designs.

What Taguchi Offers

For an example of the power of parameter design, let's look at an imaginary product-design cycle for competing U.S. and Japanese television companies. Both companies develop new TV sets. Through exhaustive system-design work, each set has been designed with many unique features, including voice-activated channel selection. Through close examination, however, an informed observer would recognize that the American design at this point holds the advantage in terms of innovation.

After system design is complete, the Americans set about engineering the various circuits so that they conform to the given specifications. In order to maintain a high-quality picture, the American engineers set certain critical tolerances very tightly. To achieve these tolerances, high-quality components are specified, and these significantly raise the consumer price for the TV.

The Japanese, after coming up with a system design, go through the parameter-design stage. During this stage, they optimize the performance of various aspects of the TV using the cheapest possible components. Because they've optimized the various circuits during parameter design, the need to specify very tight tolerances during the tolerance-design stage is greatly reduced. The Japanese utilize Taguchi's experimental-design techniques during both parameter and tolerance design to quickly and cost-effectively determine design and tolerance levels for the TV. They also discover that they can replace certain design elements with cheaper components without affecting picture quality or set reliability.

Both TVs are introduced to the market. The Japanese

TV comes to market some three months earlier than the American TV, and quickly gains a reputation as a high-quality/high-value unit. The American TV is late because various circuits had to be redesigned that were adversely affected by various ambient-temperature and humidity levels discovered during last-minute prototype testing. Cost overruns in several areas, including unanticipated production problems occurring with the voice-activated channel selector, have forced the American manufacturer to drop several of the innovative sales points from his TV—including the channel selector. The TV is quickly redesigned to feature a conventional channel tuner. The American manager is shocked to see that the Japanese TV—with voice-activated channel selector—is selling for less than the projected price of his TV. He orders his engineers to reduce the cost of the TV by respec'ing certain noncritical circuits using cheaper components. After six months on the market, the American manufacturer is inundated with customer complaints and warranty costs, because the TV's performance and reliability, when compared with its Japanese competition, aren't even in the same ballpark. Many of these warranty costs, incidentally, can be traced back to the cheaper components that were substituted at the last minute for more costly, higher-quality parts.

Many industries, including the bulk of the television-building industry, have moved out of the United States. The reason typically given for moving offshore is that the company can't compete because of the cost of the U.S. labor force. When the Japanese yen gained in value by more than 50% in the mid-1980s, everyone in the United States expected the American trade deficit with Japan to shrink considerably. In many cases, U.S. products had become as inexpensive as Japan's, the reasoning went, so

Americans should start buying U.S.-made alternatives. Instead, the U.S. trade deficit with Japan actually continued to grow for some time. Why? The Japanese have proven that consumers are willing to buy a quality product even if they must pay a premium price for it. Reducing labor costs is only a small part of the competitive equation. It's the easy part, too; that's why so many companies have hurried offshore with their products. But if low labor costs are the only thing an offshore venture is bringing to the party, its long-term competitive ability in a sophisticated market such as the United States will be a very "iffy" thing.

The more difficult, although ultimately more lucrative, route to becoming competitive starts with design.

Using It Because It Works

Dr. Genichi Taguchi's Quality Engineering techniques put maximum analytical power in the hands of design engineers. In fact, Taguchi Methods were custom-designed for engineers by a brilliant engineer, and an important ingredient of their success is the special knowledge an engineer has of a product or process. This knowledge is what makes it possible to shortcut traditional test-every-combination experiments.

In a very real sense, your successes with Taguchi Methods will be tied directly to the savvy of your engineers. Taguchi Methods allow an engineer to organize his thinking and to deal exclusively with facts. They provide a road map that leads an engineer to the optimum levels of performance a product or process can achieve without adding cost.

Traditionally, as noted above, finding the optimum level of performance for a product or process has been something of a crapshoot in American industry. A product would be designed to meet certain artificially set performance criteria. Specification limits for a product are usually set according to inherited knowledge of that product—in other words, if it worked on the last version, it'll work on this one, too. Your engineers would eventually get you close to your target, often by spec'ing closer-than-necessary tolerances and higher-performance/higher-cost critical components. Many times, that higher-cost component could have been replaced by a lower-cost device that had been optimized to its fullest.

The analogy of looking for a needle in a haystack is a good one in describing traditional product- and process-design techniques. There can be literally thousands of ways that a complex product can be put together. Testing every combination of variables is impossible in a manufacturing environment, because problems tend to be fairly complex and time is almost always in short supply. Some combinations will give you optimum results, but not for the minimum cost. Traditionally, unless an engineer performs a classical full-factorial or fraction-factorial design of experiments, with the aid of a statistician, he really has no way of knowing if the combination of design factors he chose while designing a product was the best possible combination.

Taguchi's methodology allows the design engineer to shortcut that long, drawn-out procedure, and it allows him to do it without the aid of a trained statistician.

Training

An engineer can usually grasp enough of the fundamentals of Taguchi's off-line quality-control techniques to begin performing process-related design experiments after a week's training in Taguchi Methods. Be aware, however, that it takes years for an engineer to become an expert.

Within many Japanese companies, training in Taguchi Methods is considered a necessary and continuing part of every engineer's education. A Japanese engineer without knowledge of Taguchi Methods is said to be only half an engineer. Most of this training is done in-house, and is augmented by regularly scheduled symposia during which particularly interesting and successful case studies are presented. (It's been Taguchi's philosophy that the only way to truly understand his methodology is by participating in Quality Engineering case studies.)

Within the United States, Ford is a recognized leader in promoting Taguchi Methods training—not only for its own engineers, but for those of supplier companies as well. The ITT Automotive Group also has an aggressive in-house Taguchi Methods training program. AT&T Bell Laboratories is also a leader in in-house training, as is Xerox Corp. Still, compared with leading Japanese companies, the Americans are just beginning to climb the steepest part of the Taguchi Methods learning curve. It has been estimated that many Japanese engineers complete as many as 600 hours of training in Taguchi Methods.

Nippondenso Co., Ltd., for example, despite having more than 30 years of experience in Taguchi Methods, retains a very aggressive Taguchi Methods training schedule. About 15% of Nippondenso's 6,000-person engineering staff is considered expert in the methods, and another 30% is very competent.

The rest of the engineering staff is taught and advised by 918 expert practitioners. By comparison, only a relative handful of the engineers in most leading American companies that have embraced Taguchi Methods have even gone through preliminary Taguchi Methods training. And the number of experts in Taguchi Methods in the entire United States can literally be counted on one's fingers.

At Nippondenso, all new engineering employees go through a four-day introductory course in experimental design. Nippondenso trains about 400 people per year in this course. Within three to seven years of employment, engineers are given an additional 12-day course in the use of various Taguchi Methods techniques, including orthogonal arrays and the QLF.

Within five to nine years of employment, engineers go through an advanced 11-day session of Taguchi Methods. Additionally, reliability engineers take a separate course in parameter design and tolerance design, and engineering assistant managers attend a seven-day session on the entire system.[3]

An important part of the training is to have all trainees produce case studies for critique. Nippondenso, however, is something of a special case; it's one of the premier users of Taguchi Methods in Japan, and its training program reflects this fact.

A more typical example of experimental-design training comes from the Sharp Corp., which introduced Taguchi Methods ten years ago. Sharp provides roughly nine days of Taguchi Methods training a year for its engineering staff. It also requires engineers to attend yearly design-of-experiments seminars, which are sponsored by the Japanese Standards Association and taught by Taguchi himself. Taguchi is often retained to teach his methodology at Japanese companies. Apart from formal training sessions, the bulk of real understanding concerning Taguchi Methods comes as engineers use the techniques in the course of their daily work, aided by more experienced practitioners.[4]

Theory, Computer Simulation, and Taguchi Methods

The traditional approach when undertaking a Taguchi Methods design of experiments is to lay out the experiments using an orthogonal array, perform each experiment, and then record and analyze your data. However, the advent of accessible computers allows an experimenter to perform certain parameter- and tolerance-design case studies on a theoretical level. In situations where scientific theory exists for the actions and reactions of factors, it's possible to "perform" orthogonal-array experiments totally within the circuits of a computer. Taguchi has long advocated the use of theory in his experimental-design philosophy, since it's often more cost-effective to perform experiments on paper or in a computer than it is to physically conduct experiments.

Engineers at General Motors Corp.'s Detroit Diesel Allison Division performed just such an experimental design in developing a theoretical diesel-engine design. While the program was given a proposed budget of $10,000, the entire system was run on computer for less than $400.[5]

The engineers wanted to develop a theoretical engine of the future that would identify which combination of engine-design features would generate optimum levels of fuel efficiency.

The engineers used a computer simulation program that acted in effect as their "engine." Six factors were to be evaluated, and in each case the "engine's" goal was to generate 300 horsepower at an engine speed of 1,800 revolutions per minute. The engineers also suspected that there were three interactions between three factors that could have significant effects on the performance outcome of the engine.

The engineers assigned the six main factors to a 27-experiment (L_{27}) orthogonal array and ran the experiments on their computer-simulated "engine." Each factor was to be tested at three different operating levels. A little quick math will show that to perform a full factorial experimental design, during which every possible combination of the six factors at three levels is tested, GM would have had to run 729 experiments. The engineers came to the conclusion that even using a high-speed computer, a computer simulation of a full-factorial design of experiments would take too long to accomplish.

And if GM had elected to perform 27 experiments involving structural changes to the engine, the company would have had to construct the equivalent of 27 different engine configurations. While engineers will usually use one-cylinder test engines that can be reconfigured to replicate the 27 combinations of factors, the time and money spent to do so would be many times as expensive as the computer simulation.

After running the experiments, the GM engineers analyzed the data using a commercial personal-computer software program. This program is custom-tailored for Taguchi Methods experimental-design analysis, and it does most of the tedious and exacting number crunching, thus reducing the chances of calculation error.

The optimum levels of the six factors were revealed during analysis, and a confirmation run using these factor levels proved the superior fuel efficiency of this "engine."

Best of all, the engineers calculated that the simulator-driven Taguchi Methods experimental design generated a 17-to-1 return on investment based on the cost of the project and the man-months needed to complete it.

Intelligent Orthogonal Arrays

Today, it's possible to perform parameter-design experiments via computer simulation, removing much cost and drudgery from the experimental-design process. But what about tomorrow?

Just as computers themselves have become more user-friendly over the years, recent development work at Bell Labs indicates that the full power of Taguchi's experimental-design system could soon become even more accessible to engineers.

Madhav Phadke and two colleagues, Newton Lee and Rajiv Keny, have developed an expert system for experimental-design techniques that automates the selection of an orthogonal array and the design of an experiment. The Prolog-based computer-software system uses artificial intelligence to assist less-than-expert practitioners in the design of complex experimentation.[6]

The prototype system, which was developed to assist AT&T engineers in running Taguchi Methods experiments, asks the experimenter a few questions concerning the experiment to be planned and then suggests an appropriate orthogonal-array design that could be used for the experiment.

There are 17 basic orthogonal arrays that engineers generally choose from. These 17 arrays run from the L_4, which will accommodate three two-level factors arranged in four different experiments, to the L_{81}, which will accommodate 40 three-level factors arranged in 81 different experiments.

While in many basic experiments the selection of an orthogonal array can be fairly clear-cut, some applications can be quite complicated. For example, in several arrays that can accommodate only two-level factors, it's possible to combine two columns of two-level factors, thereby creating the equivalent of a four-level factor column. There are also certain arrays that are best suited for dealing with the main effects of control factors.

Bell Labs' expert system will also assign the factors to specific columns in the orthogonal array using a computerized version of Taguchi's linear graphs. A linear graph is a one-dimensional depiction of the relationships between columns in the orthogonal array. Every column in the orthogonal array is represented by either a dot or a line drawn between two dots. The columns represented by lines indicate that those columns may be used to observe the interactions between the two dots (columns) they join. While a limited number of linear graphs are usually used for each array, an experimenter facing unique requirements may wish to tap more unusual linear-graph arrangements. The number of graphs available for certain arrays can be formidable.

The expert system is able to handle complex or simple linear graphs equally well, and commits no mental errors or silly mistakes. As it stands now, Bell Labs' software can solve roughly 85% of the real-world experimental-design problems it would face in the field.

Future goals include teaching the system "tricks," such as combining noninteractive factors on a single orthogonal-array column so that a smaller array could be used, which would reduce the number (and cost) of experiments.

Another area under study involves problem solving. For example, the system could suggest to the user that by dropping noncritical factors, the experiment could run on a smaller orthogonal array—again, with cost cutting in mind.

In addition to other refinements, the software designers are exploring the possibility of giving the system an explanation capability. This would allow the software to explain why it made certain decisions and recommendations in the layout of the experiment, thereby functioning as a teaching element. At present, AT&T has no plans to sell the system outside of the company, but such research points to the day when any moderately trained practitioner will be able to tap into expertise concerning Taguchi Methods any time a need arises.

Applying Taguchi Methods

Indiscriminate use of any quality tool can produce less-than-optimum results. As Taguchi himself has said, if you can obtain the same results by changing one factor at a time and instead you use experimental-design techniques, you're wasting both time and money.

So how do you know when and where to use Taguchi Methods? Many cases will actually shout for their use. Flex Technologies, Inc., a small automotive supplier located in Midvale, Ohio, faced a problem involving post-extrusion shrinkage of the plastic speedometer casings it manufactured for GM. The casings had been in production for more than 15 years in total at one of GM's captive-supplier divisions or at Flex Technologies. The GM captive supplier had spent a great deal of money trying to solve the shrinkage problem by changing one process factor at a time, but with little positive result.

The excessive shrinkage of the speedometer casing could cause the assembly to be noisy under certain conditions. The engineers at Flex Technologies, headed by James Quinlan, who had received training in Taguchi Methods at the American Supplier Institute, Inc., decided to run a design of experiments to reduce the shrinkage. In choosing which factors they should experiment with, Quinlan asked for opinions from everyone, including customers, production technicians, quality people, and engineers. From this information, Quinlan's team developed a cause-and-effect diagram for the experiments, listing all of the possible causes for the shrinkage problem.[7]

Instead of performing the 32,768 experiments that would have been necessary in a full-factorial experimental design, the Flex Technologies engineers assigned the 15 factors to a 16-experiment (L_{16}) orthogonal array and ran the experiments, after which four samples of the casing produced during each experiment were subjected to heat soaking to simulate the percentage of shrinkage that each experiment produced.

By applying Taguchi's Signal-to-Noise Ratio, the experimenters discovered that eight of the factors were having a significant effect on the shrinkage. By adjusting four of these, some of which meant changing basic design specifications, the engineers were able to reduce the amount of shrinkage dramatically, from 0.25% to 0.05%.

Using the QLF based on the $80 warranty cost the manufacturer would incur to replace the cable casing, Quinlan was able to document a cost per unit that dropped from $2.12 to $0.13.

This was a clear-cut example of a situation for Taguchi's techniques.

Not all cases are so obvious, however. It's relatively easy for a manufacturer to confuse the magnitude of a problem with the importance of solving that problem. For example, which is more important: solving a reject problem on a plastic part that produces noticeable amounts of scrap, but which actually costs the company a relatively modest amount, or solving a product-design problem that would not be obvious to anyone on the shop floor, but which would cost the company a fortune through a combination of downstream reengineering and process redesigns? The largest cash drains are usually the most invisible when viewed on a day-to-day basis. They usually fall through the cracks in an organization—until they start registering in the profit/loss column.

Likewise, it would be unwise for a company to spend large amounts of money, time, and effort improving a product's quality characteristics if the ultimate consumer of that product couldn't tell the difference, or possibly wouldn't even care. But how does a manufacturer spot which quality characteristics mean a lot to consumers, and which mean relatively little?

It requires vigilant attention to the marketplace and to the needs and desires of consumers. This often requires an unusual degree of sleuthing. For example, a Japanese automaker wanted to know just what sort of cargo Americans typically haul in the trunks of their cars. To find out, it sent engineers to Walt Disney World in Florida, where they actually watched what people put in and took out of their trunks. They noted which trunks seemed easiest to use, which seemed more difficult, and so on. Using this information and other surveys of car owners, they could make sure their car trunks included those features consumers wanted most: spaciousness, easy access, and so forth.

Today, the design engineer's job involves a lot more than simply sitting in front of a CAD screen designing products. He has to be in touch with the marketplace, so that he can make advantageous use of the technology he's developing. The design engineer must be keenly aware of the things customers like and don't like regarding a product, and why. He alone can seek innovations in the laboratory that could meet customer needs that even the customer isn't aware of yet. But the only way he can do this is through constant communication with the market.

The modern design engineer must be part product planner, part market researcher, part consumer, and part visionary.

Notes

1. Lance Ealey, "Man of the Year," *Automotive Industries*, Feb. 1987, p. 64.
2. Genichi Taguchi, "Specification Value and Quality Control: Japanese Quality Control and American Quality Control," transcript of lecture series, *Collection of Publications on Taguchi Methods*, 1984, Section VI.
3. "The History of Nippondenso Activities of Application of the Taguchi Method," April 1987. Provided by Nippondenso Co., Ltd.
4. Information supplied by Sharp Corp., Osaka, Japan, April 1987.
5. Jerry Roslund and Mustafa Savliwala, "A Theoretical Engine Design Using a Taguchi Factorial," presented at University of Michigan Quality Assurance Seminar, Aug. 1986, Traverse City, Michigan.
6. Telephone interview with Madhav S. Phadke, Aug. 1987. Also, Newton S. Lee et al, "An Expert System for Experimental Design: Automating the Design of Orthogonal Array Experiments," *ASQC Quality Congress Transactions*, 1987.
7. Jim Quinlan and engineering staff of Flex Technologies, Inc., "Product Improvement by Application of Taguchi Methods," 1985 Taguchi Application Award, American Supplier Institute, Inc.

11

Getting Started

The scenario is a common one: Certain middle-level individuals inside an organization embrace Statistical Process Control (SPC) and Quality Engineering on their own. Such enterprises seem to struggle along fitfully, at least as far as changing a company's quality culture is concerned.

So, too, do enterprises that may have the tacit approval of upper management, especially if upper management sees such programs as technology pills—quality enhancers that can be bought and then used without necessitating real change in the organization (see Chapter 2).

The problem is a subtle one: At the organizations most in need of Taguchi Methods and other quality tools, real change is necessary, and real change is typically bitterly opposed.

Several U.S. companies have attempted to adopt Taguchi Methods within the context of their current organizational structure and have met considerable resistance. Why?

The question can usually be answered in terms of company culture. If management offers little more than budgetary backing for the implementation of Taguchi Methods, a company will have a difficult time ahead of it.

Perhaps the most important aspect of the successful implementation of Quality Engineering is communicating the need for change throughout the organization. As we shall see, nowhere is this communication more important than at the top executive level.

The First Ten Years

As the first decade of American awareness regarding Taguchi Methods draws to a close in the late 1980s, it's striking to see just how far some of our leading companies and research facilities have come in implementing the techniques. The road hasn't always been smooth, but the successes have been noteworthy.

One of the most compelling reasons for the use of Taguchi Methods is the ease with which they can be implemented. Instead of investing millions in new technology, a company invests a fraction of that sum to train its engineering staff, and can, as has been proven time and again, avoid capital-investment costs as a result.

However, company-wide adoption of quality techniques such as Taguchi Methods requires determination and participation on the part of upper management. Only upper management has the influence and power to integrate Taguchi Methods within a large corporation. Recently, the American Supplier Institute (ASI), Inc., surveyed some of the leading companies in America regarding their implementation of Taguchi Methods. One question in particular regarding difficulties in Taguchi Methods implementation received a wide cross section of responses.

Those companies reporting few or no difficulties typically indicated a high degree of upper management support and involvement for implementation of and training in Taguchi Methods. Some pointed to the momentum created by each successful experiment, the effect of which was to win over hitherto unconvinced engineers and managers. Complaints from companies that have had a more difficult time integrating Taguchi Methods into their organization were equally enlightening. Some of the problem areas included the fact that some people within the organization came to regard Taguchi Methods as a cure-all for any engineering problem the company might have, and thus became disappointed when Taguchi Methods were not applicable to their particular problem. Some were intimidated by Taguchi Methods, or were simply reluctant to change from old, well-established ways of doing things. Perhaps most telling were such comments as "lack of management awareness and education;" "we need to bring (engineering, testing, etc.) functions together!" or "resistance within management in the form of *passive acceptance*."

These point to strategic rather than tactical implementation problems. As such, they represent a great danger within an organization in regard to a gradual falloff in the use of Quality Engineering.

This falloff can be extremely subtle. It can happen even in companies that had embraced Taguchi Methods—and experienced successful results. In several such companies, sustained interest in the use and propagation of Quality Engineering techniques actually faltered further on down the line.

The Evolution of U.S. Quality Techniques

1860s–1920s

Inspection

Begun during mass production of arms for U.S. Civil War. Introduction of uniform tolerances and gauging systems. Technique usually used was 100% inspection. System very labor-intensive but affordable because of relative wage scales at the time. System provided minimum amount of feedback to manufacturer on the control level of his equipment.

↓

1920s–Present

Statistical Process Control (SPC)

Devised at Bell Laboratories. The system, while fairly costly and complex to implement, uses sampling techniques in conjunction with a measuring system and a charting system. Used to plot a histogram of a machine's or process's tolerance performance, showing how much variation is present. Used typically to denote how much of the output was falling within a tolerance range, rather than the overall closeness of the output to a target specification. SPC was usually implemented by quality-control staffs in U.S. industry. Few machine operators were taught the technique. System not used extensively in U.S. industry before 1980. System provides fairly rapid feedback to manufacturer. Maintaining the SPC system can be difficult over the long run, however, especially if machine operators are not involved.

↓

1920s–Present

Statistical Sampling Inspection System

Perfected during World War II in defense industry. Provides a statistically valid method for gauging the quality levels of entire lots by random sampling small portions of the lots. System is still used among U.S. defense contractors and commercial industry. System provides very late feedback to manufacturer on the control of his systems, as inspection is done after the product is built, rather than during the production cycle.

1970s–Present

Just-in-Time Production

A pull-through production system wherein upstream operations build only as much product as requested by downstream operations. System forces manufacturer to achieve smooth production flow and mandates close to 100% good output if production levels are to be sustained. Reduces inventories tremendously. Extremely quick feedback for entire production system.

1980s–Present

Product and Process Optimization

Typically features Dr. Genichi Taguchi's Quality Engineering system. System optimizes products or processes so that they are not affected by variation-causing environmental or intra-product conditions. Extremely cost-effective system used off-line to systematically improve quality while reducing cost.

Why?

Taguchi Methods approach quality from a very different viewpoint in comparison with the conventional American approach. The philosophy is different, as are the goal and technique. That American engineers with 40 hours training can successfully perform Taguchi Methods experimentation points to the user-friendly nature of the system. Still, if your company is just beginning to introduce Taguchi Methods, you will likely meet with a certain amount of opposition. It's human nature to resist change. In fact, to prove that point, it just might be helpful to take a trip back in time to Japan in the late 1950s, when many Japanese companies were just beginning to embrace Taguchi Methods. At a round-table discussion on the use of orthogonal arrays and experimental-design techniques as taught by Taguchi, representatives of some of Japan's most respected companies were in attendance. The companies ranged across a wide array of industries, from paper production to oil refining, from wire making to chemical manufacture. Taguchi himself was there, representing Nippon Telephone and Telegraph Co. The date was June 29, 1959.[1]

The representative for Tatsuta Electric Wire Co. raised points regarding the application of Taguchi orthogonal arrays and experimental-design techniques as they existed at that point. "Older people, in particular, do not accept and use new things without being strongly convinced of their use," the representative said. He also pointed to the fact that "some researchers with difficult personalities don't or won't consult with more experienced team members regarding their implementation of experiments, thus resulting in ineffective results."

The representative of Showa Oil Co. indicated that, at first, engineers and researchers would come to him to discuss the layouts of their experimental designs, but because the company encouraged them to carry out experimentation on their own, they became locked in a limited-application cycle and wouldn't attempt new or unfamiliar methods in experimental design.

The representative of the Honshu Paper Co. indicated his contingent thought that the first experiment was "vitally important, since, if it failed, an introduction of experimental design would be rejected (within the company)." Said another, "Another problem comes from the fact that the academic world is so conservative. While corporations understand the situation very well, scholars at the academic associations do not understand the necessity of time and cost saving. Those people will still demand that we perform experiments where only one variable is changed while other variables are kept constant. This proves the lack of diffusion of experimental design."

The representative from the paper company also blamed the management of his company for forcing hurried acceleration of production after a process experiment was completed, which caused other quality problems to occur. He also blamed some people for thinking "that their sixth sense works better than experiments." Several participants mentioned the difficulty involved in assigning factors to the correct columns in the orthogonal array, as this was before Taguchi introduced the use of linear graphs.

Finally, one speaker talked about the two groups within the organization that had to become involved in the spread and use of orthogonal arrays and experimental design. "One is the management level, such as factory managers and chief researchers, and the other is the engineers themselves. I think that the first target is the most important one. Top management does not understand when a statement such as 'no difference in the significance level' is found in a report. They usually get upset and reject the report saying, 'Don't use stupid equations people don't understand.' This is a common problem in the beginning."

If the above sounds remotely similar to arguments you may have heard regarding Taguchi Methods in the United States, it only points to the fact that people of all cultures resist change with a vehemence that tends to be proportional to the amount of change required.

Today, Taguchi Methods are accepted to such a degree in Japan that shop-floor technicians routinely perform simple experiments on their own. Today, if you ask senior engineers of most Japanese automakers and supplier companies whether their company uses Taguchi's Quality Engineering techniques, the usual response is a rather disbelieving stare. "Of course they do," they say as politely as possible. Some simply brush the question off, as though it should be *understood* that they do; as though you were asking a question regarding whether their engineers had degrees in engineering.

Because Quality Engineering is so well-accepted and so often used in Japan today, we in America have a distinct advantage over the group arguing around that table in Osaka, Japan, in 1959. That advantage is significant: Taguchi Methods as they stand now have been tested in the crucible of Japanese industry for more than 30 years, and the techniques are more complete and much easier for a novice to use today than they were in 1959.

In fact, the situation brings to mind the great technological uproar in the automotive industry in the mid-1970s regarding emissions-control equipment for passenger cars. Car companies searched frantically for the key to reducing emissions without seriously impairing fuel efficiency or driveability. If you've ever owned a 1974-77 vintage car sold in America, you probably know all about the initial results of that search: poor performance, poor fuel economy, engine knock that could at times rival a steel drum band, and fitful driveability and starting or stopping performance. The push for emissions control made those cars some of the worst ever sold in U.S. auto history.

Ultimately, however, researchers discovered the key to efficient emissions control—the use of three-way catalytic converters and feedback fuel-delivery systems that maintained engine air/fuel ratios at precise levels. Now, with the new technology, cars run clean, and are actually more efficient and powerful than they were in the 1970s.

In recent years, the European Economic Community has adopted U.S-style automotive emissions standards in many instances. Are the Europeans having the same dramatic problems that American consumers had with their cars in the mid-1970s? Of course not. There are some unique technical problems, to be sure (such as catalytic-converter burnout under high-speed, long-distance driving conditions), but most of their problems involve human nature, not technology.

The technology is simply borrowed from that developed so painfully in the United States. The Europeans thus don't have to put up with gas-guzzling cars with horrible driving performance—they are automatically able to take advantage of the same state-of-the-art technology used in America.

The same is true of American industry regarding the adoption of Taguchi Methods. We benefit from more than

30 years of refinement and discovery that has taken place in Japanese industry, not only in terms of the technical aspects of Taguchi Methods, but in the most appropriate methods of promoting the methodology and other quality technologies inside a company.

Common Elements

There are some common elements among the quality-technology adoption tactics of successful companies, and many of them go well beyond the adoption of Taguchi Methods. The need for a high level of top-executive commitment and leadership right from the start, for example, and the need to rapidly and effectively disseminate vital information regarding not only *why* the company is adopting new quality technology, but *how* it will affect the day-to-day goings-on in the company and the entire corporate culture itself. Also, workers need to know what they can expect to gain from the new ways of thinking and working.

As mentioned, the very first experiment engineers tackled at some companies using Taguchi Methods often resulted in spectacular success, and use of the technique was propagated, only to ultimately founder and have to be rescued over the long term. Initially, such organizations tend to view Taguchi Methods as something that can be added to the company's arsenal of technology much the way a CAD system or a new stamping press can be incorporated. They don't realize that Taguchi Methods are strategic in nature rather than tactical, and that they usually require the adoption of an entirely different approach to doing business.

J. K. (Jim) Pratt, Director of Statistical Programs for ITT, mentioned that such a rite of passage occurred within his company in a speech he gave on the subject in 1987.[2]

ITT, Pratt said, began using SPC and Taguchi Methods in the early 1980s. "As time passed, to our amazement, the techniques fell into disuse or stagnated into an unproductive mode. Our investigation of this phenomenon revealed a serious conflict in objectives had caused the deterioration."

Put simply, the conflict involved management's expectations versus engineering's goals.

"Our management-system objectives of quality conformance, productivity, and cost did not fit what the practitioners were working to achieve. Frustration set in and the practitioners finally gave up and reverted to the more traditional approaches to satisfy their managers."

To combat this, ITT changed its approach in the implementation of quality technology from one of merely introducing a new technique to a much more formidable challenge: to actually change the culture of the entire company in regard to quality.

Notes Pratt: "Cultural change—even at modest levels—demands senior-management involvement. It's not enough to support the change, it's not enough to be committed to the change—involvement is required. . . . Senior management must be the constant driving force behind the transition—it's a full-time element of the management job."

The first hurdle any organization has to overcome is the need to convince management of the profit and quality potential of the new methods. Upper management has to buy into the cost-cutting, quality-enhancing philosophy of Taguchi Methods, not only in terms of the system itself, but in terms of everything the company does, from shipping to accounting.

There's also the necessity of recognizing that many of the assumptions and instincts managers have had regarding product and process quality—the belief in conformance within specification limits rather than adherence to a single, best target value—are out-of-date concepts. And upper management must set up a mechanism through which it can actively monitor progress in implementation—this naturally requires that upper management be familiar with the philosophy behind Taguchi Methods and, to some extent, with the way results are achieved.

Once organized in the mind's eye, all of the tenets of Taguchi's Quality Engineering philosophy become linked in a simple yet profound way: Continuous improvement is necessary because any deviation from the target causes an economically traceable loss, not only to the customer, but to the manufacturer as well.

ITT has refocused its attention on involving personnel, from the highest levels of the corporation right down to the factory floor, in the recreation of the company's corporate quality culture. The company has been having tremendous success, and has already tracked savings in the tens of millions of dollars through consistent application of Taguchi Methods.[3]

Ralph Reins, President and CEO of the ITT Automotive Group, has spoken lucidly on the transformation, not only in terms of Taguchi Methods, but regarding other quality and design technology as well.[4] "We learned that introduction of and emphasis on new techniques alone was not enough. Our people learned to use these tools easily and expertly in a relatively short period of time. Dramatic improvements were quickly attained. However, they were not sustained over a longer period.

"After looking more closely at this problem we finally realized the objectives of these powerful statistical tools and those of our classical management system were in conflict.

"The second lesson we learned was that making a basic cultural change in our plants required a new level of top-management involvement. Simply put, this magnitude of change is too important to delegate to subordinates."

He adds, "When you make the decision to proceed, the first step is a management seminar for the CEO and senior staff. We know that until these people fully understand what is involved—and why—and agree to their role, there is no sense going further."

In the experience of many large organizations, it seems that until top management becomes actively involved, the company is merely spinning its wheels in trying to create change.

In situations where Taguchi Methods enter a company through the engineering department, the route to sustained progress is more difficult, but achievable. The real problem in this case involves inertia and spheres of influence. It's vitally important to get as many influential people as possible interested in Quality Engineering as quickly as possible. The most obvious route is to build momentum with successful experiments. The problem is finding enough influence to begin a structured program once recognition is achieved at higher levels. There's a very real danger in these situations that upper management will view Taguchi Methods as a slick trick to be carted out every time a process goes awry and forgotten in-between times. Also, some managers may have unreal expectations regarding what Taguchi Methods can and cannot do in terms of product and process design.

An ideal method, which is difficult to implement but which generates compelling results, is to have upper management actually learn the system and teach it to underlings. The benefits are direct management involvement, intense knowledge regarding the quality situation of the company, and horizontal deployment of knowledge and recognition throughout the organization. Unfortunately, few American companies will be able to corral upper management into such an undertaking, unless of course the CEO himself decrees it.

Some Other Success Stories

The following are several examples of companies that are training their management and engineering staffs in Taguchi Methods.

Many of the early success stories in U.S. industry are found in the automotive industry, mainly through the influence of Ford Motor Co., which has been active in promoting the use of Taguchi Methods among its own suppliers, as well as within Ford's engineering organization worldwide. The company has completed hundreds of Taguchi Methods experiments to date, and has embarked on large-scale training of its engineers. One Ford executive has even said that there's no room at the company for any engineer who doesn't know Taguchi Methods. Insiders say the effect of Taguchi Methods within Ford has been substantial, in terms of everything from creating robust designs to the way people approach problems.

AT&T and Bell Laboratories have trained many engineers in the use of Taguchi Methods, although Taguchi's techniques are by no means the only quality system used. Training in Taguchi Methods isn't mandatory.

Xerox Corp. has developed its own Design Institute for Assembly and Manufacturability, which teaches Xerox engineers Taguchi Methods as a required subject of study. Taguchi himself is a member of the Design Institute's board of directors. Xerox has trained more than one-third of all its engineers in Taguchi Methods to date. Training is considered a requirement for the engineering staff. The company routinely uses Taguchi's off-line quality-control techniques, and is experimenting with on-line quality control.

ITT is acknowledged by many as being the leader in U.S. Taguchi Methods applications, having completed more than 3,000 case studies. Taguchi Methods training at ITT involves 80 hours of off-site, expert-level training in two one-week seminars. This is followed by on-site consulting assistance by ITT's own expert specialists over the next two years to develop user skills. The company's objective is to train all engineers in Taguchi Methods, and to promote the technique as a routine engineering tool in product and process design and improvement. ITT is also developing simplified forms of Taguchi's system that can be used on-line by shop-floor workers.

The Chevrolet-Pontiac-Canada Group (C-P-C) of General Motors Corp. is aggressively promoting the use of Taguchi Methods in terms of design/development, rather than simply using it to improve in-process quality.[5] In 1985, C-P-C began formalizing its plans to implement Taguchi Methods. Taguchi suggested C-P-C do two things: use the case-study approach with symposia, and develop resident consultants to help when problems develop during experimentation. (Most leading companies hold their own internal Taguchi Methods symposia.)

C-P-C thus developed a team case-study process, wherein cross-functional teams of five or more people (usually engineers but sometimes including technicians and others) are given 40 hours of training in Taguchi Methods. Each team is required to perform experimentation on a real-life project during training, and is coached by an experienced Taguchi Methods practitioner. C-P-C held its first internal Taguchi Methods symposium in 1987.

In addition, C-P-C has established a system in which

the group vice president and his staff review one case study each month. Aside from demonstrating the power of Taguchi Methods, this process makes upper management conversant in the language and philosophy of the system.

C-P-C also set up a network of resident Taguchi Methods consultants, who have developed their skills in the utilization of the technique. These internal consultants help the teams when they run into trouble. They also perform on-the-job training for less-expert associates. At Taguchi's suggestion, C-P-C is seeking to achieve a ratio of one consultant to 20 engineers.

In addition, C-P-C has developed a Taguchi Council made up of individuals who have used and understand the technique. The council selects teams to be trained, and has set fairly difficult criteria for team selection. On the average, only one out of every ten teams that apply is chosen. The council also decides which resident consultants are assigned to which teams.

The Budd Co., a large supplier of automotive parts and components, began using Taguchi Methods in the mid-1980s. The company has already held several of its own Taguchi Methods seminars, where internal case studies are reviewed and discussed. Budd started with a small number of engineers who began using Taguchi Methods in their work. Management was skeptical, and so, apparently, were some of the Taguchi Methods students. However, with the successful completion of several experiments, the group overcame the skepticism and proved to management that Taguchi Methods were focused directly on the bottom line.

The company is using Taguchi Methods not only in traditional areas such as spot welding, but also in refining stamping-press die settings to improve the surface quality of stamped parts. One effective set of experimentation involved indirect spot welding of sheet-metal flanges. These had to be welded strongly to stamped sheet-metal panels without marring the surface appearance, which is traditionally very difficult to do.

Using Taguchi Methods, Budd technicians achieved success and the company was able to significantly reduce internal repair and scrap costs. This particular experiment was carried out by a group of young technicians, many of whom were not seasoned or even trained engineers. They each had five days of Taguchi Methods training, and were able to come back to their plant and perform a successful experiment. In addition, the data for the experiment were collected by hourly workers, who were told why the data were needed and kept abreast of experimentation results.

In another experiment in the company's Wheel and Brake Division concerning the manufacture of heavy truck-brake rotors, scrap and rework were reduced by 87.5%.

Today, Budd Co. upper management is committed to the use of Taguchi Methods, with Budd Co. President and Chief Operating Officer David P. Williams actively promoting their use. Williams noted in an address, "When dealing with similar circumstances in the past, our people, while knowledgeable and dedicated, would tend to react to gut feeling. Everyone would want to jump in and tear the machine or equipment apart without significant analysis of the problem. Taguchi Methods have allowed us to achieve a better understanding of the process needs and requirements."[6]

Sheller-Globe Corp., another automotive supplier, first began using Taguchi Methods in 1984. Sheller-Globe, a leader in Taguchi Methods applications for its size, has completed more than 400 case studies.[7] The company has developed an extensive in-house training program, which includes training at ASI. Sheller-Globe also holds an annual in-house Taguchi Methods symposium, during which case studies are presented. Future goals of the corporation include implementing Taguchi Methods in upstream applications in research and development, and product and process engineering, as well as expanded in-plant applications. Sheller-Globe also actively promotes the use of Taguchi Methods among its supplier companies. The company has developed simplified Taguchi Methods that allow operators themselves to optimize processes.

Eaton Corp. has been developing Taguchi Methods since 1985. The company has developed an extensive training program at its Quality Institute. Cross-functional teams are taught together, as at GM's C-P-C Group. The institute teaches both introductory and advanced courses.

Dana Corp. netted a direct cost savings of $447,000 on its first nine Taguchi Methods experiments—which cost a total of $33,200. The company has embarked on a significant Taguchi Methods training program.[8]

Davidson Textron Co. started slowly after attending the first seminar offered by the Ford Supplier Institute. One experiment performed in 1986 eliminated the need for new equipment, generating a capital savings of $1.3 million. Today, all engineers at the company's R&D center have at least 40 hours of training in Quality Engineering.

Moving Into Tomorrow

Taguchi has economically justified quality for modern commercial industry, replacing art and "gut instinct" with measurable costs and measurable quality. He may actually have been the first person to define quality in modern industrial terms. Taguchi's concept of continuous improvement by working to reduce variation in a cost-effective way is driven by pure economics, but it's had an incredible effect on the products companies make. It has revitalized the notions of craftsmanship and quality in mass production—craftsmanship and quality without the high prices they carry with them in conventional manufacturing.

Quality Engineering is alive in the idea of tuning machinery to its highest levels of quality production, and in designing products that give real value to the consumer.

To tap into the potential of Taguchi Methods, however, most American companies will have to dramatically rethink their organization's quality ambitions.

Simply put, there's no such thing as "good enough" anymore. "Good enough" worked with varying degrees of success up to the mid-1970s for America. Today, it doesn't stand a chance, which is why the vigorously managed American company cannot hope to maintain *consistent* superiority within its field on mere innovation alone.

A company must have a solid, stable foundation upon which it builds that innovation. As automation increases and the need for cost-effective control over processes and products grows, Taguchi's methodology will be called upon more than ever.

Taguchi Methods, notably the Quality Loss Function, can be of great benefit in smoothing the way for new technology, particularly attempts to incorporate Computer-Integrated Manufacturing (CIM) systems.

Japan is on the brink of full-fledged immersion in CIM and flexible automation. America is lagging somewhat, as mentioned in Chapter 2, due to its typically short-term approach to management and lack of recognition regarding the type of corporate cultural changes needed to implement full-fledged CIM, not just the "islands of automation" some companies refer to as CIM systems. Many companies also point to the tremendous costs that are involved, which are many times difficult to justify under traditional cost-accounting methods.

Over the long term, the company that masters CIM will be to conventional manufacturers what a computer is to a mechanical adding machine. In tying an entire plant or organization together, CIM represents something very close to organic life in terms of how quickly a company can react to changes and find solutions. The benefits will be enormous, if a company's goal is to gain market share over the long term, rather than to maximize profits in the short term.

The use of CIM and real flexible automation will grant the mass-production manufacturer great latitude in custom-tailoring products to the market or even to individual consumers, latitude that's simply beyond the realm of anything they can approach today. Automobiles, for example, could be ordered on computer terminals in dealer showrooms, terminals that will link directly with factories capable of producing countless variations of car models. The deal will be "paperless," with the transaction, accounting, and reordering of inventory once the car is made, done entirely by computer. For the first time since mass production began, companies will literally be able to build products to order without special costs or waiting periods that involve the consumer.

The buyer will thus be able to custom-design the car, and with the help of CAD/CAM and flexible manufacturing systems, the car will be uniquely his. One of the problems with flexible automation is that it requires an extremely high degree of control and process stability, not to mention a thoroughly robust system design.

It seems much more than likely that tomorrow's leaders in CIM and flexible manufacturing—the companies that are looking to long-term growth and stability—will be the companies that are leaders in the use of Taguchi's Quality Engineering methods today.

American industry is being driven by highly sophisticated consumers who aren't willing to settle for good enough. Indeed, they haven't been willing for almost two decades now. The American auto industry is now a buyer's market. It will probably never be a seller's market again. The same observation can be made for countless other products in countless other industries. Whether these industries ultimately move offshore to low-cost producing countries, as many already have, or whether they stay in the United States depends largely on the commitment and degree of self-confidence U.S. companies have in their abilities to compete with the world, on the world's terms. America has been given one of the principal keys to Japan's quality/value stronghold, a key that has remained hidden the longest—perhaps because it's the most important of all.

Notes

1. Transcript of round-table meeting, "Plant Experiments Using Orthogonal Array," Osaka, Japan, June 29, 1959. Provided by Genichi Taguchi.
2. J. K. (Jim) Pratt, "Strategy for Senior Executives," ASI transcript of speech given at University of Michigan 1987 OSAT Conference, November, 1987, Dearborn, Michigan.
3. Rock Miller, "Continuing the Taguchi Tradition," *Managing Automation,* Feb. 1988, p. 34.
4. Ralph Reins, "Strategy for Senior Executives," ASI transcript of speech given at University of Michigan 1987 OSAT Conference.

5. Robert H. Schaefer, "Educating Today's Engineers," transcript of speech given at the Fifth Annual Taguchi Symposium, October 1987, Detroit, Michigan.

6. David P. Williams, "Taguchi Methods," ASI transcript of speech given at University of Michigan 1987 OSAT Conference.

7. Carl Kirkland, "Quality Program Saves Big Bucks for Sheller-Globe," *Plastic World,* Feb. 1988, p. 48.

8. L. P. Sullivan, "The Power of Taguchi Methods to Impact Change in U.S. Companies," ms. of paper printed in *Quality Progress,* June 1987.

Appendix A: The Taguchi Approach to Parameter Design

Diane M. Byrne and Shin Taguchi

"The quality of a product is the (minimum) loss imparted by the product to the society from the time the product is shipped."—Genichi Taguchi

"Loss to society" can be thought of on a much broader scale than air pollution, excessive noise caused by a car with a bad muffler, or a chemical leak from a nuclear power plant. Dr. Genichi Taguchi associates loss with every product that reaches the consumer. This loss includes, among other things, consumer dissatisfaction, added warranty cost to the producer, and the loss due to a company having a bad reputation and losing market share.

Loss Function

From an engineering standpoint, the losses of concern are those caused by a product's functional characteristic deviating from its desired target value. For example, consider an AC-DC converting circuit where the AC input is 110 volts and the circuit is to output 115 DC-volts. The output voltage is the functional characteristic of interest and its desired target value is 115 volts. Any deviation from 115 volts is considered functional variation and will cause some loss.

Suppose there are four factories producing these circuits under the same specification and their production output is as pictured in **Figure AA-1.** Suppose further that all four factories carry out 100% inspection (let's even naively assume it is 100% effective) so that only those pieces within specification are shipped out. While all four factories are shipping out circuits that meet the engineering specifications, Factory IV appears to offer a more uniform product, i.e., the variation about the 115-volt target is less with Factory IV than with the other three factories.

Loss occurs not only when the product falls outside of specifications. Moreover, the loss continually increases as the product deviates further from the target value, as indicated by the parabola (Quadratic Loss Function) in **Figure AA-2.** While a loss function may take on many different forms, Taguchi has found that the simple quadratic function approximates the behavior of loss in many cases. When the quality characteristic of interest is to be maximized, such as tensile strength, or minimized, such as part shrinkage, the Loss Function may become a half parabola. Belief in the Loss Function promotes efforts to continually reduce the variation in a product's functional characteristics. Taguchi's method of Quality Engineering can be used to attain such improvements.

Controllable Factors vs. Noise Factors

To minimize loss the product must be produced at optimum levels and with minimal variation in its functional characteristics. Two factors affect the product's functional characteristics: controllable factors and noise (or uncontrollable) factors. Controllable factors are factors that can easily be controlled, such as choice of material, cycle time, or mold temperature in an injection molding process. Noise factors, on the other hand, are nuisance variables that are either difficult, impossible, or expensive to control.

There are three types of noise factors: external noise, internal noise, and product-to-product noise. For the injection molding process, the ambient temperature and humidity may be the external noise; the aging of the machinery and tolerances on the

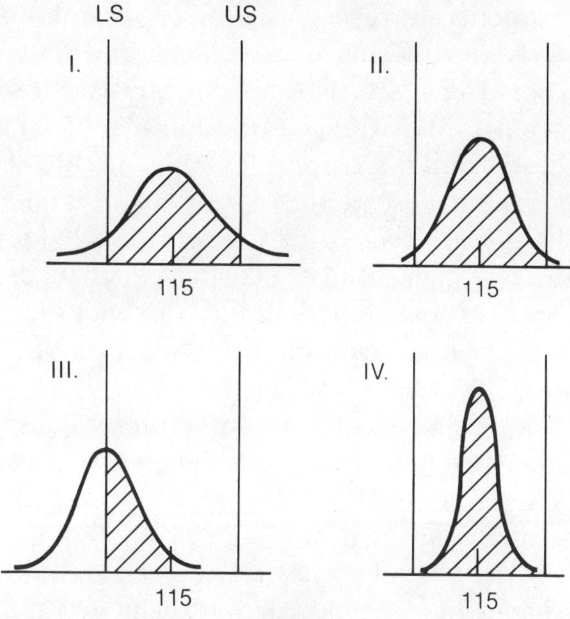

Figure AA-1

The Quadratic Loss Function

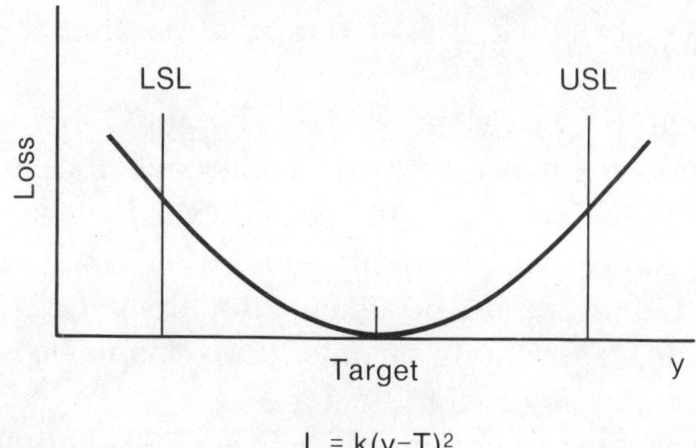

$$L = k(y-T)^2$$

L = Loss in Dollars
k = Cost Coefficient
y = Value of Quality Characteristic
T = Target Value

Figure AA-2

process factors may be the internal noises; while manufacturing imperfections are generally responsible for the product-to-product noise. Noise factors in general are responsible for causing a product's functional characteristic to deviate from its target value (see **Figure AA-3**). Is the goal then to identify the most guilty noise factors so that an attempt can be made to control them? No—controlling noise factors is very costly, if not impossible. Values should be selected for the controllable factors to make the product or process least sensitive to changes in the noise factors; that is, instead of finding and eliminating causes, as the causes are often noise factors, the impact of the causes should be removed or reduced.

For example, a mid-sized tile manufacturing company in Japan in 1953 was having a serious problem with their new $2 million tunnel kiln purchased from West Germany. The problem was extreme variation in the dimensions of the tiles that were baked stacked inside the kiln. Tiles toward the outside of the stack tended to have a different average and exhibited more variation than those toward the inside of the stack. The cause of variation was apparent uneven temperature inside the kiln. The temperature a tile received varied, depending on its location. This variable will be called N = temperature that the tile received.

To what category does this variable belong? It is a noise factor, an external noise at production. To eliminate the cause itself the company would have had to redesign the kiln—a countermeasure that may have cost them about a half million dollars. Fortunately, this company's budget did not allow such costly action, but the kiln was creating a tremendous financial loss for the company, so something had to be done.

The appropriate engineers, chemists, and others who had knowledge of the tile-manufacturing process were brought together. They brainstormed and finally identified seven major controllable factors that they thought could affect the tile dimension: A) content of limestone, B) fineness of additive, C) con-

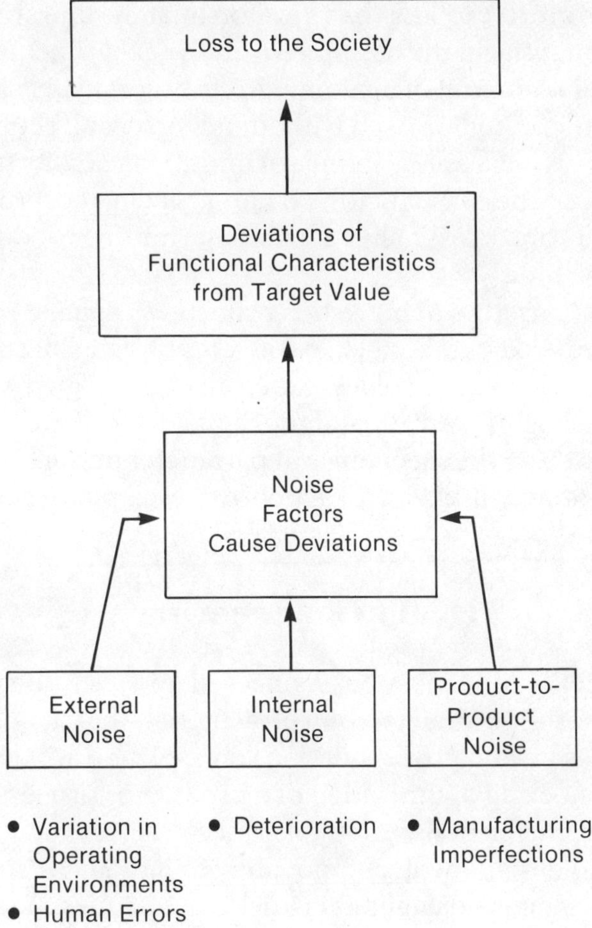

Figure AA-3

tent of agalmatolite, D) type of agalmatolite, E) raw-material quantity, F) content of waste return, and G) content of feldspar.

After testing these factors over specified levels using an orthogonal design, the experimenters discovered that Factor A, content of limestone, was the most significant factor, with other factors having smaller effects. It was found that by increasing the limestone content from 1% to 5%, and by choosing better levels for the other factors, the percentage of size defects could be reduced from 30% to less than 1%. Fortunately, limestone is the cheapest material in the tile. Moreover, the experiment revealed that a smaller amount of agalmatolite, the most expensive material in the tile, could be used without adversely affecting tile dimension. This is a classic example of improving quality (reducing the impact of the noise factor, N) and reducing cost (using less agalmatolite and drastically reducing the number of defectives) at the same time.

The tool used to achieve this robustness against noise factors and reduced cost is called parameter design. Parameter design, Taguchi style, involves experimental-design techniques utilizing orthogonal arrays and the Signal-to-Noise (S/N) Ratio. Before exploring the mechanics of parameter design, let's take a brief look at how it fits into Taguchi's overall picture of quality engineering.

Quality Engineering

Product quality must be engineered in! This is the thrust of Taguchi's off-line quality-control activities that involve both product-design and process-design stages. There are three steps in the engineering optimization of a product or process: system design, parameter design, and tolerance design.

System design involves innovation and requires knowledge from the science and engineering fields. It includes the selection of materials, parts, and tentative product-parameter values in the product-design stage and the selection of production equipment and tentative values for process factors in the process-design stage.

The tentative nominal values are then tested over specified ranges in the next step, parameter design, to determine the best combination of levels. Parameter design determines the product-parameter values and the operating levels of process factors that are least sensitive to change in environmental conditions and other noise factors. This is the key step in achieving high quality without increasing cost.

Finally, tolerance design is used if the reduced variation obtained through parameter design is not sufficient. It involves tightening tolerances on product parameters of process factors whose variations impart large influence on the output variation. Tolerance design means spending money—buying better grade materials, components, or machinery.

In the United States most engineers are conditioned to spend money to reach required product-performance levels. They jump from system design to tolerance design, omitting parameter design—the step where they can reduce costs and improve quality most efficiently.

The strategy in parameter design is to recognize controllable factors and noise factors and to treat them separately. The search for interactions among controllable factors is de-emphasized, although there are exceptions. The key to achieving robustness against noise is to discover the interactions between controllable factors and noise factors. Specific interactions between controllable factors and noise factors need not even be identified. As long as the noise factors are changed in a balanced fashion during experimentation, preferred parameter values can be determined using an appropriate S/N Ratio. This is demonstrated in the following example.

The Experiment

An experiment was conducted to find a method to economically assemble an elastomeric connector to a nylon tube that would deliver the requisite pull-off performance to be fit for use in automotive-engine components. The objective of the experiment was really twofold: 1) to minimize assembly effort and 2) to maximize pull-off force. What follows focuses on the portion of the experiment designed to maximize the pull-off force, but results from both portions of the study were considered in the final selection of factor levels.

Researchers identified four controllable factors and three noise factors that they felt could affect the assembly's pull-off force. They were searching for the levels of the controllable factors—A) interference, B) wall thickness, C) insertion depth, and D) percent adhesive—that were least influenced by changes in the noise factors—E) conditioning time, F) conditioning temperature, and G) conditioning relative humidity—and that resulted in the greatest pull-off force for the assembly. They decided to test each controllable factor at three levels and to vary each noise factor over two levels. While the noise factors are uncontrollable during normal operations, they were controlled over distinct levels during the experiment. The complete list of factors and levels is provided in **Table AA-1.**

The L_9 orthogonal array in **Table AA-2** was selected for the controllable factors since it is the most efficient orthogonal design to accommodate four factors at three levels. The L_9 array specifies nine experimental runs to be conducted, but the intent is to find the $3^4 = 81$ combinations that exist. This can be done since the design is orthogonal, a property that permits the effect of each factor to be separated out. The "ones," "twos," and "threes" in the array denote the first, second, and third levels of a factor, respectively. The first test condition in the L_9 array, for example, has all ones across the row, dictating that all the factors should be set at their lowest levels for that particular experiment.

The three noise factors were placed in an L_8 orthogonal array as shown in **Table AA-3.** For the columns labeled E, F, and G, the ones and twos in the matrix represent the levels at which those factors should be set during the experiment. The remaining columns are not referenced during the experiment, but they are used in the analysis to estimate interaction effects and experimental error. The most important use of this array is to deliberately create noise to identify the controllable factor levels that are least sensitive to it. Usually the effects of interactions among the noise factors are not estimated, but the experimenters in this case allowed for such interactions, as they felt the information might have been valuable.

Table AA-1
Factors and Levels

Controllable Factors	*Levels*		
A. Interference	Low	Medium	High
B. Connector Wall Thickness	Thin	Medium	Thick
C. Insertion Depth	Shallow	Medium	Deep
D. Percent Adhesive in Connector Pre-Dip	Low	Medium	High

Uncontrollable Factors	*Levels*	
E. Conditioning Time	24h	120h
F. Conditioning Temperature	72 °F	150 °F
G. Conditioning Relative Humidity	25%	75%

Table AA-2
L_9 Array

	Column			
No.	*A*	*B*	*C*	*D*
1	1	1	1	1
2	1	2	2	2
3	1	3	3	3
4	2	1	2	3
5	2	2	3	1
6	2	3	1	2
7	3	1	3	2
8	3	2	1	3
9	3	3	2	1

Table AA-3
L_8 Array

	Column						
No.	*E*	*F*	*E × F*	*G*	*E × G*	*F × G*	*e*
1	1	1	1	1	1	1	1
2	1	1	1	2	2	2	2
3	1	2	2	1	1	2	2
4	1	2	2	2	2	1	1
5	2	1	2	1	2	1	2
6	2	1	2	2	1	2	1
7	2	2	1	1	2	2	1
8	2	2	1	2	1	1	2

The two arrays were then combined, as shown in **Table AA-4**, to form the complete parameter-design layout. The L_9 array containing the controllable factors is called the inner array, while the L_8 array of noise factors is called the outer array. The layout also includes a data matrix, where the observations (pull-off force in pounds) are recorded.

How is the full design interpreted? Consider, for example, experimental condition #1 from the L_9 array, where all the controllable factors are set at their lowest levels. Notice the first observation is 19.1 lbs., while the second observation is 20.0 lbs. The L_8 array for noise factors shows that these observations were made with E at 120h, F at 150 °F, and G at 75%, and with E at 120h, F at 150 °F, and G at 25% respectively. Hence, the eight observations at each experimental condition of the controllable factors are not mere repetitions—each observation was made at a specific combination of noise factors. Variation due to changes in the noise factors was, therefore, deliberately induced within each set of eight responses. Through studying this variation, in addition to the mean response, researchers were able to determine the combination of controllable factor levels that could

Table AA-4
Layout by Orthogonal Arrays L_9 and L_8

									8	*7*	*6*	*5*	*4*	*3*	*2*	*1*	*No.*	L_8 ARRAY
									2	2	2	2	1	1	1	1	E	
									2	2	1	1	2	2	1	1	F	
									1	1	2	2	2	2	1	1	E×F	
									2	1	2	1	2	1	2	1	G	
									1	2	1	2	2	1	2	1	E×G	
									1	2	2	1	1	2	2	1	F×G	
									2	1	1	2	1	2	2	1	e	
									120h	*120h*	*120h*	*120h*	*24h*	*24h*	*24h*	*24h*	*Cond. Time (E)*	
									150F	*150F*	*72F*	*72F*	*150F*	*150F*	*72F*	*72F*	*Cond. Temp. (F)*	
L_9 ARRAY *No.*	*A*	*B*	*C*	*D*	*Inter-ference (A)*	*Wall Thickness (B)*	*Ins. Depth (C)*	*Percent Adhesive (D)*	*75%*	*25%*	*75%*	*25%*	*75%*	*25%*	*75%*	*25%*	*Cond. R. H. (G)*	*S/N Ratio (dB)*
1	1	1	1	1	Low	Thin	Shallow	Low	19.1	20.0	19.6	19.6	19.9	16.9	9.5	15.6	—	24.025
2	1	2	2	2	Low	Medium	Medium	Medium	21.9	24.2	19.8	19.7	19.6	19.4	16.2	15.0	—	25.522
3	1	3	3	3	Low	Thick	Deep	High	20.4	23.3	18.2	22.6	15.6	19.1	16.7	16.3	—	25.335
4	2	1	2	3	Medium	Thin	Medium	High	24.7	23.2	18.9	21.0	18.6	18.9	17.4	18.3	—	25.904
5	2	2	3	1	Medium	Medium	Deep	Low	25.3	27.5	21.4	25.6	25.1	19.4	18.6	19.7	—	26.908
6	2	3	1	2	Medium	Thick	Shallow	Medium	24.7	22.5	19.6	14.7	19.8	20.0	16.3	16.2	—	25.326
7	3	1	3	2	High	Thin	Deep	Medium	21.6	24.3	18.6	16.8	23.6	18.4	19.1	16.4	—	25.711
8	3	2	1	3	High	Medium	Shallow	High	24.4	23.2	19.6	17.8	16.8	15.1	15.6	14.2	—	24.832
9	3	3	2	1	High	Thick	Medium	Low	28.6	22.6	22.7	23.1	17.3	19.3	19.9	16.1	—	26.152

EXPERIMENTAL CONDITIONS

give maximum (or at least increased) pull-off force while achieving robustness against noise.

The Analysis

Data from a designed experiment are traditionally used to analyze the mean response. Taguchi, however, stresses the importance of also studying the variation of the response using the S/N Ratio. In its simplest form, the S/N Ratio is the ratio of the mean (signal) to the standard deviation (noise). The formula used to compute the ratio, however, depends on the situation; the S/N Ratio is directly tied to the Loss Function. While there are many different S/N formulas, three of them are considered standard and are generally applicable when the response can be classified as "larger-the-better," "smaller-the-better," or "nominal-the-best." Regardless of the type of characteristic, the transformations are such that the S/N Ratio is always interpreted the same way: the larger the S/N Ratio, the better.

The procedure for analyzing the pull-off force was as follows:

1. S/N Ratios were computed for each of the nine experimental conditions.
2. The levels for the controllable factors were selected based on the S/N analysis. For a given factor, the level corresponding to the highest average S/N Ratio was selected.
3. While the S/N analysis is generally sufficient, experimenters in this case also examined the mean response to aid in the selection of factor levels.

The pull-off force of the present example is a larger-the-better characteristic, since the pull-off force was to be maximized. The standard S/N formula for this type of response is

$$\text{S/N (in dB)} = -10 \log \left[\frac{1}{n} \left(\frac{1}{y_1^2} + \frac{1}{y_2^2} + \dots + \frac{1}{y_n^2} \right) \right]$$

where $y_1, y_2, \ldots, y_n$ refer to the n observations within an experimental condition of the controllable factors. This formula offers a built-in tradeoff between the mean response (highest pull-off force is best) and the variation in the response (least variation is best), but it is considerably more sensitive to the mean. The far right column in **Table AA-4** contains the nine S/N Ratios computed for each of the nine experimental conditions.

Since the experimental design is orthogonal (i.e., balanced), it is possible to separate out the effect of each factor. In the following analysis, the factor effects are separated out in terms of the S/N Ratio and in terms of the mean response.

There are several ways to approach this analysis. One common way is to do a statistical analysis of variance (ANOVA) and perform F tests to see which factors are statistically significant. Taguchi often teaches engineers to analyze their experiments using a conceptual approach that involves graphing the effects and visually identifying the factors that appear to be significant, without using ANOVA.

Taguchi's Analysis

The average S/N Ratios for each level of the four controllable factors are plotted in **Figure AA-4.** The graphs reveal that Factors A and C are more significant than Factors B and D. Clearly, the A_2 (medium) level appears to be the best choice for the Factor A, since it corresponds to the highest average S/N Ratio. As for Factor C there does not seem to be much difference between the C_2 (medium) level and the C_3 (deep) level, meaning that the two levels are equally good when the mean response and the variation in the response are simultaneously considered. The experimenters examined the mean response plot of Factor C (see **Figure AA-5**) to aid in their decision. The mean response revealed C_3 to be best in terms of the average pull-off force, suggesting that C_2 is best in terms of variation (variation is less at C_2 than at C_3). Therefore, when the experimenters decided to use C_3 over C_2 because it had a higher pull-off force, they were over-

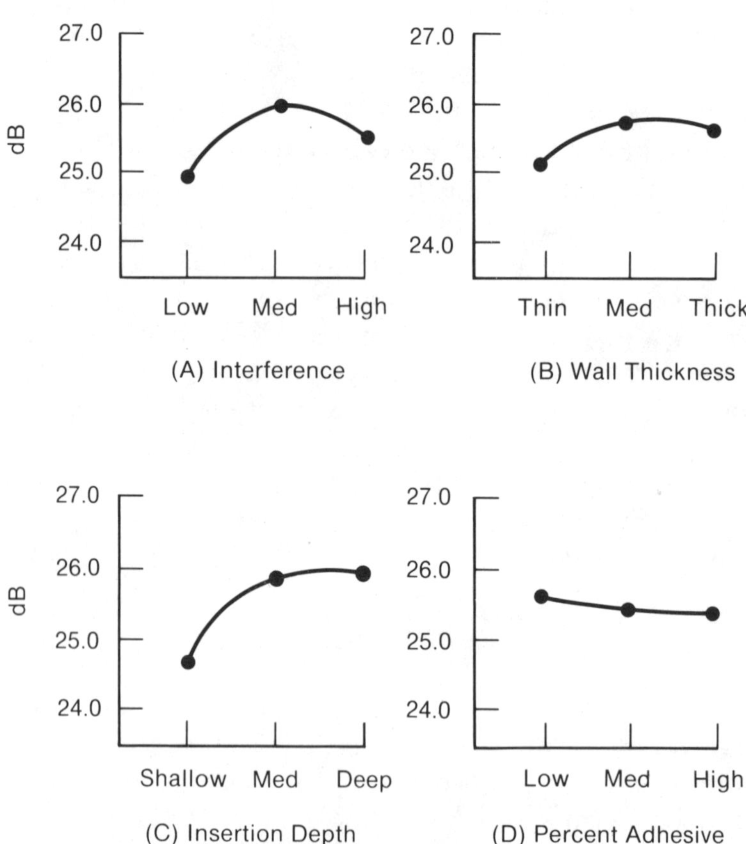

Figure AA-4

riding the built-in trade-off offered by the S/N Ratio and leaning even more toward the mean.

Factors B and D appear to have little significance with respect to the S/N Ratio (see **Figure AA-4**). The S/N analysis for Factor B, however, suggests that Levels B_2 and B_3 are a little better than B_1. Regardless, the researchers ultimately decided to use B_1 from a cost consideration (thin wall is less expensive than thick).

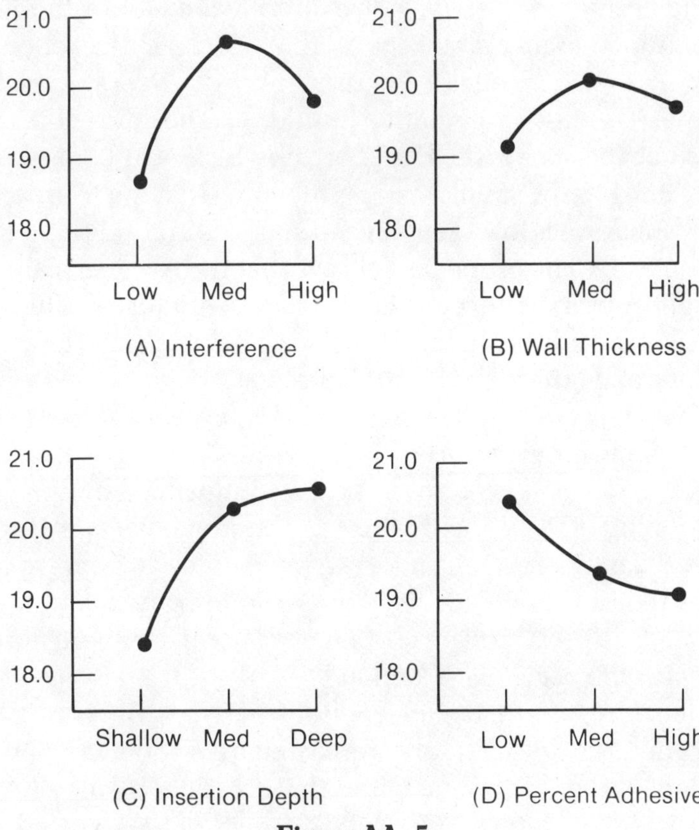

Figure AA-5

Similarly, the S/N analysis for Factor D suggests that the D_1 level may be a little better than D_2 and D_3. Experimenters decided to use the D_1 level. Factor D is particularly interesting in that the mean response (see **Figure AA-5**) at D_1 was much greater than at D_2 or D_3, while the S/N analysis made little distinction. This points out that smaller variations can be found at the higher levels of Factor D by the same argument that was made in the discussion of Factor C.

Performing the S/N analysis generally eliminates the need

for investigating the specific interactions between controllable factors and noise factors. Nevertheless, such investigation may provide additional insight. For example, the plot of the A × G interaction in **Figure AA-6** shows that a strong interaction does exist between Controllable Factor A (interference) and the Noise Factor G (conditioning relative humidity). The interaction is evident, since the lines in the figure are nowhere near being parallel. The A_2 line has the smallest slope, meaning that the A_2 (medium) level of Factor A is least sensitive to changes in conditioning relative humidity. The graph also shows that the A_2 level resulted in the highest pull-off force over the range of interest. Thus A_2 is obviously the preferred level for Factor A, which agrees with the decision made through the S/N analysis.

The interaction between Factors D (percent adhesive) and E (conditioning time) pictured in **Figure AA-7** also proved interesting. The D_2 level of D seems to be least influenced by changes in conditioning time, as the D_2 line has the smallest slope. But over almost the entire range of interest, the D_1 level appears to result in the highest pull-off force. From examining this plot, D_1 was chosen as the preferred level of Factor D, which once again coincides with the previous selection.

All of the two-factor interactions between the controllable factors and the noise factors were similarly examined. The plots for many of them contained lines that were nearly parallel, indicating a lack of interaction. A few others demonstrated some slight interaction, but it did not alter the levels selected for maximizing pull-off force—A_2, B_1 (cost consideration), C_3, D_1—as determined through the S/N and mean response analysis.

Summary of Results

Recall that the research involved two objects—assembly effort was to be minimized and pull-off force was to be maximized. While the experiment relative to assembly effort was not discussed here, the results of the assembly effort were also consid-

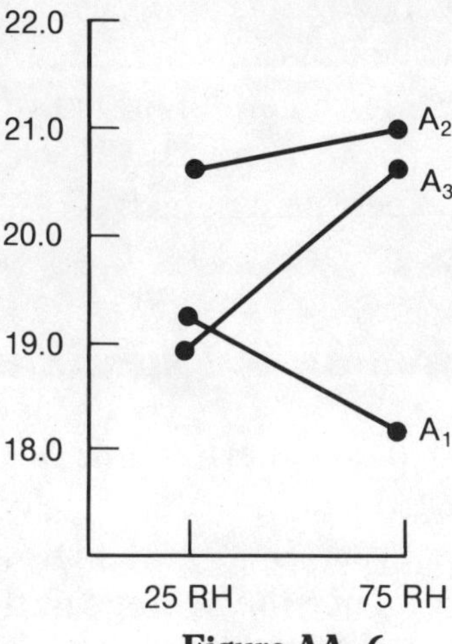

Figure AA-6

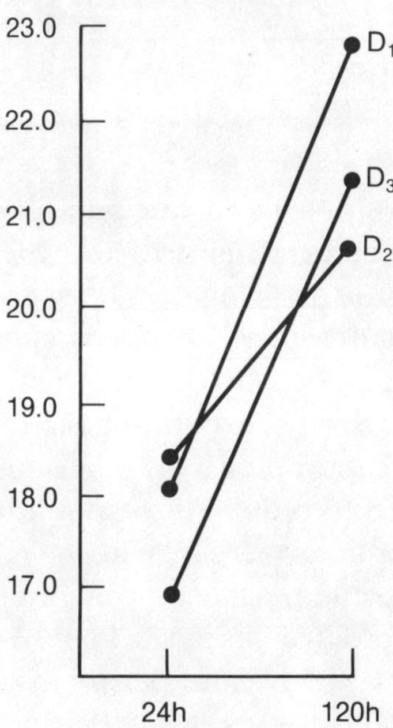

Figure AA-7

ered in the final choice of factor levels. **Table AA-5** shows that, at times, the objectives were conflicting. In selecting the best levels some trade-off was involved. As indicated in the far right column of **Table AA-5**, the optimum combination of factor levels was determined to be A_2, B_1, C_2, and D_1. This combination was never run during the experiment, which is often the case when highly fractionated designs are used.

Confirmation of Experiment

An important step in an experiment is the confirmation of the results. In this case, five additional samples were constructed and tested at the levels of A_2, B_1, C_2, and D_1, and conditioning levels of E_1, F_1, and G_1. Since the average of these samples fell within a predetermined 90% confidence band, the experiment was confirmed. Another confirmation took place on the line as workers experienced ease of assembly after changing to the new levels.

Alternative Design Layouts

In the previous example regarding pull-off force, the experimenters chose to use an L_8 outer array for the three noise factors, which allowed the surfacing of interactions among noise factors as well as the interactions between controllable factors and noise factors. Combined with the L_9 inner array, this design required a total of $9 \times 8 = 72$ experiments. In terms of cost and time, this size of an experiment was realistic. Should the researchers have desired to reduce the amount of experimentation, however, some options were available.

The researchers could have used an L_4 outer array to contain the three noise factors as shown in **Table AA-6.** This design would have required $9 \times 4 = 36$ experiments, half the original amount. With this layout, interactions among noise factors could not have been determined, but such information is not generally

Table AA-5
Summary of Results

Factors	*Levels*	*Assembly Effort*	*Pull-Off Force*	*Cost Rating*	*Performance Rating* Assy.	Pull	*Overall Rating*
Interference	1 Low	8.1	18.7	Least	Best	Worst	
(A)	2 Medium	8.3	20.7	—	—	Best	X
	3 High	8.7	19.8	Most	Worst	—	
Wall	1 Thin	—	—	Least	—	—	X
Thickness	2 Medium	—	—	—	—	—	
(B)	3 Thick	—	—	Most	—	—	
Insertion	1 Shallow	7.7	18.4	Least	Best	Worst	
Depth	2 Medium	8.3	20.3	—	—	—	X
(C)	3 Deep	9.1	20.6	Most	Worst	Best	
Percent	1 Low	8.3	20.5	Least	Best	Best	X
Adhesive	2 Medium	8.4	19.5	—	Worst	—	
(D)	3 High	8.4	19.2	Most	Worst	Worst	
Conditioning	1 24h	—	17.8	—	—	Worst	(O)
Time	2 120h	—	21.7	—	—	Best	(O)
(E)							
Conditioning	1 72 °F	—	18.2	—	—	Worst	(O)
Temp	2 150 °F	—	21.2	—	—	Best	(O)
(F)							
Conditioning	1 25%	—	—	—	—	—	(O)
R.H.	2 75%	—	—	—	—	—	(O)
(G)							

Table AA-6
L_9 by L_4 Layout

	Column				*2*	*2*	*1*	*1*	*E*
					2	*1*	*2*	*1*	*F*
No.	*A*	*B*	*C*	*D*	*1*	*2*	*2*	*1*	*G*
1	1	1	1	1					
2	1	2	2	2					
3	1	3	3	3					
4	2	1	2	3					
5	2	2	3	1					
6	2	3	1	2					
7	3	1	3	2					
8	3	2	1	3					
9	3	3	2	1					

needed. The primary purpose of the outer array is merely to create noise during the experiment to aid in the selection of controllable factor levels. Specific interactions between controllable factors and noise factors could still be identified using this design.

The experiment could also have been reduced to 18 runs if the experimenters had been willing to sacrifice two pieces of information: 1) interactions among noise factors and 2) specific interactions between controllable factors and noise factors. By using the S/N Ratio analysis, it is not really necessary to identify the specific interactions between controllable factors and noise factors. A reduction to 18 runs could also have been done by compounding the noise factors to two noise levels as shown in **Table AA-7.** Generally, when the intent is to maximize or minimize a response, the two noise levels should represent a "nominal" and a "worst" condition.

Processes are oftentimes subject to many noise factors that, in combination, strongly influence the variation of the response. For extremely "noisy" systems, it is not generally necessary to identify specific noise factors and to deliberately control them during experimentation. It is sufficient to generate repetitions at each experimental condition of the controllable factors and analyze them using an appropriate S/N Ratio.

Alternative Analysis

The researchers could have chosen a different route in the analysis if they had felt that the trade-off offered by the standard larger-the-better S/N Ratio was not appropriate. They could have developed an S/N Ratio with a trade-off that better fit their needs, but this is often difficult to do. A more common alternative is to analyze the data in two steps:

1. Identify the factors that influence the variation in the response and choose their levels to minimize variation.

Table AA-7
Layout with Noises Compounded

	Column				*Noise* N_1			N_2		
No.	*A*	*B*	*C*	*D*	$(E_1,$	$F_1,$	$G_1)$	$(E_2,$	$F_2,$	$G_2)$
1	1	1	1	1						
2	1	2	2	2						
3	1	3	3	3						
4	2	1	2	3						
5	2	2	3	1						
6	2	3	1	2						
7	3	1	3	2						
8	3	2	1	3						
9	3	3	2	1						

2. Identify the factors that minimally influence the variation but strongly influence the mean response (such factors are called adjustment factors) and choose their levels to adjust for the mean.

This two-step approach is the method used to target a nominal response, but it may also be used to maximize or minimize a response. The analysis may be performed by examining the S/N Ratio and mean-response plots, where the appropriate S/N Ratio is S/N (in dB) = $20 \log (\bar{y}/s)$. The $\bar{y}$ and s refer to the mean and standard deviation, respectively, of data from a given experimental condition.

Factor levels corresponding to the highest S/N Ratios would be selected to minimize variation. Factors that don't appear significant in the S/N analysis are candidates for adjustment factors and, in the present example, their levels would be selected on the basis of highest pull-off force. This approach puts the most weight on variation, while the standard larger-the-better S/N Ratio leans heavily toward the mean.

Parameter Design Is the Key

While the Taguchi method of Quality Engineering encompasses all stages of product development, the key element for achieving high quality and low cost is parameter design. Through parameter design, levels of product and process factors are determined, such that the product's functional characteristics are optimized and the effect of noise factors is minimized. Orthogonal arrays and the S/N Ratio are important tools in this methodology.

Parameter design is still often neglected by U.S. engineers as they continue to foster the idea that higher quality must cost more money. Emphasis should be placed on initially optimizing with low-cost materials and components (parameter design), spending money on higher-cost items (tolerance design) only when necessary.

Acknowledgments

The authors would like to thank Baylock Manufacturing Corp. for allowing this discussion of their research and Ford Motor Co. for granting permission to reproduce graphs and tables pertaining to the Baylock example.

Diane M. Byrne is a staff member of the American Supplier Institute, Inc., in Dearborn, MI. She was formerly a specialist in the Corporate Product Quality Assurance Department at Eaton Corp. in Southfield, MI. She is also a statistical specialist with the Department of Business and Industry Programs at Schoolcraft College in Livonia, MI. Byrne received her BS in mathematics from the University of Michigan and has pursued graduate studies in statistics. An ASQC member, Byrne is the Assistant Chairperson, Eastern Region Councilors.

Shin Taguchi is the director of Taguchi Methods at the American Supplier Institute (ASI), Inc., in Dearborn, MI. Prior to working at ASI, Taguchi was a researcher at the Quality Research Lab in Tokyo, Japan, and at the Indian Statistical Institute in Bangalore, India. Taguchi is an ASQC member.

Bibliography

Baylock Mfg. Corp. engineering staff. "Experiment to Optimize the Design Parameters of an Elastomeric Connector and Tubing Assembly," transactions from the Supplier Symposium on Taguchi Methods, April 10, 1984.

Phadke, M. and Raghu Kackar. "An Introduction to Off-Line and On-Line Quality Control Methods." International QC Forum, February 1985.

Taguchi, Genichi and Yuin Wu. "Introduction to Off-Line Quality Control." Nagoya, Japan: Central Japan Quality Control Association, 1980.

Appendix B: The Quality Loss Function

Dr. Duane Orlowski and Shin Taguchi

The evaluation of quality, as taught by Dr. Genichi Taguchi, is based on two major tools: the Signal-to-Noise (S/N) Ratio, which measures the performance of a quality characteristic in the face of noise factors, and the Quality Loss Function (QLF), which measures quality loss due to deviation of a quality characteristic from its target value.

The QLF is the philosophical cornerstone of Taguchi's approach to quality. Taguchi defines quality as the characteristic that avoids loss to society from the time a product is shipped (see **Figure AB-1**). When a product reaches the customer, to the extent that it fails to function as expected, it imparts a loss. This loss is realized by the customer in costs associated with repair, replacement, and dissatisfaction with the product. It is eventually experienced by the manufacturer in warranty costs, customer complaints, poor company reputation, and eventual loss of market share. Taguchi has developed the QLF in order to quantitatively evaluate the impact of product quality on the customer, in terms of this loss.

According to this concept, loss occurs not only when a product is outside of specifications, but also when it falls within specifications. Taguchi argues that there is very little difference between a 60% student and a 59% student, between a product just within specification limits and one just outside those limits. But there is a great deal of difference between the 60% student and the 99% student. The way to reduce this loss is not with go/no go specifications, but by reducing deviation from target values.

"THE QUALITY OF A PRODUCT IS THE (MINIMUM) LOSS IMPARTED BY THE PRODUCT TO THE SOCIETY FROM THE TIME THE PRODUCT IS SHIPPED."
-Dr. Genichi Taguchi

Figure AB-1

Customers are sensitive to variation around a target value even when a product characteristic is within engineering specifications. A 1979 article in the *Asahi,* a Japanese newspaper, reported that subsidiary Sony plants in San Diego and Tokyo had been built to manufacture TV sets for the U.S. market. Both plants used identical designs and tolerances. Yet, the American consumer displayed a marked preference for the Japanese-made sets.

Examining the color density of the screen helps explain why (see **Figure AB-2**). There was a greater number of Japanese-made sets around the desired target value, whereas a great percentage of American-made sets were out near the edge of the tolerance limits. If you were looking at this comparison in terms of A's, B's, and C's, then you would have to say that the Japanese sets had more A's than the American sets. By getting the distribution closer to the target value, the Japanese were getting closer to the "voice of the customer."

The QLF quantitatively evaluates quality loss due to functional variation. This is a more realistic and useful measure of quality than engineering specifications, which may not be meaningful in terms of customer perceptions and may only inhibit working toward continuous improvement. Finally, the QLF can be directly related to quality improvement in experimental design. It is mathematically related to the S/N Ratio, a metric ideally suited to engineering applications. This allows evaluations of quality in engineering terms (S/N Ratio) to be easily converted into financial estimates (the QLF). The QLF provides a common language for management, engineering, and manufac-

Performance Variations

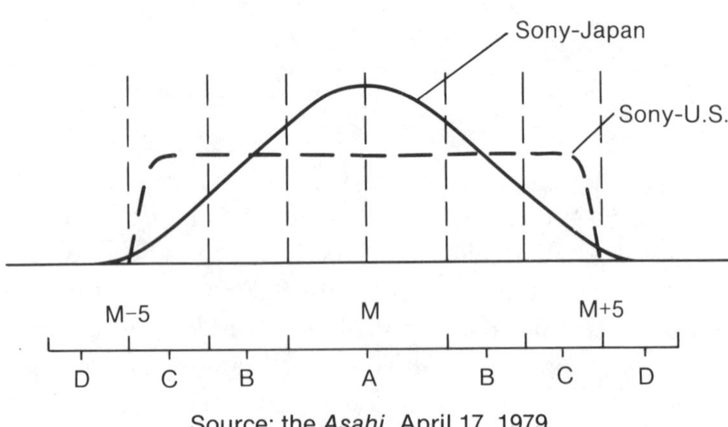

Source: the *Asahi*, April 17, 1979

Distribution of Color Density in TV Sets

Sony TV

Factory	Percent Defective	Standard Deviation	Process Capability	Variance	Loss
Japan	0.27%	$\frac{10}{6}$	1.00	$\left(\frac{10}{6}\right)^2$	\$8.33
U.S.	0.00	$\frac{10}{\sqrt{12}}$	0.58	$\frac{10^2}{12}$	\$25.00

Quality Loss Analysis
U.S. vs. Japan

Figure AB-2

turing, and encourages more effective horizontal and vertical communication within a company.

The Quadratic Loss Function

In principle, for each quality characteristic we can define a mathematical function that uniquely expresses the relationship between economic loss and the deviation of that characteristic from its target value. But the time and resources required to derive such a relationship for each item would be prohibitive. Taguchi has found that a quadratic representation of the QLF is an efficient approximation that allows us to realistically assess loss due to poor quality (deviation from a target value).

The QLF is a quadratic function. It is an approximation of a Taylor Series expansion around the target value, m:

$$
\begin{aligned}
L(y) &= L(m + y - m) \\
&= L(m) + \frac{L'(m)}{1!}(y - m) + \\
&\quad \frac{L''(m)}{2!}(y - m)^2 + \ldots \text{ higher order terms}
\end{aligned}
$$

where L = loss; m = target value; y = value of the quality characteristic; and $y - m$ = deviation from the target value at y. For every value of our characteristic, y, we can express loss as a function of $y - m$. Let us assume that this loss is minimal at the target, m. If we take loss as minimal at the target value, m, then $L'(m)=0$. If we are only evaluating losses due to variation, then at the target value, m, $L(m)=0$. Finally, we can ignore the higher order terms.

With these three assumptions, the Taylor Series expansion reduces to:

$$L(y) = \frac{L''(m)}{2!} (y - m)^2$$

$L''(m)/2!$ is a constant for a given quality characteristic. We can call this constant k. It represents the proportional financial importance of the quality characteristic to the customer in terms of the target value. Thus we have:

$$L(y) = k(y - m)^2$$

As shown in **Figure AB-3**, the constant, k, and the target value, m, completely define the QLF curve where L(y)=loss in dollars when the value of the quality characteristic is equal to y; y=value of the quality characteristic (length, width, concentration, surface finish, flatness, etc.); m=target value; and k=proportionality constant. The value of k depends on the financial importance of the quality characteristic.

Taguchi thus recognizes that loss is a continuous function. It does not occur suddenly. His quadratic representation of the QLF, L(y), has the following characteristics: L(y) is minimum at y=m; L(y) increases as y deviates from m; L(y) increases slowly while y is in the neighborhood of m and begins to increase more rapidly the further y deviates from m; and L(y) is expressed in monetary units.

Taguchi has developed standard loss-function formulas for each of the three types of continuously measurable characteristics (see **Table AB-1**). These have found extensive application in many Japanese and American industries for quantifying the financial benefits achieved by reducing variability around a target, for justifying an investment in improved quality, for prioritizing product improvement, and for defining realistic, customer-related tolerances that strike a balance between cost and quality.

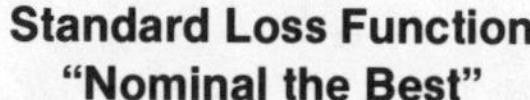

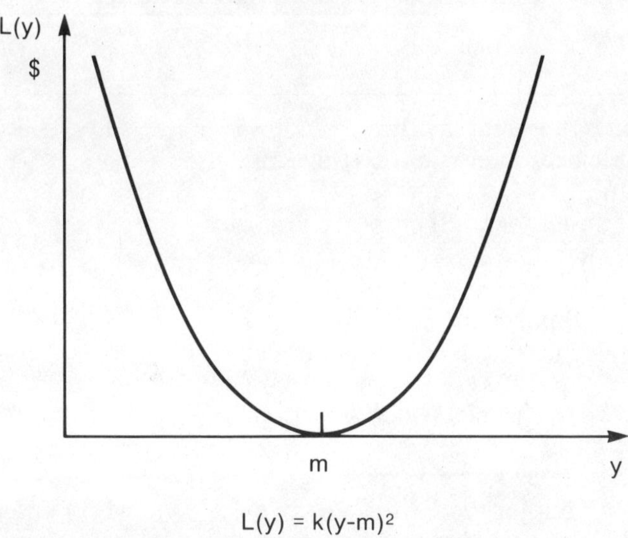

Note: 1) k is a constant
2) y – m is deviation from the nominal
3) Loss is proportional to the square of the deviation from the nominal value.

Figure AB-3

The Coefficient k

The QLF is derived from consumer information. This is the key to deriving the appropriate QLF equation for the appropriate situation.

Product performance or process variation is more critical to the consumer for some instances than for others. The rate of loss increase depends on the financial importance of the quality characteristic. For example, if the characteristic is a critical dimension of a safety device on a nuclear reactor, the loss will increase very quickly as the characteristic deviates from the target

Table AB-1
Standard QLF Formulas
for Continuously Variable Characteristics

Type of Characteristic	*QLF Formula*
"Nominal the Best" Measurable characteristic with a specific target value. *Example:* dimension, shift pressure, viscosity	$L(y) = k(y - m)^2$
"Smaller the Better" Measurable characteristic with a target of zero. *Example:* wear, shrinkage, deterioration, noise	$L(y) = k\,y^2$
"Larger the Better" Measurable characteristic with a target of infinity. *Example:* tensile strength, fuel efficiency, product life	$L(y) = k\,\frac{1}{y^2}$

value. A QLF equation should be developed to reflect the seriousness of the consequences of variation to the consumer.

The question to ask, then, is "What is the financial importance of the quality characteristic?" In terms of the QLF, this question becomes "How quickly does loss increase as we move away from the target value?" Mathematically, the question becomes "What is the steepness of the slope of the parabola?" (See **Figure AB-4**.)

The first step in applying the QLF is the determination of the coefficient, k, for a particular quality characteristic. This represents the proportional financial importance per deviation from the target for the customer:

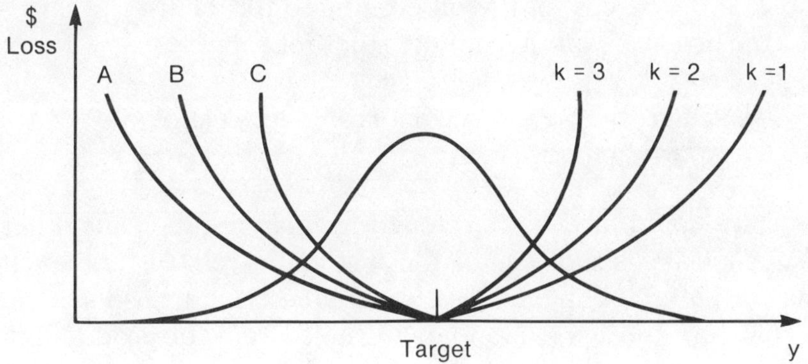

Loss increases more quickly with Function C than with Function A.

The financial importance of Curve C is greater than that for Curve A.

Figure AB-4

$$k = \frac{\text{consumer's loss}}{\text{functional tolerance}} = \frac{A_0}{\Delta_0}$$

The *functional tolerance* (Δ_0) is the value of the maximum permissible deviation from the target value for a characteristic at which the average product does not function. This represents an average customer viewpoint. It is important to remember that the functional tolerance is not a specification limit.

The *consumer's loss* (A_0) is the average loss generated when the value of the characteristic exceeds the functional tolerance. It represents the average cost to the consumer for replacement or repair of the product, with its associated dissatisfaction, at the functional tolerance.

What costs should be included in (A_0), the average customer loss due to poor quality? Usually included are items such as cost of repairing or replacing a product. Many Japanese companies also include the cost of the time required for the user to transport the product to and from the store for repair.

> A_0 = average cost to repair + average cost of transporting to repair, etc.

Data could also be developed to include other customer costs, such as gas and wear on the customer's vehicle, time spent waiting, potential damage to clothing or self in transporting a product, or time lost from not being able to use the product (including the cost of rental or loaner products).

Both the functional tolerance (Δ_0) and the average cost for trouble (A_0) can be determined from marketing, dealer, service, and customer-relations information (see **Figure AB-5**). Sources include warranty claims, product returns, customer complaints, and service records. Customer feedback groups, focus groups where customers can discuss and be tested on their experiences with products, are an important source of information.

Most American companies are not accustomed to providing this type of information to engineering and manufacturing personnel. Nor do most engineers know how to ask for it. As these conditions change, proportionality constants can be developed and updated for critical quality characteristics and the QLF applied more effectively in evaluating product and process improvement in U.S. industry. This would represent an important change in the way U.S. manufacturers think about cost, quality, the customer, and continuous improvement.

Example: "Nominal the Best"— A Television Power Supply

Let us set up the QLF for a TV-power-supply circuit. The nominal output voltage is 115 volts. When the output voltage varies from the nominal by more than 20 volts (is more than 135 volts or less than 95 volts), customers take action at an average

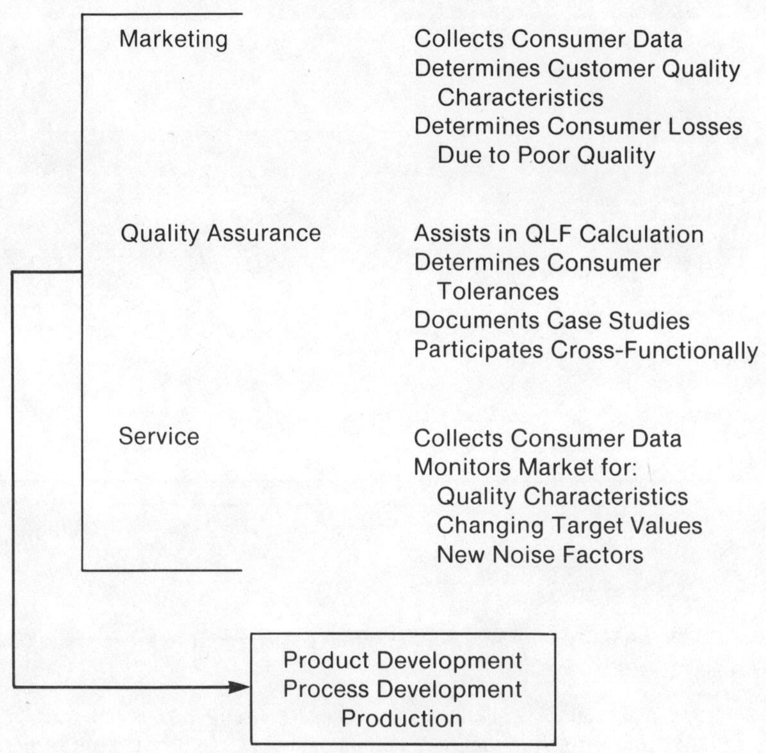

Figure AB-5

cost of \$100 (see **Figure AB-6**). To apply the QLF and determine a realistic manufacturing tolerance, we must find the proportionality constant, k.

$$\text{Functional Tolerance } (\Delta_0) = 115 \pm 20 \text{ volts}$$

$$\text{Average Consumer's Cost } (A_0) = \$100$$

$$\text{Target} = 115 \text{ volts}$$

$$k = \frac{A_0}{\Delta^2} = \frac{\$100}{(20\text{v})^2} = \$0.25 \,/\, \text{volt}^2$$

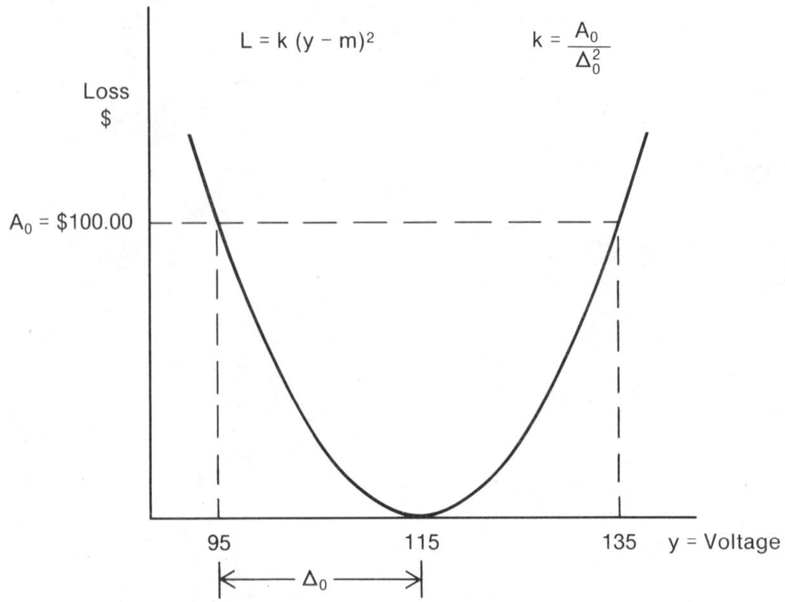

What is the y value (voltage) that corresponds to the average cost to the customer, i.e., $100?

This value is called the Functional Tolerance (or LD-50) and represents the functional limits of acceptable product performance from the viewpoint of the average customer.

Figure AB-6

Knowing this, we can estimate the average loss to society (see **Figure AB-7**). When the output voltage reaches 95 or 135 volts, somebody is paying $100. As long as the output voltage is at 115 volts, society's financial loss is minimized.

What is society's loss for a poor-quality TV-power-supply circuit? Suppose a circuit is shipped with an output voltage of 110 volts without being reworked. It is imparting a loss of:

$$\begin{aligned} L(y) &= \$0.25\,(110 - 115)^2 \\ &= \$6.25 \end{aligned}$$

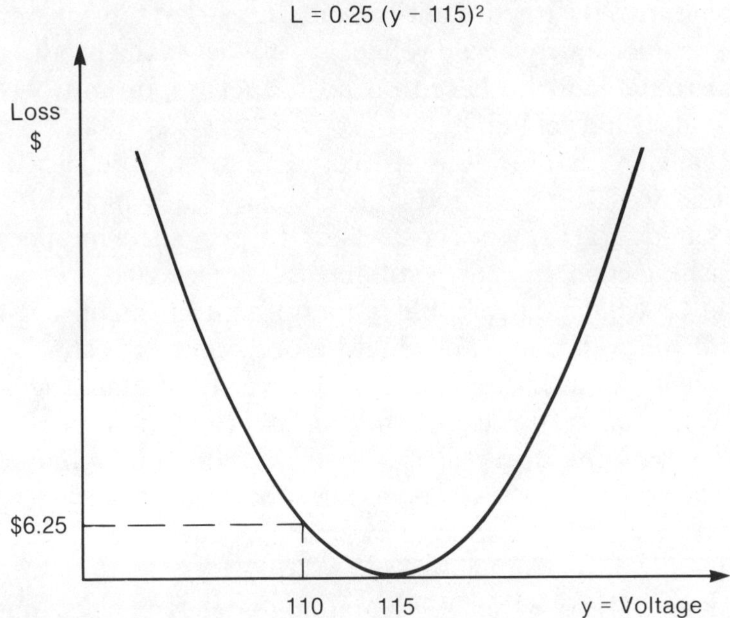

Circuit shipped at 110 volts has quality loss of $6.25.

Figure AB-7

On the average, somebody is paying $6.25. This is a rough approximation of the loss due to inferior quality. It will be experienced by the customer as loss associated with A_0. It will be experienced by the manufacturer as customer dissatisfaction, added warranty costs, and so forth.

Customer-Based Tolerances

Tolerancing is the determination of manufacturing/shipping specifications for product characteristics at all points in the manufacturing pipeline. As traditionally established, tolerances do not ensure quality. Rather, they dictate the limits of product functionality as specified by the engineer. Two products can both function adequately, but one can still be better than the other in terms of functionality and in the eyes of the consumer. Realistic tolerances should reflect the impact of the product on the customer and be based on a product's optimum performance at the target value.

Realistic customer-based tolerances should be based on customer loss, the deviation from the target at which this loss occurs, and scrap/rework costs. The QLF provides a method for establishing economically justifiable tolerances.

Up to what point should a manufacturer spend a given amount to fix (repair) a product before shipment? This is the break-even point, in terms of loss, between the manufacturer and the customer. It is called the manufacturing tolerance.

The manufacturing tolerance includes the functional tolerance, the consumer's loss, and the cost of scrap/rework.

If A = cost of scrap/rework and Δ = the manufacturer's tolerance, then anything outside the limits m +/− Δ is a scrap/rework loss. We use the QLF equation to determine the manufacturer's tolerance:

$$L(y) = (y - m)^2$$

where

$$k = \frac{A_0}{\Delta_0^2} \text{ and } \Delta = y - m$$

Therefore

$$A = \frac{A_0}{\Delta_0^2} (\Delta)^2$$

Solving for Δ we have

$$\Delta = \sqrt{\frac{A}{A_0}} (\Delta_0) \text{(manufacturer's tolerance)}$$

Suppose the output voltage of the TV sets can be recalibrated at the end of the production line at a cost of $2 per set. What is the manufacturer's tolerance? (See **Figure AB-8**.)

$$
\begin{aligned}
A_0 &= \$100.00 \\
\Delta_0 &= 20 \text{ volts} \\
A &= \$2.00 \\
\Delta &= \sqrt{\frac{A}{A_0}}\,(\Delta_0) = \sqrt{\frac{2.00}{100.00}}\,(20 \text{ v}) \\
&= 2.83 \text{ volts} \Rightarrow \quad 3 \text{ volts}
\end{aligned}
$$

As long as the output voltage, y, is within 3 volts of the target (115 +/−3 volts), the manufacturer should not spend $2 per set for recalibration. The manufacturer's tolerance sets the limits for shipping the product. At that point, either the manufacturer or the customer can, on average, spend $2 for quality. Beyond that point, the customer's loss increases beyond acceptable limits.

Suppose the factory ships a TV-power-supply circuit with an output voltage of 110 volts without rework. In the short run, the factory saves $2 by not reworking the circuit, but it is imparting a loss of $6.25 to the customer.

The QLF can also be applied to derive tolerances for subsystems, subcomponents, parts, and materials from suppliers. Here the manufacturer becomes the customer and we must determine the relationship between quality characteristics critical to the manufacturer's process and those used by the supplier. (For example, in producing stamped products from sheet metal, a critical dimension in a stamped product is affected by the hardness of the sheet metal. We must determine the relationship expressing the effect of sheet-metal hardness on the critical dimension.)

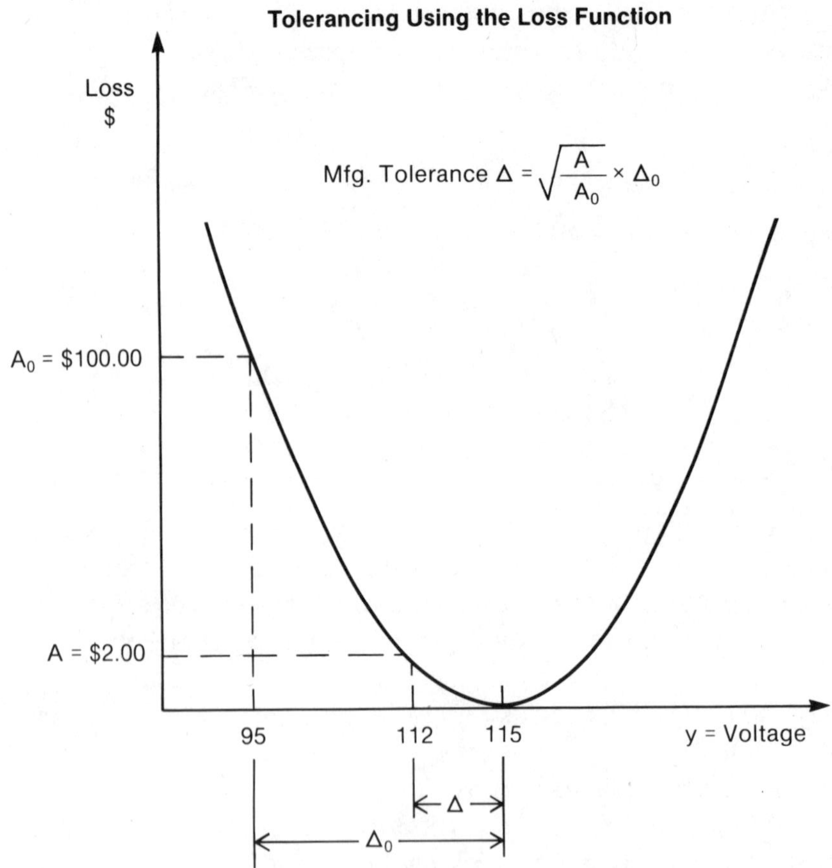

Rework cost is $2. The manufacturer's tolerance is 3 volts. If y measures more than 3 volts, the plant should spend $2 for rework.

Figure AB-8

Evaluating the Quality of More Than One Piece

We have applied the QLF to determine the manufacturing tolerance for one piece of a product. More often, manufacturers need to evaluate the average quality of all their products over a given period of time. This can be done, with respect to a given quality characteristic, using the average of $(y - m)^2$, which is called the Mean Square Deviation (MSD).

$$\text{MSD} = \frac{(y_1 - m)^2 + (y_2 - m)^2 + \ldots + (y_n - m)^2}{n}$$

$$= \sum_{i=1}^{n} \frac{(y_i - m)^2}{n}$$

$$\text{MSD} = \frac{(y_1 - \bar{y})^2 + (y_2 - \bar{y})^2 + \ldots + (y_n - \bar{y})^2}{n} + (\bar{y} - m)^2$$

$$= \sum_{i=1}^{n} \frac{(y_i - \bar{y})^2}{n} + (\bar{y} - m)^2$$

where m = target value; y_i = measured value of the characteristic; and $\bar{y}$ = the mean.

$$\bar{y} = \sum_{i=1}^{n} \frac{y_i}{n}$$

The variance around the mean is computed by

$$\sigma^2 = \sum_{i=1}^{n} \frac{(y_i - \bar{y})^2}{n}$$

Here the population variance (σ^2) is used instead of the sample variance (s^2), even though we are using the sample size, n. Thus we have:

$$\text{MSD} = \sigma^2 + (\bar{y} - m)^2$$

MSD is a measure of the variance (variability around the mean) and the deviation of the mean from the target value, m. We can now evaluate the quality of all of our outputs:

$$L = k\,(MSD)$$
$$= [\sigma^2 + (\bar{y} - m)^2]$$

↑ Variance (Variability around the mean)

↑ (Shift of the mean from the target value)

To reduce the average loss due to poor quality, we must reduce the MSD. This can be accomplished by reducing variability around the average (σ^2) and adjusting the mean to the nominal $(y - m)^2$.

Justifying Quality Improvement

U.S. companies must be competitive in cost as well as quality. Therefore, product and process designs must improve both cost and quality for all products and all processes, not just those with obvious quality deficiencies. This concept can be translated into operation through the QLF.

For a process that is producing, say, 96% of the product inside specifications, traditional thinking with regard to quality costs would focus on the 4% outside specifications. Yet it is the 96% that is more important. The QLF allows us to quantitatively evaluate quality on the entire population (100% of the product).

Most U.S. companies are managed by financially oriented executives who have imposed short-term financial payback guidelines that improvement actions must meet. By using the QLF, however, we can often justify a long-term investment in improved quality.

Consider the now well-known example of the four factories. All are producing the same product under the same engineering specifications, with a desired target value of m. All four factories carry out 100% inspection and ship only products within specification limits. Factory IV seems to be the preferred supplier. It offers more products at or near the desired target and exhibits less piece-to-piece variability (see **Figure AB-9**).

Let us take a sample size of only 13 pieces. In reality, we would want to use a larger sample in estimating loss (see **Table AB-2**).

For a "nominal the best" characteristic with a derived proportionality constant of k=0.25, we can calculate the MSD and the loss per piece of a product for each factory. We have:

$$
\begin{aligned}
m &= 115 \\
k &= 0.25 \\
L &= k[\sigma^2 + (\bar{y} - m)^2] \\
&= k[\text{MSD}] \\
&= k\left[\sum_{i=1}^{n} \frac{(y-m)^2}{n}\right] \\
&= k\left[\frac{(y_1-m)^2 + (y_2-m)^2 + \dots + (y_n-m)^2}{n}\right]
\end{aligned}
$$

For Factory I:

$$
\begin{aligned}
L &= 0.25\left[\frac{(112 - 115)^2 + (113 - 115)^2 + \dots + (118 - 115)^2}{13}\right] \\
&= \$0.73/\text{piece}
\end{aligned}
$$

In other words, as a rough approximation, one randomly selected piece shipped from Factory I is, on the average, imparting a loss of $0.73. The $0.73 is spent by somebody—a customer, the company itself, an indirect consumer, etc.

The QLF can help justify a decision to invest in improving a process that is already capable of meeting specifications. Suppose, for example, that you are an engineer at Factory II, and you tell your boss that you would like to spend $20,000 to raise the quality level of your process to that of Factory IV. Re-

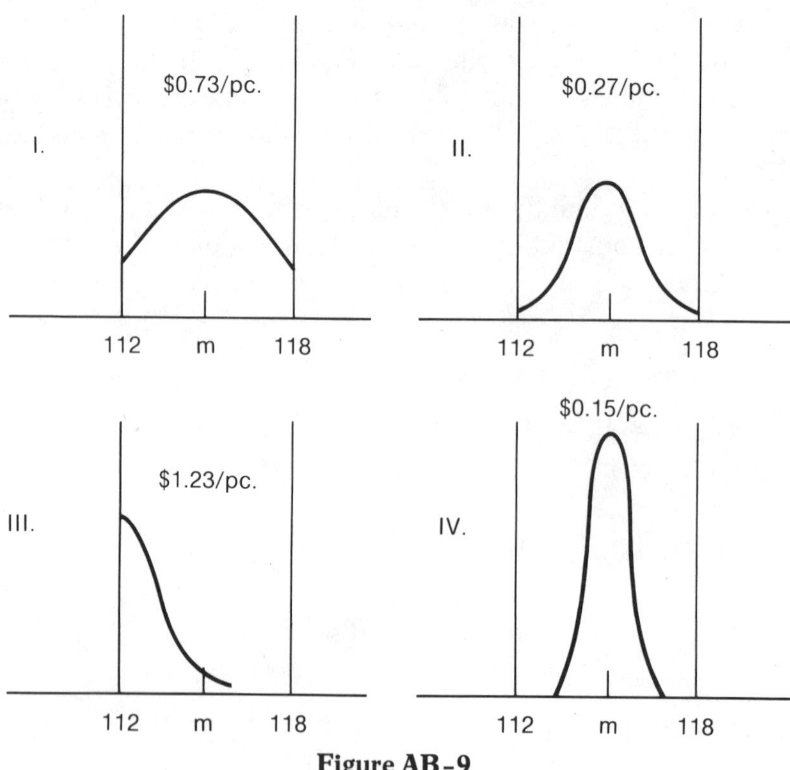

Figure AB-9

member, 96% of your output is already within specifications and your boss is reasonably satisfied. How would you justify your proposal?

Let us assume that your monthly production is 100,000 pieces. Using the QLF, the improvement (Factory II to Factory IV) would provide savings of:

$$\$(0.27 - 0.15)/\text{piece} \times 100{,}000 \text{ pieces/month}$$
$$= \$12{,}000/\text{month}$$

More and more Japanese companies are using the QLF to justify quality improvement. At Nippondenso, for example, the estimated savings from three quality-improvement projects was

Table AB-2
Data for Four Factories

Factory	*Data*	*MSD*	*Loss*
I	113 113 113 114 114 115 115 116 116 117 117 115 118	2.92	\$0.73/piece
II	113 114 114 114 115 115 115 115 115 116 116 117 113	1.08	\$0.27/piece
III	112 113 112 113 112 113 114 115 112 113 114 112 114	4.92	\$1.23/piece
IV	114 114 116 114 115 116 114 115 116 114 115 116 115	0.62	\$0.15/piece

calculated by traditional methods and then by the QLF. According to the traditional method, three improvements in a machine-rotor-shaft press-fit process would have saved a total of \$55,000. QLF calculations, however, revealed a savings of \$548,000—almost a tenfold increase.

Evaluating Supplier Quality

When customers purchase an automobile, they expect a warm, comfortable interior, whether driving on an expressway on a windy day or parked in a rain or dust storm. They expect the car to be well-sealed. An automobile-door weatherstrip is a component part that is intended to aid in vehicle sealing without unduly compromising door opening and closing. The width of the weatherstrip bulb is a quality characteristic that ensures that the weatherstrip functions effectively.

Dr. W. H. Moore of Ford Motor Co. describes an application of the QLF to the evaluation of weatherstrip quality that motivated the application of the Taguchi approach for quality improvement at Ford.

Three weatherstrip suppliers reported the following production statistics in which process capability was calculated (see **Table AB-3**). Process capability is a measure of how capable a process is at meeting specifications. It is also a measure of whether a process is centered on the target value and the variability of the process around the target value. The capability index (Cpk) was determined for each manufacturer:

Table AB-3
Weatherstrip Bulb Dimension
Specification y = 20 ± 4 mm

Supplier	$\bar{y}$	*Variance* (s^2)	*Cpk*
I	20.0	$(4/3)^2$	1.0
II	18.0	$(2/3)^2$	1.0
III	17.2	$(2/5)^2$	1.0

Cpk = The minimum of USL − $\bar{y}/3\sigma$ or $\bar{y}$ − LSL/3σ where USL = upper specification limit; LSL = lower specification limit; $\bar{y}$ = the process average; and 3σ = three times the standard deviation.

Cpk has been considered an excellent basis for comparing the quality of different producers or the quality of a single producer over time. However, Cpk is a function of preset specifications that may or may not be meaningful. It assumes that all products within specifications are equally good. As we can see from the weatherstrip-bulb-dimension data, this can lead to the wrong conclusion (all have a Cpk of 1.0; all appear to be equivalent.)

Applying the QLF resolves this problem. The QLF measures loss in monetary units as a function of deviation from the target value. It is not dependent on specifications.

Based on field data and in-plant testing, the weatherstrip was predicted to fail at a width deviation from the target of

5 mm. At 15 mm, the bulb is small and the door does not seal well. About 50% of the customers will not only complain, but will insist that the bulb be replaced at a cost of \$50. At 25 mm, door-closing efforts are objectionable, and the average customer asks to have the problem resolved. Thus,

$$k = \frac{A_0}{\Delta_0^2} = \frac{\$50}{5\ \text{mm}^2} = 2.0$$

For the three suppliers, the loss through variability around the target per unit was calculated using the following equation:

$$\text{Average Loss} = k[\sigma^2 + (\bar{y} - m)^2]$$

$$\text{Supplier I} \quad L_1 = 2.0 \left[\left(\frac{4}{3}\right)^2 + 0^2\right] = \$3.55\ /\ \text{unit}$$

$$\text{Supplier II} \quad L_2 = 2.0 \left[\left(\frac{2}{3}\right)^2 + 2^2\right] = \$8.88\ /\ \text{unit}$$

$$\text{Supplier III} \quad L_3 = 2.0 \left[\left(\frac{2}{5}\right)^2 + 2.8^2\right] = \$16.00\ /\ \text{unit}$$

Notice that the suppliers that appeared to have equivalent quality now appear to be very different (see **Table AB-4**). Sourcing decisions on loss by defects (as measured by the Cpk) are different from those based on loss due to variability around the target (as measured by the QLF).

Based on *loss by defects,* Suppliers II and III are equivalent and the best choice. However, using *loss by variability* based on the QLF, Supplier I produces the best quality, followed by Supplier II, and then Supplier III. In terms of long-term customer-related loss and considering all units produced, Supplier III—previously considered to be one of the best—is as bad as fictitious Supplier IV, with a Cpk of only 0.471 and 16% of its parts out of specification (defective).

This application of the QLF motivated weatherstrip engineers and manufacturing personnel at Ford's Automotive Body and Assembly Division to be trained in this new way of thinking and the application of Taguchi Methods. It motivated the pursuit of continuous quality improvement.

Table AB-4
Weatherstrip Dimension

Specification $\bar{y} = 20 \pm 4$mm; customer loss per unit $A_0 =$ \$50.00; functional tolerance $\Delta_0 = \pm$ 5mm; annual production = 250,000 units.

Supplier	$\bar{y}$	σ	*Cpk*	*Defects %*	*Loss* *Defects \$*	*Loss* *Dispersion \$*
I	20.0	4/3	1	0.270	\$ 33,750	\$ 887,500
II	18.0	2/3	1	0.135	\$ 16,875	\$2,220,000
III	17.2	2/5	1	0.135	\$ 16,875	\$4,000,000
IV	20.0	2.82	0.471	16.000	\$2,000,000	\$4,000,000

Conclusion

Today, worldwide competition has increased, and customers have become more concerned about value and total product cost. Survival has become a real issue for companies. Customer satisfaction must be a part of the cost equation that drives the decision process in development and production of products.

Exposure to SPC has provided U.S. manufacturers with an awareness of the importance of reducing variability and centering important characteristics around a target value. However, the question still remains—how can we carry these ideas over into making effective, cost-justified decisions regarding product and process quality? The QLF allows us to evaluate the total cost impact of alternative decisions regarding quality improvement

Loss Function Summary

1. "Nominal the Best"

$$L = \begin{cases} k\,(y - m)^2 & k = \dfrac{A_0}{\Delta_0^2} \\ k\,(\mathrm{MSD}) \end{cases}$$

$$\mathrm{MSD} = \frac{1}{n} \sum_{i=1}^{n} (y_i - m)^2$$

$$= \sigma^2 + (\bar{y} - m)^2$$

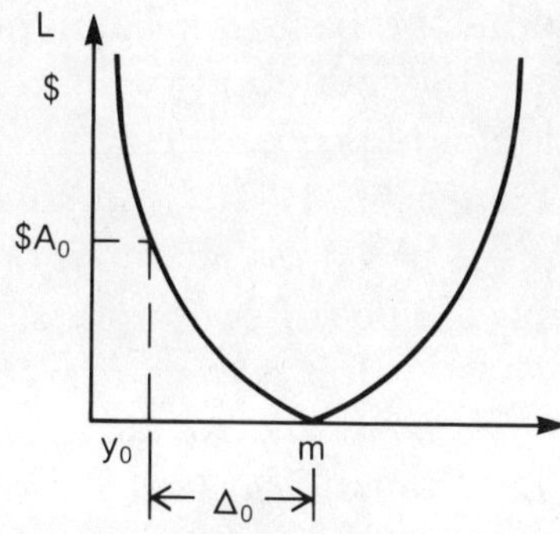

2. "Smaller the Better"

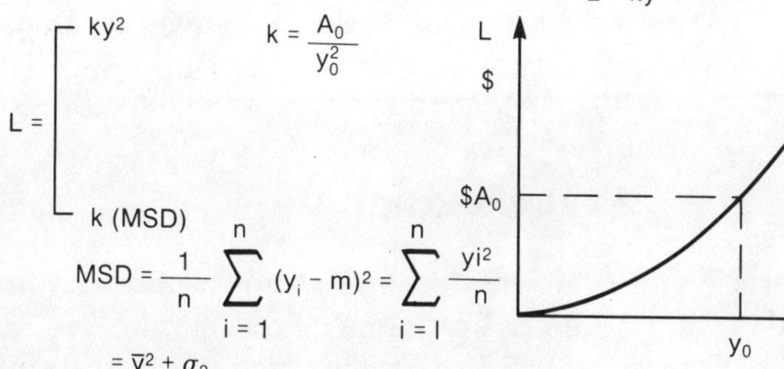

$$L = \begin{cases} ky^2 & k = \dfrac{A_0}{y_0^2} \\ k\,(\mathrm{MSD}) \end{cases}$$

$$\mathrm{MSD} = \frac{1}{n} \sum_{i=1}^{n} (y_i - m)^2 = \sum_{i=l}^{n} \frac{yi^2}{n}$$

$$= \bar{y}^2 + \sigma_2$$

3. "Larger the Better"

$$L = \begin{cases} k\,\dfrac{1}{y^2} & k = A_0 y_0{}^2 \\ k\,(\mathrm{MSD}) \end{cases}$$

$$\mathrm{MSD} = \frac{1}{n} \sum_{i=1}^{n} \frac{1}{y_i^2}$$

$$= \frac{1}{\bar{y}^2} \left(1 + 3 \times \frac{\sigma^2}{\bar{y}^2}\right)$$

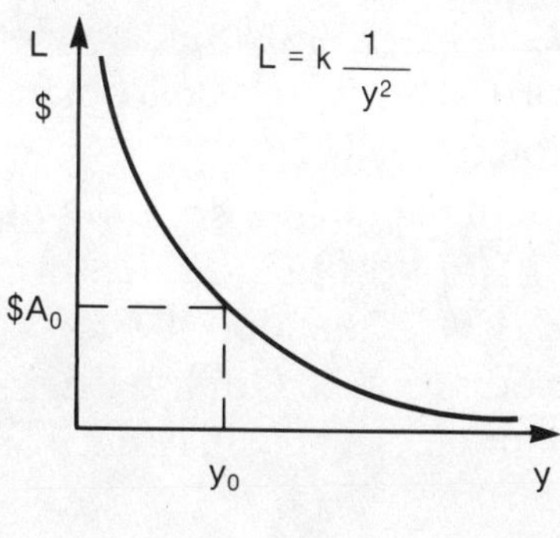

Figure AB-10

in a way that captures difficult-to-quantify customer-related costs and considers the long-term economic well-being of a company. As we have seen, it is an ideal evaluator of quality and provides the basis for Taguchi's approach to quality improvement—the reduction of loss through development of robust product and process design.

Figure AB-10 summarizes the relevant QLF formulas for one piece of a product and more than one piece of a product for the three types of continuously variable quality characteristics.

Dr. Duane Orlowski is manager of technical writing at the American Supplier Institute (ASI), Inc., in Dearborn, MI. He was previously Assistant Professor of Anthropology in the Department of Science and Technology Studies at Rensselaer Polytechnic Institute in Troy, NY.

Bibliography

Jessup, Peter T. "The Value of Continuous Improvement." International Communications Conference Proceedings, "ICC '85," June 1985. Copyright 1985, Institute of Electrical and Electronics Engineers.

Moore, W. H. "Ford Has a Better Idea: Quality Engineering at Ford Motor Co." Dearborn: Body and Chassis Division, Ford Motor Co., 1986.

Taguchi, Genichi. *Introduction to Quality Engineering: Designing Quality into Products and Processes.* Tokyo: Asian Productivity Organization, 1986.

"Introduction to Quality Engineering," five-day seminar course manual. Dearborn: American Supplier Institute, Inc., 1988.

Appendix C: Signal-to-Noise Ratio

Dr. Don Clausing

The evaluation of performance is critical to the rapid optimization of new products and processes, essential to achieve good quality and to greatly reduce product-development time. If performance is evaluated by simply compiling a list of detailed and specific problems, the improvement of the product or process will be ad hoc and diffuse, with quality improvement very uncertain. To be an international leader in quality and rapid development, it is imperative to develop compact metrics for the efficient evaluation of performance.

In defining metrics that measure the performance that is the output from a system, we consider both the output that we wish to achieve and the undesirable output that we would prefer not to have present. We want a metric that provides one number that appropriately encompasses both desirable and undesirable aspects of performance. We think of the desirable performance as the signal and the undesirable performance as the noise. This is analogous to the original use of the term Signal-to-Noise (S/N) Ratio in the field of electronic communications.

We want the S/N Ratio to have several characteristics besides the one mentioned in the first paragraph of being a good measure of performance that takes into account both desirable output and undesirable output. These desired characteristics are:

1. If several factors, A,B,C, each individually have an effect on the performance, then we'd like the total effect of all

three factors simply to be the sum of the individual effects. This property is called additivity.

2. The maximization of the performance metric should correspond to the minimization of quality loss.
3. The optimization of the performance metrics should be independent of the adjustment of the performance value. Often, after the design is optimized, we may wish to adjust the performance to some preferred value. This adjustment should not upset the optimization.

To summarize, we want the performance metric to have economic significance and to facilitate optimization procedures.

Nominal-the-Best Characteristics

Many systems have output that can be characterized as "nominal-the-best." There is some nominal value for the output that is the preferred value. Any values that are different from the nominal value are less desirable. Examples are production processes. Usually production processes are intended to create some nominal value of a dimension or other characteristic. Another example is a power supply. If we have a 24-volt power supply, we very much prefer that it put out 24 volts. Both 23 and 25 volts are much less desirable.

If we measure the performance of a system in several experiments, we can then calculate the mean value and the value of the standard deviation from these data. Suppose you were asked: "The standard deviation is one. Do you like it?" What would you answer? Of course, there is no way to give a sensible answer with the information that has been provided. First of all, we don't know the dimensions of the quantity. Secondly, we have no reference point by which to judge the magnitude. If we are told that the mean value is 10, we are likely to think that the standard deviation of 1 is excessive. However, if the mean value is 100, we may think that a standard deviation of 1 is quite good, and if the mean value is 1,000, we're almost certain to like the standard deviation of 1. This suggests that the ratio of the mean value divided by the standard deviation is a good performance metric. This ratio will immediately cause the dimensions to cancel and we needn't worry as to the actual dimensions of the performance measurement. Also, this ratio contains a reference by which we can achieve a reasonable perspective on the magnitude of the standard deviation. Therefore, this ratio seems like a reasonable performance metric.

It also tends to give the property of making the performance metric independent of subsequent adjustment. Consider the data for three different designs that are summarized in **Figure AC-1.**

The distinct designs, 1, 2, 3, have each been tested under several conditions of noise and the mean values and standard deviations calculated for each design. These are the points that are plotted in **Figure AC-1.** Based on the data that are shown in **Figure AC-1**, which design do you prefer? Many people initially think that Design 1 is preferable because it has the smallest standard deviation. However, the target value is shown as M in **Figure AC-1**, and we see that Design 1 happened to be tested under circumstances that gave output much less than the target value. Therefore, we must adjust the system to increase the output so that the mean value for Design 1 is as close as possible to the target value. Usually, adjusting the mean value to the target is quite easily done. In fact, a more significant concern is that engineers are all too ready to adjust the performance to the target in order to make the product look good under one set of conditions. Engineers having demonstrated much ingenuity in this respect, we can be confident that adjustment of the mean to the target will be easily accomplished. Now, what is going to happen to the standard deviation of Design 1 when the mean is adjusted to the target? Adjustment is most conveniently done with an adjustment factor that changes the mean and the standard deviation in the same proportion, keeping their ratio constant. Thus, when

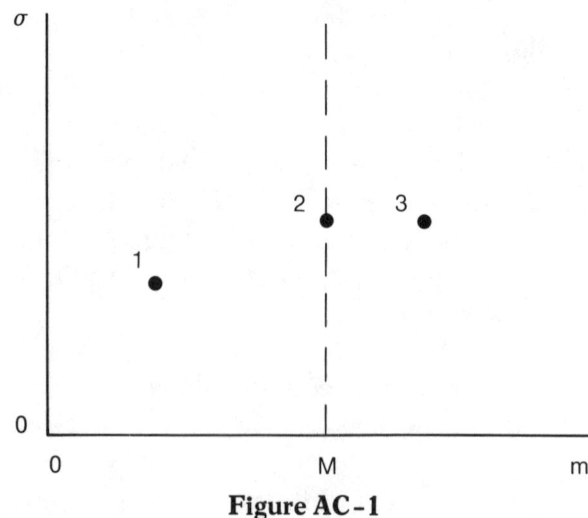

Figure AC-1

the mean for Design 1 is adjusted to the target, our most realistic expectation is that the standard deviation will increase to the value plotted as 1′ in **Figure AC-2.**

Similarly, the standard deviation for Design 3 will be reduced to the value 3′. Thus we see that the performance for Design 3 is actually the best. This leads us to want to take the ratio of mean to standard deviation in optimizing the performance. From the plots in **Figures AC-1** and **AC-2**, we see that achieving the best ratio of mean divided by the standard deviation will give us the smallest value of standard deviation after the mean has been adjusted to the target value.

By basing the nominal-the-best S/N Ratio on the ratio of the mean value to the standard deviation, we are creating a performance metric that will remain constant during adjustment to the target if the assumption of constant ratio of mean value to standard deviation is satisfied. Therefore, when performing adjustments to the target, we can check the S/N Ratio over the range of the adjustment. If the experimentally determined S/N Ratio is almost constant over the range of adjustment, then we can be confident that the optimization by which the standard

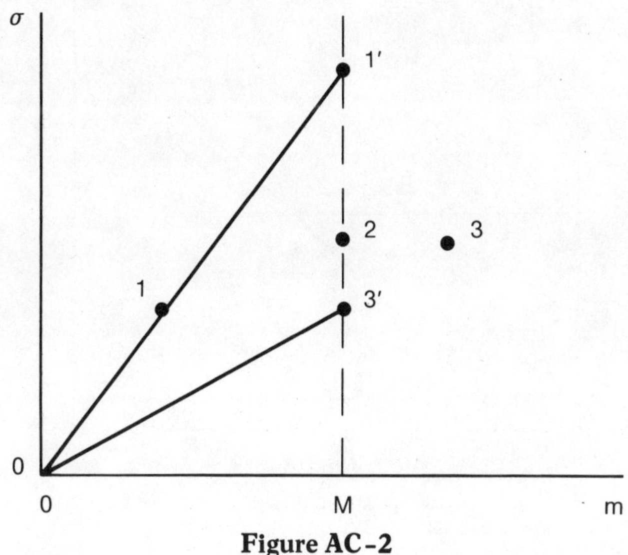

Figure AC-2

deviation has been minimized will remain valid even after the mean value has been adjusted to the target. Therefore, after conducting the optimization experiments and plotting the data, we search for an adjustment factor that has the characteristics that are shown in **Figure AC-3**.

In **Figure AC-3** the plotted data show that the S/N Ratio is constant. This justifies our assumption that the ratio of the mean value to the standard deviation will remain constant during adjustment of the mean value to the target. Also, we see in **Figure AC-3** that the mean is linear in its relationship with the adjustment factor. From **Figure AC-3** we can easily change the value of the adjustment factor to bring the mean to the target without in any way disturbing the optimization that has minimized the value of standard deviation. We can be confident that if we use this adjustment factor to adjust the performance values for each of the designs to the target, the one that we choose as optimum on the basis of the S/N Ratio will actually have the smallest standard deviation. Of course, in actual experimentation, we will not find data that conform to our assumptions as well as is indicated

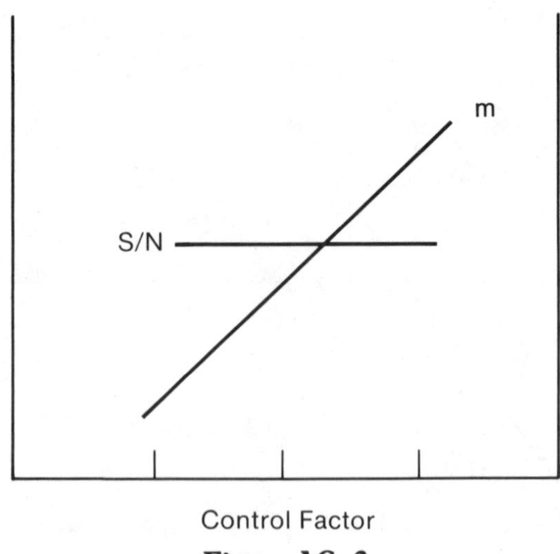

Control Factor

Figure AC-3

in **Figure AC-3**. However, often we find a control factor that has characteristics that are approximates, as shown in **Figure AC-3**. Then this control factor will make a good adjustment factor. If the S/N Ratio changes by an amount greater than we would prefer, we can always compare the new standard deviation after adjustment. This can be done easily by simply taking the new value of the S/N Ratio. In this way, even if the S/N Ratio changes by a significant amount, the definition of the S/N Ratio for a nominal-the-best characteristic will enable us to quickly find the optimum design. Therefore, the S/N Ratio for the nominal-the-best system is:

$$SN = 10 \log E \left[\frac{m^2}{\sigma^2} \right] \tag{1}$$

$$SN = 10 \log \frac{\frac{1}{n}(Sm - V)}{V}$$

$$Sm = \frac{(\Sigma y)^2}{n} \qquad V = \frac{1}{n-1}(\Sigma y^2 - Sm)$$

Here E indicates the expected value, and y represents the data points for performance. Commonly the n data points are obtained under n different conditions of noise. (Noise here refers to undesirable but inevitable deviations from nominal in the parts of the system and in the environment in which it is used.) The logarithm is used because it usually improves additivity. The multiplier of 10 is simply the usual convention in electronics and acoustics of using the unit of decibels. The nominal-the-best S/N Ratio is used for many engineering systems.

For some performance characteristics negative values are possible. Then it may occur that the mean value is smaller than the standard deviation. For such situations it is usually best to take 10 log (1/V) in Equation 1.

Many performance characteristics that are simple to consider as nominal-the-best are actually dynamic characteristics (described later in this appendix). For example, a power supply that has an advertised output of 24 V is not expected to produce this output if the input voltage is zero; the output depends on the input. However, over the usual range of input voltage (approximately a constant value) it is reasonable to consider that the output has a fixed target of 24V. Actual performance characteristics should be carefully analyzed as to whether they have a static target value, or are dynamic characteristics.

Smaller-the-Better Characteristics

Many performance measures have zero as the desired value. Examples are background density on a copy, wow on a turntable, and unbalance in car wheels. A little thought suggests that the reason that these characteristics have zero as the preferred value is that the characteristics are, themselves, noises. In many cases it is expedient to treat the characteristics as "smaller-the-better." In this case the performance metric is simply the variance from zero. In other words, this is the mean square error from zero. (Of course, the term "variance" more specifically means the mean square error from the mean value.) This performance characteristic is given simply by the following equation:

$$SN = -10 \log \frac{1}{n} \Sigma y^2 \qquad (2)$$

The negative sign must be used because the metric that is being measured is undesirable. As its value decreases we want the S/N Ratio to increase.

We should consider the possibility that the smaller-the-better characteristic might be best integrated into another type of characteristic. For example, wow might be made the noise in a nominal-the-best characteristic. Background density on a copy is the output noise when the input signal is zero. It would be better to consider the full range of inputs from white to black, rather than concentrating on one value of input. It may be that the smaller-the-better characteristic is seldom, if ever, the best performance metric. However, for many applications it is convenient to use, particularly for initial applications.

Larger-the-Better Characteristics

"Larger-the-better" characteristics are characteristics such as strength. A little thought will show that the inverse of a larger-the-better characteristic is simply the smaller-the-better characteristic that we considered in the previous section. Therefore, if we have a larger-the-better characteristic y, then we can simply take the reciprocal of y as a smaller-the-better characteristic. This directly leads to the following equation for the larger-the-better S/N Ratio:

$$SN = -10 \log \frac{1}{n} \Sigma \frac{1}{y^2} \qquad (3)$$

Static Characteristics

The three S/N Ratios that have been described above are all static characteristics. In other words, the value that we want is a constant, which can be defined before we start the experiments. In many cases the performance characteristic is not so simple and cannot be represented by a constant value. These dynamic characteristics are described in the following section.

Dynamic Characteristics

There are four basic types of dynamic characteristics:

1. Input-variable/output-variable
2. Input-variable/output-digital
3. Input-digital/output-variable
4. Input-digital/output-digital

Here we will only consider the first case where both the input and output are continuous variables (analog signals). The most important fact about digital signals to keep in mind in creating the appropriate performance characteristics is that digital signals are actually continuous variables (analog signals) coupled with a protocol that distinguishes zeros from ones.

An example of input-variable/output-variable dynamic systems is the steering system of an automobile. The intended turning radius is not a constant: it depends on the angle that the driver imparts to the steering wheel. (See Chapter 10 of *Introduction to Quality Engineering.*[1]) For such a system we can define the desired performance as a linear relationship between turn-

1. Genichi Taguchi, *Introduction to Quality Engineering: Designing Quality into Products and Processes,* Asian Productivity Organization, 1986.

ing radius and the steering-wheel angle. If all data points lie on a straight line, then the performance is perfect. Define the best straight line as:

$$y_\beta = m + \beta(M-\overline{M}) \tag{4}$$

where m = mean of y value; β = slope of line; M = signal factor; and $\overline{M}$ = average value of signal factor.

Actual data will not lie exactly on a straight line. We define the discrepancy from the best straight line as error.

The best line is the one that minimizes the sum of the square of the errors.

$$\sum_{1}^{n} e^2 = \sum\{y - [m + \beta(M-\overline{M})]\}^2 \tag{5}$$

The S/N Ratio is

$$SN = 10 \log \frac{\frac{1}{\Sigma(M-\overline{M})^2}(S_\beta - V)}{V} \tag{6}$$

$$S_\beta = \Sigma \left\{ [M-\overline{M}] \left[\frac{\Sigma y(M-\overline{M})}{\Sigma(M-\overline{M})^2} \right] \right\}^2$$

Here n is the total number of data points. Again, the performance evaluations are commonly done while subjecting the system to several noise conditions. For example, **Figure AC-4** might result from six noise conditions at each of three signal values, for a total of 18 data points.

As for the nominal-the-best static case, the performance must be adjusted to the target after the design values that produced the largest S/N value have been selected. Now the straight line must be adjusted to coincide with the design-target straight line. Two parameters, m and β, must be adjusted, so two adjustment factors must be found among the design parameters.

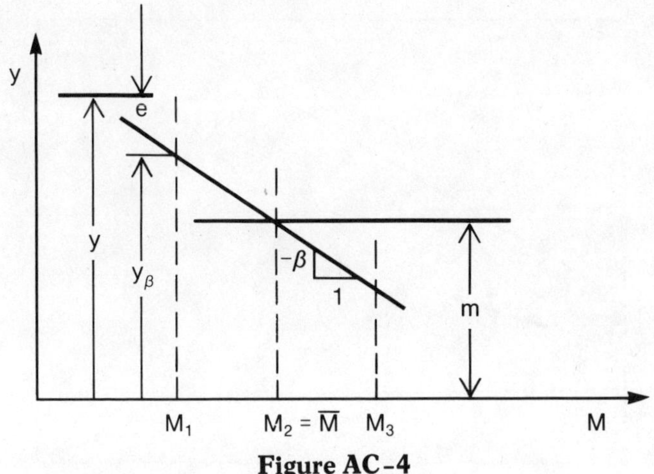

Figure AC-4

In general, that part of performance that will be adjusted will be decided on the basis of what is easy to adjust. In some systems it might be easy to adjust a bilinear response. Then the S/N Ratio should be based on the best bilinear fit to the data.

In **Figure AC-5**, Curve 2 has the least dispersion. If it is easy to adjust the bilinear curve to coincide with the target performance, then the design that leads to Curve 2 should be selected. It should not be penalized by comparing the data with a single straight line. Three adjustment factors will be needed.

The dynamic S/N Ratios are more important and more powerful than the static S/N Ratios. Most devices transform input energy into output energy. The best performance characteristic quantifies the dynamic relationship between output and input, as influenced by noises. Often the use of a static characteristic is a way station on the road to the development of a powerful dynamic characteristic.

Derivation of Dynamic S/N Ratio

The best values for m and β are found by differentiating $\sum e^2$ (Equation 5) with respect to m and β and setting the derivatives equal to zero.

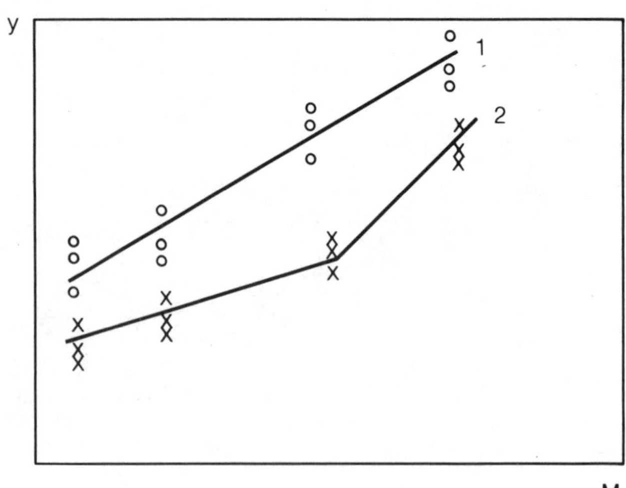

Figure AC-5

$$\frac{\partial}{\partial m} \sum e^2 = \frac{\partial}{\partial m} \sum\{y - [m + \beta(M-\overline{M})]\}^2 = 0 \quad (7)$$

$$- 2 \sum\{y - [m + \beta(M-\overline{M})]\} = 0$$

$$\sum y = nm + \beta \sum(M-\overline{M})$$

$$\sum y = nm + 0$$

$$m = \frac{\sum y}{n} \quad (8)$$

$$\frac{\partial}{\partial m} \sum e^2 = \frac{\partial}{\partial m} \sum\{y - [m + \beta(M-\overline{M})]\}^2 = 0 \quad (9)$$

$$- 2 \sum\{y - [m + \beta(M-\overline{M})]\} \{M-\overline{M}\} = 0$$

$$\sum(y - m)(M-\overline{M}) = \beta \sum(M-\overline{M})^2$$

However,

$$m \sum (M - \overline{M}) = 0 \tag{10}$$

Therefore

$$\beta = \frac{\sum y(M - \overline{M})}{\sum (M - \overline{M})^2}$$

$$\sum e^2 = \sum \left\{ y - m - (M - \overline{M}) \frac{\sum y(M - \overline{M})}{\sum (M - \overline{M})^2} \right\}^2 \tag{11}$$

The average value of $\sum e^2$ per data point is

$$V = \frac{\sum e^2}{n - 2} \tag{12}$$

There are two adjustable constants, m and β, so the value of $\sum e^2$ for two (or fewer) data points is zero. Therefore, V is the average incremental increase in $\sum e^2$ per additional data point (above two).

Equation 12 is the average incremental value of $\sum e^2$ (called variance) for y. What is the variance for M? When e is added to Equation 4, the complete equation for y is

$$y = m + \beta(M - \overline{M}) + e \tag{13}$$

Solving for M

$$M = \frac{1}{\beta}(y - m + \beta\overline{M}) - \frac{e}{\beta} \tag{14}$$

The first term on the right is the estimate of M based on the measured value y.

$$\hat{M} = \frac{1}{\beta}(y - m + \beta\overline{M}) \tag{15}$$

The variance of M is

$$V' = \overline{(M - \hat{M})^2} \tag{16}$$

$$V' = \frac{\overline{e^2}}{\beta^2} \tag{17}$$

$$V' = \frac{V}{\beta^2} \tag{18}$$

The value of β^2 is found from Equation 10. However, this experimental determination overestimates the actual value of β^2 because it includes the effect of error. Therefore, a small correction is made.

$$E(S_\beta) = V + [\Sigma(M - \overline{M})^2]\beta^2 \tag{19}$$

$$\beta^2 = \frac{1}{\Sigma(M - \overline{M})^2}[S_\beta - V] \tag{20}$$

Where

$$S_\beta = \beta^2 \Sigma(M - \overline{M})^2 \tag{21}$$

$$S_\beta = \left[\frac{\Sigma y(M - \overline{M})}{\Sigma(M - \overline{M})^2}\right]^2 \Sigma(M - \overline{M})^2 \tag{22}$$

Combining Equations 18 and 20

$$V^1 = \frac{\frac{V}{1}}{\Sigma(M-\overline{M})^2} [S_\beta - V] \quad (23)$$

S/N is defined

$$S/N = 10 \log \frac{1}{V^1} \quad (24)$$

$$S/N = 10 \log \frac{\frac{1}{\Sigma(M-\overline{M})^2} [S_\beta - V]}{V} \quad (25)$$

Conclusion

Utilization of the S/N Ratio to concisely measure performance and focus the activities to optimize the values of the critical parameters is essential in order to achieve strongly improved quality and shorter development time. By combining physics, economics, and deep knowledge of engineering practice, the S/N Ratios are a great advance over common expressions of performance. The reader is encouraged to further study performance evaluation in the works mentioned in the bibliography.

Dr. Don Clausing is Bernard M. Gordon Adjunct Professor of Engineering Innovation and Practice at Massachusetts Institute of Technology, Cambridge, Massachusetts. He was previously Manager and then Principal Engineer in the Advanced Development Activities at Xerox Corp.

Bibliography

Taguchi, G. *Introduction to Quality Engineering: Designing Quality into Products and Processes*. Asian Productivity Organization, 1986 (available in North America, the United Kingdom and Western Europe from the American Supplier Institute, Inc., and UNIPUB/Kraus International Publications, White Plains, New York).

Taguchi, G. *Systems of Experimental Design*. UNIPUB/Kraus International Publications, White Plains, New York and American Supplier Institute, Inc., Dearborn, Michigan, 1987 (Specifically Chapters 18, 19, 22, 23, 24 and 40.4).

Taguchi, G., and M.S. Phadke. *Quality Engineering Through Design Optimization*. Proceedings of IEEE GLOBECOM-84 Conference, November 1984, Atlanta, Georgia, pp. 1106–1113.

Phadke, M.S., and G. Taguchi. *Selection of Quality Characteristics and S/N Ratios for Robust Design*. Proceedings of IEEE GLOBECOM-87 Conference, November 1987, Tokyo, Japan.

Appendix D: On-Line Quality Control

Dr. Duane Orlowski and Shin Taguchi

Quality Engineering stresses the need for reducing variability in products and processes at the design stage. This improves quality by making the product robust against the many uncontrollable and changing conditions encountered during both manufacture and customer use. However, even after optimum conditions have been determined using off-line methods, the following sources of variability still remain at the production level: variability in materials and purchased components; tool wear, drifting of process parameter levels, and machine fatigue; variability in the execution of production processes; measurement error; and human error.

In order to reap the benefits of off-line quality and cost improvements, these sources of production variability must be cost-effectively controlled. They are dealt with by quality-control techniques applied during normal production—in other words, by real-time, on-line methods. Dr. Genichi Taguchi has developed a system of on-line quality-control methods based on the conceptual framework of the Quality Loss Function (QLF). As the following examples illustrate, these methods are a way to monitor and maintain quality at the lowest possible cost.

Off-Line and On-Line QC

In March 1985, a group of Ford Motor Co. and supplier engineers participated in a one-day awareness seminar on Taguchi's Quality Engineering techniques. Several applications resulted, including the evaluation and optimization of an automobile-door system using the QLF and off-line and on-line quality-control techniques.

Through the use of the QLF, the engineers found that the process capability (how well the process meets the product's target value) of three weatherstrip manufacturers was much different than they had thought.

A comprehensive off-line design-optimization study of the processes used in the production of a trimmed automobile door was soon begun. The study, which included some 25 control factors, was broken into a number of individual investigations, including weatherstrip-bulb optimization. Weatherstrip-bulb extrusion parameters that might affect door fit were then identified and optimized. Application of Taguchi's on-line quality-control techniques resulted in the economic optimization of the loss associated with door margins. The resulting on-line quality-control study showed that by spending \$0.03 more per part on inspection and \$2.38 more per part on machine adjustment, a loss of \$11.36 per part could be prevented.[1]

Through such applications, Ford and supplier engineers experienced the full force and impact of Taguchi Methods, from off-line optimization to on-line quality-control methods. This allowed them to cost-effectively maintain the potential gains of the off-line or "upstream" effort.

A Loss-Minded System

In designing any on-line quality-control system, two things must be considered: 1) the frequency at which a product characteristic should be observed or measured, and 2) the adjustment limit, which indicates that a process has drifted far enough from its target to require immediate action.

1. W. H. Moore, "Ford Has a Better Idea: Quality Engineering at Ford Motor Co., 1986.

Taguchi tells of an automated control system developed almost 20 years ago by Toyota Motor Corp. With this system, immediately after each production process, each product was measured by an automatic measuring device calibrated with a built-in standard. Whenever a deviation from target was detected, the machine automatically adjusted the tool and machine setting. When a defect was found, the system automatically stopped the process and an operator was alerted by a light or bell.

The Toyota-type system, which inspects every unit and adjusts with every deviation, is said to be "quality-minded"—it produces very high quality, but may also be expensive to implement. A system based on tolerance limits is said to be "cost-minded"—adjustments are made only when a process is out of specification limits; variability within tolerance limits isn't addressed. Such a system is inexpensive to implement, but quality is likely to suffer.

The on-line quality-control system developed by Taguchi considers both quality and cost—it can be described as "loss-minded." Taguchi's on-line quality-control system seeks to minimize the cost of quality by balancing the expense of quality control with the actual additional profits resulting from the control. It looks for the most desirable observation intervals and adustment limits and seeks an optimum solution to the problem of quality control during production. In fact, both Toyota and Fuji Photo Film Co. are reportedly using on-line quality control today.[2]

Total loss due to variation during production includes loss due to manufacturing variance and the costs associated with inspection, scrap and repair, and adjustment. Any on-line reduction in variability comes from changing process equipment, process parameters, inspection frequencies, equipment-adjustment intervals, and checking or adjustment levels. All of these proce-

---

2. Thomas B. Barker and Don P. Clausing, "Quality Engineering by Design: The Taguchi Method," *Collection of Publications on Taguchi Methods*, 1984.

dures have associated costs. The system takes these costs into account to determine how often a characteristic should be measured and what the adjustment limits should be. This allows manufacturers to make economically informed decisions about production-control measures, rather than simply regarding such measures as a necessary but expensive evil.

Control Charting and On-Line QC

W. Edwards Deming reintroduced American manufacturing to statistical thinking and Statistical Process Control (SPC) in the late 1970s and early 1980s. Control charts provide production with benchmarks for action (control limits), indicate the nature of process variability (due to special or common causes), and facilitate the assessment of process capability (allow an operator to assess the degree to which a process is capable of meeting product specifications).

Control charts, however, do not identify ways to cost-effectively reduce variability. Production-control feedback is faster with SPC than with traditional inspection. But control charts are difficult to implement and maintain, and SPC isn't considered to be a cost-based system. Taguchi's on-line quality-control techniques enable machine operators simply to measure and adjust—activities they already know how to do. By applying on-line methods they can determine how often to do so in order to maintain the balance between cost and quality as defined by the QLF.

There are three categories of on-line quality control: *measurement and disposition, diagnosis and adjustment,* and *prediction and correction.* Each technique is based on a determination of the costs and losses associated with control during production. The first, measurement and disposition, deals with the product, while the last two deal with the production process.

Measurement and Disposition

Measurement and disposition, also known as go/no go inspection, is a system whereby products are inspected and determined to be either acceptable and shipped or unacceptable and discarded or repaired (see **Figure AD-1**). Inspection methods range from zero end-of-the-line inspection to 100% inspection of every unit that comes off the line. In between are many different acceptance sampling plans developed by scientists at AT&T Bell Laboratories during World War II, including skip sampling, chain inspection, and others. Most of these inspection plans weed out defective products and product lots *after* manufacture. While such plans generally increase quality levels, they are expensive to use and maintain and don't contribute to defect prevention or productivity improvement. Even 100% inspection isn't entirely effective. A motivated inspector working under good conditions and doing repetitive industrial measurement will typically fail to notice up to 20% of all defects. Even when inspection is automated, defects creep through. Experience in the electronics industry—where components and circuits are easily tested by computer—shows that it's not unusual to find rejects at automated inspection stations of 5 to 10%.

Taguchi dismisses the value of inspection sampling plans. He argues that if inspection is used, it must be used on 100% of a production line's output. According to Taguchi, the only alternative to 100% inspection is 0% end-of-the-line inspection.

How do you decide whether to use 100% or 0% inspection? Taguchi provides a set of mathematical formulas with which the losses associated with both 100% and 0% inspection can be estimated. In the case of 0% inspection, the QLF is used. This provides the manufacturer with an estimate of how much each defective product shipped is costing him. This cost is then compared with the cost of doing 100% inspection. The formula for 100% inspection includes the cost of inspection; the cost of adjustment,

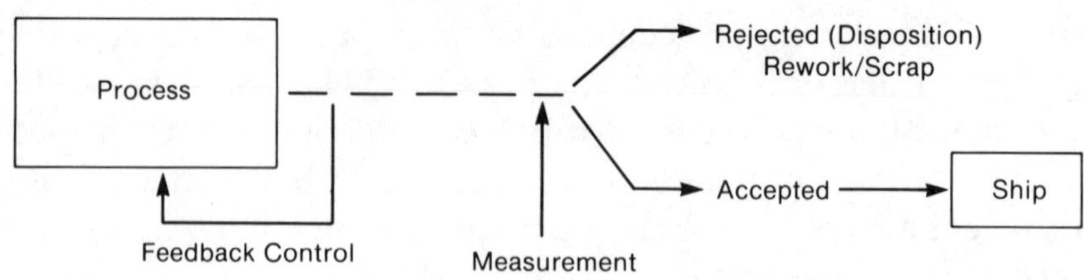

- Inspection is a decision regarding whether or not to ship a product.
- Taguchi recommends either 0% or 100% inspection.

Figure AD-1

scrap, and rework; and the number of defective products that exist.

Example

The specification limit for toxic components in automobile exhaust for a certain vehicle is 2.4 gms. The cost of inspection is \$6. Automobiles that fail inspection are reworked before inspection at a cost of \$90.

When toxic components were measured on 15 automobiles, the results in gms. were:

1.6	1.2	1.5	2.1	2.8	$n = 15$
1.7	2.0	1.8	1.4	1.0	$A_0 = \$90$
1.5	2.5	2.2	1.4	1.8	$\Delta_0 = 2.4$ gms.

We calculate and compare the profit and loss resulting from 0% inspection and 100% inspection.

The Cost of 0% Inspection

The loss when there is no inspection is $L_0 = k[\text{MSD}]$.

Here MSD is the mean square deviation from the target value of zero (ideally we want no toxic components in the exhaust).

$$\text{MSD} = \frac{1}{n}\left(y_1^2 + y_2^2 + ... + y_n^2\right)$$

$$= \frac{1}{n}\left(1.6^2 + 1.2^2 + ... + 18^2\right)$$

$$= 3.34$$

$$k = \frac{A_0}{\Delta_0^2} = \frac{90}{2.4^2} = 15.625$$

The loss per unit with no inspection is $L_0 = 15.625[3.34] =$ \$52.19/unit.

The Cost of 100% Inspection

With 100% inspection we assume that the MSD of reworked units will be about the same as those that pass inspection. If two units out of the 15 inspected were defective, then costs include: inspection cost = \$6.00; scrap/rework cost = \$90.00; and loss for units passing inspection = k [MSD] = \$52.19; the fraction rejected = 2/15.

L = Inspection cost + (rework/scrap cost × fraction rejected) + loss for units passing inspection

$$= 6 + \left(90 \times \frac{2}{15}\right) + 15.625 \times \frac{1}{13}\left(1.6^2 + ... + 1.8^2\right)$$

$$= \$61.28$$

The manufacturer can then make an informed decision as to the most cost-effective method. Comparing L_0 and L we see that 100% inspection turns out to be unprofitable. Quality control should be targeted at the process through diagnosis and adjustment, and prediction and correction. Why does selecting the most cost-effective inspection method ensure quality? Because the decision is biased toward high-process capability. In other words, the better a process is controlled, the less likelihood there is of 100% inspection costing less than 0% inspection. Therefore, it puts a premium on keeping a process in control.

If your process is loosely controlled, you might find 100% inspection to be the less expensive method. However, this probably means that you haven't attempted to optimize your process or product design using off-line quality-control methods. In some cases, if 100% inspection turns out to be cheaper than 0% inspection, you can assume that there are major process-control problems. If 0% inspection turns out to be less costly than 100% inspection, the next step is to proceed to real-time process control using either diagnosis and adjustment or prediction and correction.

Diagnosis and Adjustment

The goal of diagnosis and adjustment is to check the production process at certain economically justifiable intervals (as illustrated in **Figure AD-2**). If the process is operating within desired limits, production is allowed to continue. If an abnormality is found, 1) production is stopped, 2) the cause of the abnormality is determined and eliminated or adjustment is made, 3) the first piece produced after adjustment is checked and, if found to be good, 4) production resumes.

The assumption of this system is that once a process begins to produce abnormalities, it will continue to do so. Compared with SPC, where a number of production averages are plotted

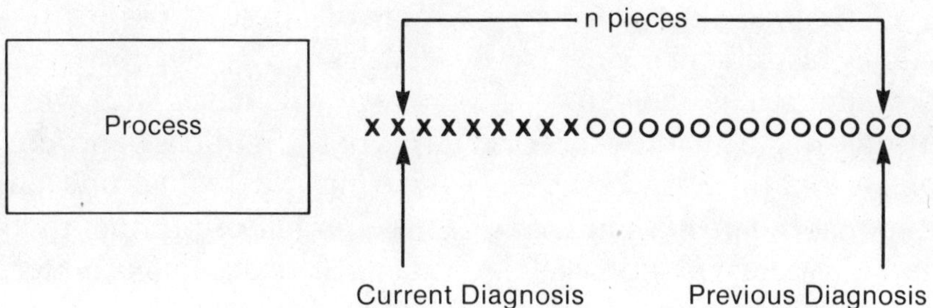

1. Diagnose every n pieces.
2. If a piece is found to be abnormal, restore the normal condition.
3. Otherwise, continue.

Figure AD-2

over time, diagnosis and adjustment occurs in real production time and requires response at the first sign of trouble.

The key to the cost-effectiveness of diagnosis and adjustment is the determination of an optimum diagnostic interval. This is a measurement or checking interval that provides an optimum balance between measurement and adjustment costs and quality loss caused by piece-to-piece product variation. Before determining the optimum diagnostic interval, a manufacturer must consider the following variables in estimating total production-control costs: the cost of diagnosis per unit; the loss due to producing a defective product (scrap/rework cost); the cost of adjusting a product within normal limits and recovery of normal production; the time lag between the diagnosis of a defective product and stopping the process; the scrap/rework cost due to defective products that are produced during this time lag; and the current diagnostic interval.

With diagnosis and adjustment, the costs incurred with

checking and adjusting the manufacturing process are minimized by determining and using the optimum diagnostic interval.

The following parameters are involved: A = loss for producing a defective unit (scrap/rework); B = diagnosis cost; C = adjustment cost; $\bar{u}$ = the average frequency with which trouble occurs in the process in terms of the number of product units; ℓ = time lag between diagnosing a defective unit and stopping the process in terms of the number of product units; and n = diagnosis interval, i.e., the number of units produced between each diagnosis.

The cost function for diagnosis and adjustment is:

$$L = \underbrace{\frac{B}{n}}_{\text{Diagnosis cost per piece}} + \underbrace{\left[\frac{n+1}{2}\left(\frac{A}{\bar{u}}\right)\right]}_{\text{Scrap/rework cost per piece}} + \underbrace{\frac{C}{\bar{u}}}_{\text{Adjustment cost per piece}} + \underbrace{\ell\left(\frac{A}{\bar{u}}\right)}_{\text{Scrap/rework cost due to time lag}}$$

We determine the optimum diagnosis interval by considering the average frequency of defective products, the cost of diagnosis, the loss for producing a defective product, and the cost of adjusting the process. The formula for the optimum checking interval is obtained by differentiating the cost function and setting it equal to zero.

$$n = \sqrt{\frac{2(\bar{u} + \ell)B}{A - \frac{C}{\bar{u}}}}$$

Optimum diagnosis interval

After the optimum diagnosis interval is determined, savings per unit from the new interval can be estimated. This is done by calculating the new cost of diagnosis and comparing it with the old cost of diagnosis. An estimate of annual savings can then be easily determined.

Example

Ten holes are reamed at once and all of them have to be good. A departure of 10 μm makes the cylinder block defective. It is scrapped at a loss of \$60.00 (A). The cost of measuring the holes is \$3 (B). Every 30th block is diagnosed (n = 30). When a defective cylinder is found the process is stopped and the reamer replaced. One block is reamed and checked. The tool cost, labor cost, and costs associated with stopping the process come to \$150 (C). Eighteen-thousand units were produced during the preceding half year, during which time seven failures were diagnosed. The average interval between failures ($\bar{u}$) is: 18,000 ÷ 7 = 2,570 units.

- A = \$60
- B = \$3
- C = \$150
- n_0 = 30 units
- ℓ = 1 unit
- $\bar{u}$ = 2,570 units

$$L_0 = \frac{B}{n_0} + \frac{n+1}{2}\left(\frac{A}{\bar{u}}\right) + \frac{C}{\bar{u}} + \ell\left(\frac{A}{\bar{u}}\right)$$

$$= \frac{3}{30} + \frac{30+1}{2}\left(\frac{60}{2{,}570}\right) + \frac{150}{2{,}570} + \frac{1(60)}{2{,}570}$$

$$= \$0.541 \ / \ \text{piece}$$

This is the quality-control cost per piece at the current diagnosis interval, n_0. If annual production is 36,000 units per year, the cost is \$19,476/yr.

The optimum diagnosis and adjustment interval is:

$$n = \sqrt{\frac{2(\bar{u} + \ell)B}{A - \frac{C}{\bar{u}}}}$$

$$= \sqrt{\frac{2(2{,}570 + 1)3}{60 - \dfrac{150}{2{,}570}}}$$

$$\approx 16 \text{ units}$$

The quality-control cost with the optimum diagnosis interval is:

$$L = \frac{3}{16} + \frac{16 + 1}{2}\left(\frac{60}{2{,}570}\right) + \frac{150}{2{,}570} + \frac{1 \times 60}{2{,}570}$$

$$= \$0.47 \ / \text{ piece}$$

The savings come to:

$$\begin{aligned} L_0 - L &= \$0.54 - \$0.47 \\ &= \$0.07/\text{piece} \end{aligned}$$

This represents an annual savings of $2,520.

Once the optimum diagnosis interval is known, the other variables in the formula can be manipulated to further reduce costs. For example, rework or diagnosis methods might be improved without affecting quality. To increase the diagnostic interval the manufacturer might consider implementing periodic tool changes, using tools with longer life, more off-line process optimization, and so forth. If the scrap/rework cost is large, the manufacturer may want to check more frequently. If the diagnostic cost is great, the manufacturer may want to check less frequently. Preventive maintenance may be an option.

Prediction and Correction

Prediction and correction, called feedback control in the United States, involves measuring a process or product feature, predicting another, and making corrections based on the predicted value and its deviation from the target. It is similar in some ways to Walter A. Shewhart's control-charting system in that it plots the stability of a process and indicates when corrections to the process mean should be made, as shown in **Figure AD-3**. The differences between this method and traditional control charting, however, are significant.

Traditional control charting corrects a process only when causes of variation move the process out of control. It does so by identifying these causes for corrective action. Otherwise, the variability around the target value is assumed to be relatively constant, and no action is taken. Taguchi, on the other hand, seeks countermeasures to the causes of variation. These include his off-line and on-line techniques for quality control.

Prediction and correction assumes that any process left alone without adjustment will eventually drift: It is only a matter of time before the process begins to produce products out of control limits. It assumes that the MSD resulting from process drift is proportional to time. The more pieces produced, the wider the deviation.

The objective of prediction and correction is to maintain uniformity around the target specification through continuous, optimum measurement of a quality characteristic and correction, not the search for and elimination of special causes of variation. Prediction and correction is a feedback-control system in which measurements are made at predetermined, cost-efficient intervals. So long as the process is within predetermined optimum control limits, production continues. If the process is outside of control limits, the process mean is adjusted back to the target.

The cost and time involved in measuring and correcting the process are taken into account during prediction and correction. Three cost factors—measurement cost, correction and process-adjustment cost, and loss due to piece-to-piece variation—are considered in determining the optimum measurement interval, optimum control limits, and how much to correct the process.

The costs for prediction and correction include the follow-

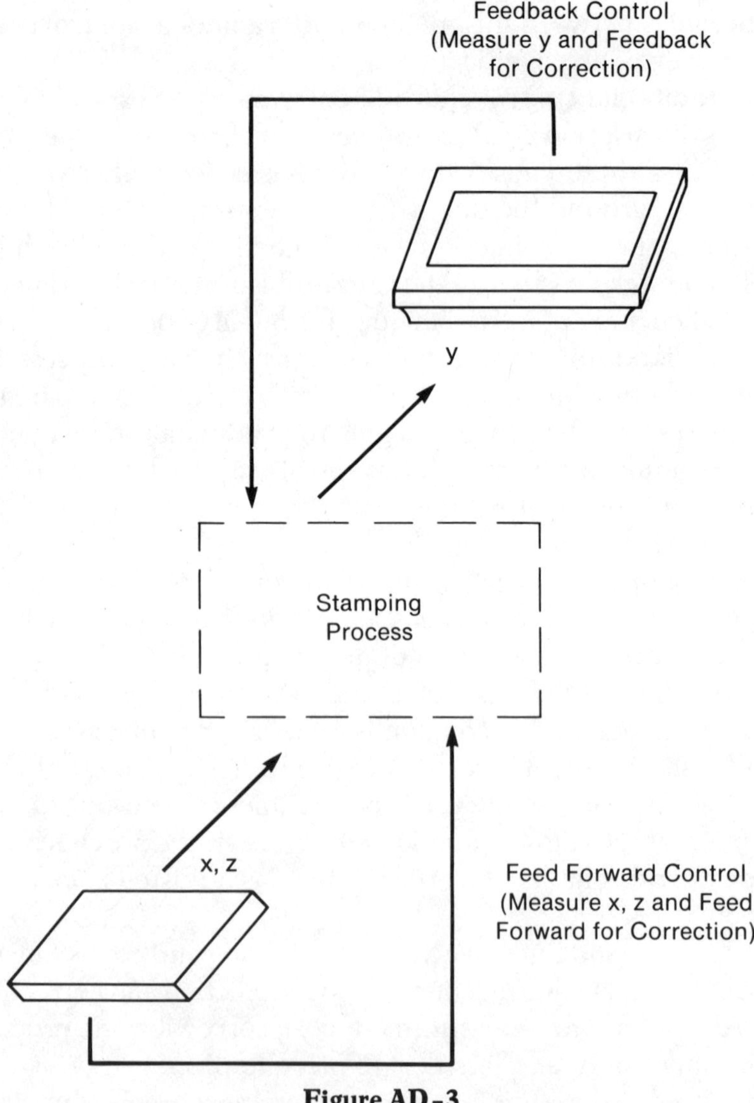
Prediction and Correction
Feedback Control
(Measure y and Feedback
for Correction)
y
Stamping
Process
x, z
Feed Forward Control
(Measure x, z and Feed
Forward for Correction)

Figure AD-3

ing: A = loss due to a defective piece; B = cost of measurement; and C = cost of correction of the process.

This method assumes that, without any correction, a process will drift, and the MSD is proportional to time (increases with the number of pieces produced). MSD can be approximated by:

$$MSD = \frac{D^2}{3} + \left[\frac{n+1}{2} + \ell\right]\left(\frac{D^2}{u}\right)$$

where D = the control limit; n = the measurement interval (number of units between each measurement); u = the average correction interval; ℓ = the time lag (number of units between measurement and stopping the process); and Δ = the tolerance limit.

The cost for prediction and correction is given by:

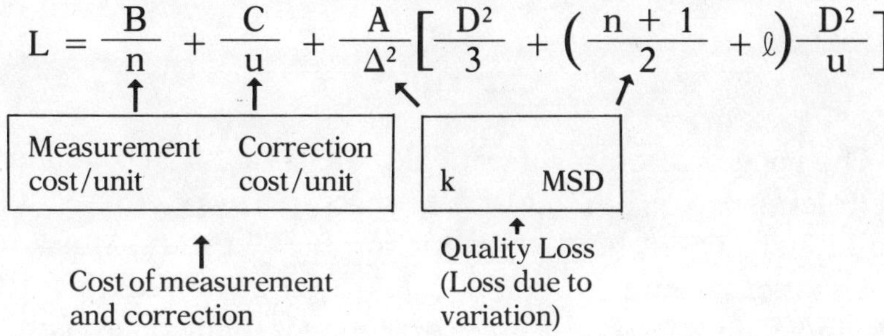

Prediction and correction is based on the ability to optimize the measurement interval and the necessary control limits of a process in relation to the costs involved. The optimum measurement interval and control limits are derived on the basis of the QLF.

The current average correction interval is:

$$u_0 = \frac{\text{total number of products produced}}{\text{number of corrections conducted}}$$

Let A be the scrap/rework cost, u_0 the current average correction interval, and D_0 the current control limit. To obtain an optimum measurement interval, n, and optimum control limit, D, we take the derivative of the cost function for prediction and correction and set L equal to zero.

$$n = \sqrt{\frac{2u_0B}{AD_0^2}} \times \Delta$$

Optimum measurement interval

$$D = \left[\frac{3C}{A} \times \frac{{D_0}^2}{u_0} \times \Delta^2\right]^{1/4}$$

Optimum control limit

The manufacturer can use the prediction and correction cost calculation to compare the new and current per-piece quality-control costs in order to estimate monthly or yearly savings.

Example

The specification for a critical dimension of a component part (tolerance Δ) is ± 15 μm. Loss for scrap/rework (defectives A) is $1.30. Current hourly production is 300 pieces. Measurement is taken every 2 hrs. and the measurement cost (B) is $1.10. The control limit (D) is ± 5 μm. Correction is made once per day and the correction cost (C) is $9.00.

- Δ = 15 μm
- A = $1.30
- B = $1.10
- C = $9.00
- Current Measurement Interval, n_0 = 300 × 2 = 600 pieces
- Average Correction Interval, u_0 = 300 × 8 = 2,400 pieces

- Current Control Limit, $D_0 = 5\ \mu m$
- Time lag, $\ell = 5$ pieces

To determine the optimum control system we determine the optimum measurement interval and control limit and compute the savings.

Optimum measurement interval n and control limits D:

$$n = \sqrt{\frac{2u_0B}{A\,D_0^2}} \times \Delta$$

$$= \sqrt{\frac{2(2{,}400)\,(1.10)}{1.30\,(5^2)}} \times 15$$

$$= 191 \Rightarrow \quad 200 \text{ units}$$

$$D = \left[\frac{3C}{A} \times \frac{D_0^2}{u_0} \times \Delta^2\right]^{1/4}$$

$$= \left[\frac{3 \times 9.00}{1.30} \times \frac{5^2}{2{,}400} \times 15^2\right]^{1/4}$$

$$= 2.6 = 3.0$$

Savings with optimum n and D: The current quality-control loss is:

$$L_0 = \frac{B}{n_0} + \frac{C}{u_0} + \frac{A}{\Delta^2}\left[\frac{D_0^2}{3} + \left(\frac{n_0 + 1}{2} + \ell\right)\frac{D_0^2}{u_0}\right]$$

$$= \frac{1.10}{600} + \frac{9}{2{,}400} + \frac{1.30}{15^2}\left[\frac{5^2}{3} + \left(\frac{600 + 1}{2} + 5\right)\frac{5^2}{2{,}400}\right]$$

$$= \$0.0717 \,/\, \text{piece}$$

The new average correction interval is estimated as:

$$u = u_0\left(\frac{D^2}{D_0^2}\right)$$

$$= 2{,}400\left(\frac{3^2}{5^2}\right) = 864 \text{ units}$$

The optimum quality-control loss is:

$$L = \frac{B}{n} + \frac{C}{u} + \frac{A}{\Delta^2}\left[\frac{D^2}{3} + \left(\frac{n+1}{2} + \ell\right)\frac{D^2}{u}\right]$$

$$= \frac{1.10}{200} + \frac{9}{864} + \frac{1.30}{15^2}\left[\frac{3^3}{3} + \left(\frac{200+1}{2} + 5\right)\frac{3^2}{864}\right]$$

$$= \$0.0396$$

The quality-control cost per piece is improved by:

$$L_0 - L = \$0.0717 - \$0.0396$$
$$= \$0.0321 \text{ per piece}$$

The annual savings based on 2,000 hrs. is:

$$\$0.0321 \,/\, \text{piece} \times 300\,\frac{\text{pieces}}{\text{hr.}} \times 2000\,\frac{\text{hrs.}}{\text{yr.}} = \$19{,}260 \,/\, \text{yr.}$$

Summary

Taguchi Methods are first and foremost aimed at obtaining and maintaining quality at the lowest possible cost. Taguchi's on-line quality-control system is a cost-driven, downstream, real-time production-control system. Off-line quality-control techniques should be applied as far upstream as possible, resulting in quality that is *designed in.* By optimizing the monitoring and control of production processes using on-line quality control in conjunction with off-line design optimization, a manufacturer can reap the full economic benefits of Taguchi's system.

Bibliography

Moore, W. H. "Ford Has a Better Idea: Quality Engineering at Ford Motor Co." Dearborn: Body and Chassis Division, Ford Motor Co., 1986.

On-Line Quality Control: A Cost-Driven System of Production Control Developed by Dr. Genichi Taguchi. Three-day seminar course manual. Dearborn: American Supplier Institute, Inc., 1988.

Taguchi, Genichi. *On-Line Quality Control During Production.* Tokyo: Japanese Standards Association, 1981.

———. "Specification Value and Quality Control." *The International Quality Control Forum,* Vol. II, 1985.

Bibliography

Altshuler, Alan, et al. *The Future of the Automobile.* Cambridge: MIT Press, 1984.

AT&T Technical Journal. Bimonthly.

Automotive Industries. Monthly.

Automotive Industries Insider. Biweekly newsletter.

Automotive News. Weekly.

Box, Joan Fisher. *R. A. Fisher, The Life of a Scientist.* New York: John Wiley & Sons, 1978.

Busch, Noel F. *The Horizon Concise History of Japan.* New York: American Heritage Publishing Co., 1972.

Business Week. Weekly.

Car. Monthly.

Chrysler Corp. Annual reports.

Clark, Ronald W. *The Life of Ernst Chain.* New York: St. Martin's Press, 1985.

Cochran, William, and Gertrude Cox. *Experimental Designs.* New York: John Wiley & Sons, 1957.

Cole, Robert E., editor. *Automobiles and the Future: Competition, Cooperation, and Change.* Ann Arbor: University of Michigan Press, 1983.

____, editor. *The Japanese Automobile Industry: Model and Challenge for the Future?* Ann Arbor: University of Michigan Press, 1981.

Collection of Publications on Taguchi Methods. Dearborn: American Supplier Institute, Inc., 1984.

Consumer Reports. Monthly.

Cusumano, Michael A. *The Japanese Automobile Industry.* Cambridge: Harvard University, 1985.

Feigenbaum, A. V. "Total Quality Control." *Harvard Business Review,* November-December 1956, pp. 93-101.

____. *Total Quality Control.* Third edition. New York: McGraw-Hill, 1983.

Fisher, R. A. *The Design of Experiments.* Edinburgh: Oliver and Boyd, 1960.

Collection of Publications on Taguchi Methods. Dearborn: American Supplier Institute, Inc., 1984.

Ford Motor Co. Annual reports.

General Motors Corp. Annual reports.

Harbour and Associates, Inc. "Comparison of Japanese Car Assembly Plant Located in Japan and U.S. Car Assembly Plant Located in the U.S." Berkley, Michigan: Report prepared for the U.S. Department of Transportation, 1980.

Harvard Business Review. Bimonthly.

Human Resources Quarterly. Biennially.

Industrial Engineering. Monthly.

Industrial Quality Control. Monthly.

Ishikawa, Kaoru. *Guide To Quality Control.* Tokyo: Asian Productivity Organization, 1982.

Juran, J. M. *Quality Control Handbook.* New York: McGraw-Hill, 1979.

Kamiya, Shotaro. *My Life With Toyota.* Translated by Thomas I. Elliot. Nagoya: Toyota Motor Sales Co., 1976.

Kowalick, James. "The Importance of Quality Considerations In The Ammunition Technology Stage," transcript of presentation given at the 1987 ADPA Gun and Ammunition Technical

Meeting, Naval Post Graduate School, Monterey, CA. Aerojet Ordnance Co., 1987.

Lacey, Robert. *Ford: The Man and the Machine.* New York: Little, Brown and Co. Inc., 1986.

Monden, Yasuhiro. "What Makes the Toyota Production System Really Tick?" *Industrial Engineering,* January 1981, pp. 36–46.

____. *Toyota Production System.* Atlanta: Institute of Industrial Engineers, 1983.

Moore, W. H. "Ford Has a Better Idea: Quality Engineering at Ford Motor Co." Dearborn: Body and Chassis Division, Ford Motor Co., 1986.

Motor Vehicle Manufacturers Association. *Motor Vehicle Facts and Figures.* Annual.

____. *World Motor Vehicle Data Book.* Annual.

Nemoto, Masao. *Total Quality Control for Management.* Translated by David Lu. Englewood Cliffs: Prentice Hall, Inc., 1987.

The New York Times.

Nippondenso Co., Ltd. "The History of Nippondenso's Activities of Application of the Taguchi Methods," April 1987.

On-Line Quality Control: A Cost-Driven System of Production Control Developed by Dr. Genichi Taguchi. Three-day seminar course manual. Dearborn: American Supplier Institute, Inc., 1988.

Pinchot, G. *Intrapreneuring.* New York: Harper & Row, 1985.

Schonberger, Richard J. *Japanese Manufacturing Techniques: Nine Lessons in Simplicity.* New York: The Free Press/Macmillan, 1982.

____. *World Class Manufacturing: The Lessons of Simplicity Applied.* New York: The Free Press/Macmillan, 1986.

Sloan, Alfred P., Jr. *My Years with General Motors.* New York: Anchor/Doubleday, 1963.

Suzaki, Kiyoshi. *The New Manufacturing Challenge.* New York: The Free Press/Macmillan, 1987.

Taguchi, Genichi. *On-Line Quality Control During Production.* Tokyo: Japanese Standards Association, 1981.

———. "Specification Value and Quality Control." *The International Quality Control Forum,* Vol. II, 1985.

Taguchi, Genichi, and Yuin Wu. *Introduction to Off-Line Quality Control.* Nagoya: Central Japan Quality Control Association, 1979.

Toyota Motor Corp. Annual reports.

Toyota Motor Corp. In-house publications.

The UMTRI Research Review. Bimonthly.

U.S. Dept. of Commerce, Bureau of the Census. *Statistical Abstract of the United States,* 1980–86.

The Wall Street Journal.

Ward's Auto World. Monthly.

Yates, Brock. *The Decline and Fall of the American Automobile Industry.* New York: Empire Books, 1983.

Index

NOTE: The symbols (F) and (T) are used to indicate that information is presented in figures or tables, respectively.